Contracting *for* Public Sector Services

Lawrence L. Martin, Ph.D. *and*
John R. Miller, CPPO

Prepared for NIGP: The Institute for Public Procurement.
All rights are conveyed to NIGP upon completion of this book.

Contracting *for* Public Sector Services

Information in this book is accurate as of the time of publication and consistent with generally accepted public purchasing principles. However, as research and practice advance, standards may change. For this reason, it is recommended that readers evaluate the applicability of any recommendation in light of particular situations and changing standards.

National Institute of Governmental Purchasing, Inc. (NIGP)
151 Spring Street
Herndon, VA 20170
Phone: 703-736-8900; 800-367-6447
Fax: 703-736-9639 Email: education@nigp.org

This book is available at a special discount when ordered in bulk quantities. For information, contact NIGP at 800-367-6447. A complete catalog of titles is available on the NIGP website at www.nigp.org.

Copyright ©2006 by NIGP, Inc. All rights reserved. Printed in the United States of America. Except as permitted under the United States Copyright Act of 1976, no part of this publication may be reproduced or distributed in any form or by any means, or stored in a database or retrieval system, without the prior written permission of the publisher.

ISBN 1-932315-08-X
    978-1-932315-08-0

This book was set in Berkeley Oldstyle
Design & production by Vizual, Inc.
Printed & bound by HBP.

Acknowledgements

Eric Hoffer, renowned philosopher, stated that "in a time of drastic change, it is the learners who inherit the future". Public purchasers must be life-long learners and it is my hope that this text will increase the body of knowledge that enables us to effectively carry out our duties and responsibilities.

I would be remiss if I did not thank my family for their support. They have always been my motivation to reach for new challenges. My wife, Barbara, especially deserves big thanks for understanding that the time devoted to this effort was something I really wanted to do.

Rick Grimm and Carol Hodes deserve specific recognition for their continuing efforts to improve the organization and the public procurement profession.

Public purchasing is indeed a noble profession and it has been my honor and privilege to have interacted over the years with so many dedicated men and women who have been an inspiration to me.

John R. Miller, CPPO

I would like to echo the comments made by my co-author, John Miller, particularly with respect to the great support we received from NIGP and its staff.

I would also like to thank my wife, Lella Martin, for her support and encouragement while this book was being written.

Lawrence L. Martin, Ph.D

Contents

Chapter 1. Contracting for Public Sector Services 1
    Introduction 1
    A Brief History of Contracting for Public Services 2
    Advantages and Disadvantages of Contracting for Public Services 4
        Advantages 4
        Disadvantages 5
    What the Research Suggests 6
        Service Costs 6
        Service Quality 8
        Public Employees 8
        Salaries and Wages 9
        Competition 10
    Services Most Frequently Contracted 12
        Public Works and Transportation Services 13
        Health and Human Services 14
        Public Safety Services 14
        Parks, Recreation, Arts, and Cultural Services 14
        Support Services 15
    The Legal and Regulatory Context of Contracting for Public Sector Services 15
        U.S. Supreme Court Decisions 16
        State Supreme Court Decisions 17
    Ethical Issues in Contracting for Public Sector Services 18

Chapter 2. Deciding To Contract 23
    Introduction 23
        Make-or-Buy Situations 23
        Inherently Governmental Functions 24
        Core Versus Ancillary Services 26
    Conducting a Make-or-Buy Decision 28
        Market Strength 28
        Political Resistance 29
        Service Quality 29
        Impact on Public Employees 29
        Legal Barriers 30
        Risk 30
        Resources 30
        Control 31
        Cost 31
    Making Cost Comparisons Between In-House and Contract Service Delivery 34
        Determining the Cost of Contract Service Delivery 36
            Contract Administration and Monitoring Costs 36
            One-Time Conversion Costs 39
            Other Costs/Revenues 39

    Determining the Cost of In-House Service Delivery 39
      The Accuracy of the Allocation Method 40
      Determining Which Indirect Costs are Avoidable and Unavoidable 40
    Comparing the Costs of In-House Versus Contract Service Delivery 41
      The Fully Allocated Costs Approach 41
      The Avoidable Costs Approach 42
      The State of Texas Approach 44
    Other Cost Comparison Issues 45

Chapter 3. Public-Private Competition 49
    Introduction 49
      Public Employees as Competitors 50
      What is Public-Private Competition? 51
      Advantages of Public-Private Competition 52
      Disadvantages of Public-Private Competition 53
    Are In-House Departments and Public Employees Competitive
    with the Private Sector? 53
    Selecting Services for Public-Private Competition 55
      Core Versus Ancillary Services and Inherently Governmental Services 56
      Hard Versus Soft Services 56
      Stand-Alone Versus Interrelated Services 57
      Service Segmentation 57
      Service Precedents 58
      Private Sector Interest 58
      Private Sector Competitiveness 59
      In-House Department Interest 59
      In-House Department Competitiveness 60
      Political Opposition 61
    Public-Private Competition Checklist 61
    Level Playing Field Issues in Public-Private Competition 62
      Process Issues 65
      Costing Issues 66
      Contract Administration Issues 68
      Using and Interpreting the Level Playing Field Checklist 69
    Separation of the Purchaser and Provider Functions 70
    Ethical Issues in Public-Private Competition 71
      The Basic Concept of Public-Private Competition 71
      Market Testing 71
      After-the-Fact Notification 72
      Conflicts with Open Records, Statutes, and Ordinances 72
      Separation of the Purchaser/Provider Functions 72
      Level Playing Field Issues Versus Best Interests of the Government 73

Chapter 4. The Request For Proposal Document 75
    Introduction 75
    Request for Proposal (RFP) and Invitation for Bids (IFB)/
    Invitation to Tender (ITT) (CN) 76
    Opening the Bid/Tender/Proposal 78

The Request for Proposal Team 79
    Project Manager 80
    Contract Manager 80
    The Procurement Office as Contract Manager 81
    The Consultant as Contract Manager 81
    The Circuit-Riding Contract Manager 81
    Contract Administrator 81
    Field Manager 82
    Consultants 82
The RFP Draft 83
The RFP Outline 83
    General Information 85
    Introduction/Overview 85
    Purpose/Objective 85
    Background/History 85
    Contact with Jurisdictional Staff 86
    Pre-Proposal Conference 86
    Contractor Qualifications 87
    Boilerplate 87
    Applicable Documents 88
    Evaluation Process/Methodologies 90
Statement of Work/Scope of Work 91
    Planning the Statement/Scope of Work 91
    Statutes/Ordinances 92
    The Unambiguous SOW 93
    Security Controls 94
    Technical Requirements 94
    Understanding Deliverables 94
    Quality Control Program 95
    Work Schedule 95
Supporting Information 96
    Personnel Qualifications 96
    Evaluation of Performance 97
    Performance Standards 97
    Liquidated Damages 98
    Evaluation of Non-Quantitative Service Areas 98
    Special Conditions 99
    Format for Technical/Price Proposals 102

Chapter 5. Performance-Based Contracting 105
Introduction 105
    Principal/Agent Theory 105
    The Context of Government Performance Accountability 107
    The Government Performance and Results Act of 1993 107
    The Government Accounting Standards Board 108
    GPRA, GASB SEA Reporting and Contracting for Public Sector Services ... 108
Defining Performance-Based Contracting 109

Does Performance-Based Contracting Work? 111
    Office of Federal Procurement Policy Study 111
    Performance-Based Contracting for Human Services 111
Performance-Based Statements of Work 112
    Performance Specifications 113
    Expanded Systems Model 113
The Elements of a Performance-Based Statement of Work 114
    Service Definition 116
    Specification of Tasks/Statement of Objectives 117
    Performance Measures/Performance Requirements 117
    Performance Standards/Acceptable Quality Levels (AQLs) 118
    Incentives/Penalties 119
    Monitoring/Quality Assurance Plan 122
Contract Types 124
Other Approaches to Performance-Based Contracting 128
    Milestone Contracting 128
    Revenue Enhancement and Share-in-Savings Contracting 130
    Award Fee Contracting 131
Performance-Based Contracting and Auditing Considerations 131

Chapter 6.   **Proposal Evaluation And Contract Award 135**
Introduction 135
The Evolving Service Contracting Process 135
Evaluation and Award 136
Best-Value Evaluation Process 137
Evaluation Committee 138
    Mission of the Evaluation Committee 140
    Administrative/Procedural Duties 141
Attendance 142
Special Responsibilities of the Evaluation Committee 142
Evaluation Process for a Competitive Negotiation 142
Evaluation Process for Multi-Step Offers 143
Evaluation Process for Competitive Sealed Bids 144
Evaluation Process—Decision Rule for Competitive Sealed Proposals 144
    Fixed Weights 147
    Variable Weights 148
    Trade-Off Analysis 148
    Go/No-Go 149
    Lowest Priced Acceptable Proposal 149
Drafting the Contract 150
Contract Format 151
    Purchase-Order Contract 151
    Short-Form Contract 152
    Standard-Form Contract for Contractors 153
    Formal Contract 154
    Exhibits 154
    American Bar Association Clauses 157

	Contract Incentives and Penalties	157
Chapter 7.	**Protests And Disputes**	**161**
	Introduction	161
	Protests	161
	Sources of Protests	164
	Debriefing	165
	Responding to Protests	166
	Alternative Dispute Resolution	167
	Protest Avoidance Strategies	167
	Disputes	168
	The Disputes Clause	168
	Assertion of Claims	169
	The Role of the Contracting Officer	169
	Appeals	170
Chapter 8.	**Contract Administration And Monitoring**	**173**
	Introduction	173
	Contract Administration	173
	The Nature and Purpose of Contract Administration	174
	Monitoring	175
	Performance Standards	177
	Monitoring Strategies	178
	Creating Trust	178
	Outsourcing Manager	179
	Outcome Monitoring	180
	Poor Performance	180
	Action Plan for Addressing Poor Performance	181
	Suspension and Debarment	182
	Termination	182
	Termination for Default	183
	Consequences of a Default Termination	183
	Alternatives to a Default Termination	183
	The Right to Terminate for Default	184
	Cure Notice	185
Chapter 9.	**Extensions, Renewals, And Transitional Contract Issues**	**187**
	Introduction	187
	Contract Renewal Terms	187
	Renewal and Extension Issues	188
	Strategies to Consider	189
	Unsolicited Proposals	191
	Publicization	192
	Partnering for Successful Service Contracting	192
	Principles of Partnering	194
	Contract Interruptions	194
	Final Report	195
	Transitional Issues	196

Appendix A.	ICMA's National Surveys (1982, 1988, 1992, 1997, 2003) Of Service Contracting By U.S. Local Governments (Tables 1 – 5)	199
Appendix B.	Privatization Profile Summary Form (Without Weights)	204
Appendix C.	Privatization Profile Summary Form (With Weights)	205
Appendix D.	Public-Private Competition Checklist	206
Appendix E.	Level Playing Field Checklist	207
Appendix F.	Examples Of Alternative Surety	208
Appendix G.	Standard Clauses Included In The RFP Boilerplate	210
Appendix H.	Performance-Based Statement Of Work Template	217
Appendix I.	Guideline Template For Scoring Of Oral And Written Presentations	218
Index		221

Chapter 1

Contracting for Public Sector Services

Governments at all levels (federal, state, and local) are making large, and increased, use of contracting for public sector services. By fiscal year 2000, federal government contracting for public services reached $88 billion in the United States, surpassing all other types of federal contracting, according to the Commercial Activities Panel of the U.S. General Accounting Office (GAO, 2001a, p. 4). Moreover, about one-half of state departments and agencies reported increased use of public service contracting when responding to a national survey conducted by the Council of State Governments in 1998 (Chi & Jasper, 1998, p. 4). Internationally, significant use of public service contracting is also occurring. In the United Kingdom, for example, contracting for public services by local governments was estimated to exceed 2.5 billion pounds annually (Kavanagh & Parker, 2000, p. 3). Also, Canadian federal, provincial and local governments, have increased use of public service contracting, according to a Bank of Canada (1997) report. Federal departments' and agencies' use of public service contracts represented almost half of all contracted dollars in 1998, based on data from the Treasury Board of Canada Secretariat (n.d., p. 1). About two-thirds of municipal and county governments worldwide were considering increased use of contracting, according to a survey conducted by the International City/County Management Association (ICMA) (Martin, 1999a, p. 12).

Several factors have contributed to the increased interest in contracting for public services, according to E.S. Savas (2000), a well-known scholar in the field of privatization and contracting. These include: pragmatic, economic, philosophic, commercial, and populist forces. Savas notes, for instance, that one pragmatic way for governments to respond to citizen demands for increased services, while experiencing smaller government staffs and lower taxes, is to increase efficiency by contracting for public services. Economically, Savas argues that because service demands of citizens are continually changing, contracting increases the flexibility of governments to respond more rapidly by adding, deleting, or otherwise altering service mixes. Philosophically, Savas points out that, as citizens' perceptions of the appropriate roles and responsibilities of governments evolve over time, contracting for public services affords a way to transcend boundaries between public and private services, as well as governments and businesses, including not-for-profit organizations. From a commercial perspective, Savas suggests, given that governments spend billions of dollars annually on services, the business community increasingly views such services as a growth market which they would like to see opened permanently. Finally, Savas cites the appeal of contracting for public services, especially with small community-based businesses or not-for-profit organizations, as a way to appease people (generally referred to as populists) who generally oppose big, centralized, bureaucratic government solutions to social problems in favor of smaller, decentralized, community-focused solutions. (pp. 5-14)

A Brief History of Contracting for Public Sector Services

Governments have contracted for public services as long as anyone can remember. Over the past several decades, however, governments have expanded the concept and applied it to service areas not previously considered (Kettl, 1993), spawning what can be called a "service contracting revolution". Today, governments may refer to contracts for public services as privatization, contracting out, sourcing, outsourcing, tendering, competitive tendering, or alternative service delivery. Regardless of their appellation, such contracting activities should strive to achieve the same noteworthy goals, such as increased efficiency and flexibility.

The intellectual antecedents of the service contracting revolution date from the late 1960s and early 1970s with the writings of Peter Drucker, the famous management theorist and consultant, and the research of E. S. Savas. In 1969, Drucker, published a book entitled *The Age of Discontinuity*, which had a major impact on the thinking of many people in Canada, the United States, and elsewhere. Drucker argued that government growth was due to the failure to consider private sector alternatives. He pointed out that businesses routinely make determinations whether to make a product or service in-house or to buy it from a supplier, commonly referred to as: *make-or-buy* decisions. Such decisions are generally based upon price, quality, supplier reliability, and other factors. Drucker argued that governments generally did not conduct make-or-buy decisions but, rather, confronted each new need as an opportunity to enlarge their bureaucracies. He was the first person to use the term *reprivatization*, which was later shortened to *privatization*. Shortly after Drucker's book appeared, Savas began conducting and publishing research on municipal solid waste collection services (Savas, 1971, 1977a, 1977b), which demonstrated that Canadian and U.S. cities that contracted for solid waste collection services had lower service delivery costs than cities providing such services in-house with public employees. While Drucker coined the term privatization, Savas arguably did as much as anyone to popularize the concept.

Of note, the Federal Government's service contracting policy predates the work of Drucker and Savas (Kettl, 1993; Martin, 1998). In 1955, the Federal Bureau of the Budget (BOB) issued Bulletin 55-4, stating that "The Federal Government will not start or carry on any commercial activity to provide a service or product for its own use if such product or service can be procured from private enterprise through ordinary business channels" (Kettl, 1993, p. 41). BOB Bulletin 55-4 was not so much a privatization policy as it was a contracting policy and one that covered services as well as supplies, materials, and equipment. Subsequently, BOB was renamed the Office of Management and Budget (OMB) and BOB Bulletin 55-4 evolved into OMB Circular A-76 (Ewoh, 1999). Today, OMB Circular A-76 is much more than a contracting policy, in that it provides a structured approach to conducting make-or-buy decisions (OMB, 2003), as well as articulating the Federal Government's approach to public-private competition.

In the 1980s, at the national level, privatization and contracting for public sector services were major policy initiatives of the Reagan Administration. However, as Donahue (1989) has correctly pointed out, the policy was more rhetoric than action. Nevertheless, this rhetoric stimulated interest in privatization and contracting. Through the 1980s and continuing into the 1990s, several state governments began establishing commissions to promote privatization and contracting for public sector services (Chi & Jasper, 1998, p. 6). Of note, the first public service procurement to use the term *outsourcing* was conducted in 1988 when the Wisconsin Department of Administration decided to contract for facilities management (Keene, 1998, p. 13). In addition, during the late 1980s at the international level, the conservative government of Prime Minister Margaret Thatcher introduced public-private competition (called "compulsory competitive tendering") to governments in the United Kingdom (Walsh & Davis, 1993). Soon thereafter, the Commonwealth of Australia followed suit with its own "competitive tendering" program (Domberger & Rimmer, 1994).

Public-private competition... allows in-house departments to compete with private sector firms...

Throughout the 1990s, Osborne and Gaebler's (1992) seminal work, *Reinventing Government*, kept privatization and contracting on the minds of government officials and citizens. Osborne and Gaebler consciously avoided using the term privatization in their book, choosing instead to talk about alternative service delivery, competition, and public-private sector partnerships. Their work had a direct influence on Vice President Al Gore and his "Reinventing Government" initiative (1993) and also helped to popularize the concept of public-private competition. Public-private competition, also referred to as managed competition, differs from traditional approaches to contracting for public sector services in that it allows in-house departments to compete with private sector firms to provide government services.

The City of Phoenix, Arizona's, experimentation with public-private competition for solid waste collection services in the late 1970s and early 1980s (Jensen, n.d., 1987) received considerable national attention. During the 1980s and 1990s, several other large local governments adopted public-private competition. These included the cities of Indianapolis, Indiana (The Civic Federation, 1996); Charlotte, North Carolina (1995); Philadelphia, Pennsylvania (Rendell, 1994); and the County of San Diego, California (1998). By the end of the 1990s, some 33% of city and county governments had at least experimented with public-private competition (Martin, 1999b, p. 17).

Today, privatization, contracting for public sector services, and public-private competition have become part of the theories and tools that comprise "The New Public Management" (Dobel, 2001; Riccucci, 2001) and are taught as part of the curricula of schools of public administration and public policy in Australia, Canada, the United Kingdom, the United States and elsewhere (Henry, 1999).

Advantages and Disadvantages of Contracting for Public Sector Services

The subject of contracting for public sector services has generated a considerable amount of public policy debate. Proponents of contracting maintain that this form of service delivery has numerous advantages over direct government service delivery (Savas, 2000). Opponents, such as the American Federation of State, County and Municipal Employees (AFSCME) (n.d.), argue that contracting for public sector services has more disadvantages than advantages. The debate can be heated at times and is frequently driven by politics and ideology rather than by research and data. The purported advantages and disadvantages of contracting for public sector services have not changed much over the last 25 years (Chi & Jasper, 1998; Fisk, 1982; Fisk, Kiesling, & Muller, 1978; Hatry, 1983; Savas, 2000), which suggests that research and data have unfortunately had little impact on the public policy debate.

Advantages

Proponents cite numerous advantages said to be associated with contracting for public sector services. The advantages most frequently cited are:

- *Lower Service Delivery Costs.* Contracting results in reduced service delivery costs.
- *Introduction of Competition.* Contracting promotes competition in government service delivery. Competition is said to lead to more efficient, effective and higher quality government services.
- *Smaller Government.* Contracting enables governments to provide more services

and address new challenges without adding additional public employees, facilities, or equipment.

- *Increased Flexibility.* Contracting provides governments with the flexibility to adjust the types and amounts of public services provided and to terminate programs more easily when such programs no longer add value or purpose.
- *Greater Experimentation.* Contracting facilitates experimentation with new and different service delivery approaches without the need to make changes in basic day-to-day government operations.
- *Access to Outside Expertise.* Contracting enables governments to access outside expertise and talent that might not otherwise be available.
- *Promotion of Public-Private Sector Cooperation.* Contracting provides a mechanism by which governments can join forces with private sector organizations (for-profit and not-for-profit) to address community and citizen needs such as economic development and the provision of human services (job training, child day care, etc.).
- *Avoidance of Large Start-up Costs.* Contracting avoids the large, up-front, capital costs associated with certain public sector services (e.g., transportation, street lighting, etc.). Private sector contractors are frequently willing and able to defray the up-front capital costs when governments cannot.

Disadvantages

Just as proponents ascribe numerous advantages to contracting for public sector services, opponents cite several disadvantages. Some of the most frequently noted disadvantages are:

- *Higher Service Delivery Costs.* Contracting results in higher service delivery costs. Opponents argue that because of transaction costs and the fact that the private sector must make a profit on government contracts, the real cost must be higher. Transaction costs refer to the added expenses incurred by governments in awarding, administering, and monitoring contracts.
- *Lower Quality Services.* Contracting leads to lower quality services. In order for contractors to earn a profit, they must provide lower quality services.
- *Displacement of Public Employees.* Contracting leads to the displacement of large numbers of public employees and has a disparate impact on minority public employees.
- *Lower Salaries and Wages.* Contractors frequently pay their employees less than governments pay public employees. Thus, downward pressure is exerted on both public and private sector salary and wage scales.
- *Increased Chances for Corruption.* Contracting leads to an increase in corruption as

elected officials, contractors, and others attempt to influence decisions about how contracts are awarded through the use of political patronage, kickbacks, and bribes.

- *Illusory Competition.* Competition does not take place for most government service contracts. In many instances, contracting simply replaces a public sector monopoly with a private sector monopoly.
- *Loss of Government Control.* Contracting leads to a loss of government control over service delivery. Relationships between governments and contractors must be interpreted through the mechanism of the contract.
- *Contracting is Simply Not Needed.* In-house departments can achieve the same positive results attributed to contracting if public employees were empowered to redesign and reengineer service delivery systems.

What the Research Suggests

The advantages and disadvantages of contracting for public sector services listed above raise the obvious questions: Who is correct? Are the proponents of contracting right about the advantages? Are the opponents right about the disadvantages? Some of the purported advantages and disadvantages have been the subject of considerable scholarly research in the United States and other countries. The advantages/disadvantages that have received the most research attention can be classified into five categories: service costs, service quality, public employees, salaries and wages, and competition. A significant amount of this research consists of case studies. Numerous case studies demonstrate how contracting has been successful for certain services in certain situations. Conversely, an equally large number of other case studies demonstrate how contracting has been unsuccessful for certain services in other situations. Any attempt to interpret the research findings on contracting for public sector services must look beyond individual case studies and focus on the identification of overall patterns. Does the research suggest a pattern?

The advantage most frequently ascribed to contracting for public sector services is that it leads to lower service delivery costs.

Service Costs

The advantage most frequently ascribed to contracting for public sector services is that it leads to lower service delivery costs (e.g., Martin, 1997; McDavid, 1996, 2001; Stone, Bell, & Poole, 1997). This aspect of service contracting has received the most research attention.

However, sorting out the research findings is not an easy task. Individuals or organizations that appear to have either pro-privatization or anti-privatization perspectives have conducted much of the research on this topic. It is difficult to determine the full cost, or total cost, of direct government service delivery (GAO, 1994; Industry Commission, 1996; Martin, 1992), which makes comparisons with private sector service delivery costs problematic. Most of the credible evidence from studies conducted in the Commonwealth of Australia (Domberger & Rimmer, 1994; Industry Commission, 1996), Canada (McDavid, 1996, 2001); the United Kingdom (Rao & Young, 1995; Walsh, 1995; Walsh & Davis, 1993), and the United States (Dilger, Moffett, & Struyk, 1997; GAO, 1997; Kettner & Martin, 1996; Martin, 1997) as well as multi-country studies (Hinke, 1993) suggests that contracting for public sector services generally results in lower service delivery costs.

The amount of cost savings that results from contracting for public sector services varies depending upon the type of service, the degree of competition present in the procurement, the location of service provision (urban/rural), and other factors. Not every instance of contracting leads to lower service delivery costs; in many instances contracting has actually resulted in higher service delivery costs. In a meta-analysis (a study of studies) of 28 examples of contracting for a variety of different public sector services in five different countries, the researcher concluded that contract service delivery resulted in lower overall service delivery costs of between 8% and 14% (Hodge, 1999, p. 461; 2000, p. 129). The researcher also noted that none of the 28 studies included the cost of contract administration and monitoring (transaction costs) in the cost of contract service delivery, which means that the cost savings were probably overstated. Other research suggests that on average, governments usually save between 5% and 20% by contracting for public sector services (Chi & Jasper, 1998, p. 10; Domberger & Rimmer, 1994, pp. 447-448; Industry Commission, 1996, p. 128; Walsh, 1995, p. 37; Walsh & Davis, 1993, pp. 141-154; Wilson & Game, 1994, p. 333).

A related issue is whether cost savings are short term only or if the savings continue over time. Four major studies have addressed this question. In a 20-year time series analysis of contracting for solid waste collection services in Canadian and U.S. cities, the researchers concluded, "Cost increases for refuse collection in competitive service cities were held to levels substantially below increases in the consumer price index" (Ammons & Hill, 1995, p. 22). The caveat here is that the contractors included not only private sector firms but also in-house contractors that had won public-private competitions. A U.S. study conducted by the Center for Naval Analysis found that cost savings continued over several years (Gansler, 2002, p. 10). Likewise, a New Zealand study found that the cost savings continued over the life of the contract (Domberger, Jensen, & Stonecash, 2002). However, the results of a more recent Canadian study (McDavid, 2001) suggest that the magnitude of overall cost savings attributable to contracting for public sector services may be declining over time as government service delivery becomes more efficient.

Service Quality

Much less research has been done on the subject of the quality of contracted services. The lack of research in this area may say something about how difficult it is to define and measure quality for many government services. Most of the credible evidence from studies conducted in Australia, the United Kingdom, and the United States suggests that contract service delivery is generally of equal or better quality than direct government service delivery (Dilger et al., 1997; Industry Commission, 1996; Kettner & Martin, 1996; Walsh & Davis, 1993).

In a study of America's 100 largest cities, survey respondents reported that contracting resulted in improved service quality in most instances (Dilger et al., 1997). Similar findings were reported for a major national study of contracted human services in the United States (Kettner & Martin, 1996). A large national study of local government's use of contracting in the United Kingdom (Walsh & Davis, 1993) concluded that contract service quality was generally equal to or better than government service delivery. However, a review of prior studies of contracting for public sector services in Australia, conducted by the Industry Commission (1996, p. 102), produced more diverse results. The studies reported on by the Industry Commission found that service quality increased in some instances, declined in others, and remained constant in still others. The meta-analysis study also considered the issue of service quality; the researcher found no quality distinctions between contract service delivery and government service delivery (Hodge, 1999).

Public Employees

Virtually every study that has considered the effect of service contracting on public employment has found that the numbers of public employees have decreased. With the exception of new public services that have never been offered by a government, it is almost a tautology that contracting for public sector services results in fewer public employees. The more important question is: What happens to those employees? Do they find other government jobs? Do they go to work for contractors? Or do they find themselves terminated?

The majority of credible evidence suggests that most public employees affected by contracting for public sector services find other jobs with the same government agency. Significant proportions go to work for contractors; and, unfortunately, significant proportions also find themselves terminated. For example, a study showing the effects service of contracting had on public sanitation employees working for Alabama cities found that 41% transferred to other jobs with the same government; 17% took jobs with contractors; 4% accepted other non-government jobs; 4% retired; and 33% were terminated (Smith, 1996, pp. 60-64). Conversely, a study of municipal governments in Illinois found that of 296 public employees affected by contracting, only 3% terminated (Johnson & Walzer, 1996, p. 30). A review of the effect of contracting for public sector services on employees of commonwealth, state, and local government departments in Australia found that of approximately 11,600 affected employees, 71% were transferred to other positions within the same government or were hired by contractors, and 29% were terminated (Industry Commission, 1996, p. 162). The National Commission for Employment Policy (NCEP) (1988) conducted the most comprehensive study of the effect of contracting on public employees in the United States. The NCEP study looked at two large government agencies, the U.S. Department of Defense and Los Angeles County, California. According to the study, of the nearly 4,000 public employees affected by service contracting in these two government agencies, 75% were placed in other government jobs, another 8% went to work for contractors; 12% either retired or left government voluntarily; and less than 5% were terminated (pp. 18-19).

A related issue here is the contention that service contracting has a disparate impact on minority public employees. Most of the credible evidence on this topic supports the conclusion that contracting for public sector services has no such effect (Industry Commission, 1996; NCEP, 1988; Smith, 1996; Suggs, 1986). For example, an early study of contracting for public sector services in 10 U.S. cities specifically looked at this issue and found no evidence of disparate treatment in terms of contractor hiring practices. According to the author of the study, the Joint Center for Political Studies, "displaced minority workers were hired by private service providers in about the same proportion as they had been by city departments" (Suggs, 1986, p. 14). In both the Alabama and the NCEP studies cited above, no difference was found in the numbers of ethnic, minority public employees who were terminated vis-à-vis non-minority public employees (NCEP, 1988; Smith, 1996). Redundancies, or terminations, due to contracting for public sector services in Australia have been reported to have a disparate impact on women, people with less education, and people whose native language is not English (Industry Commission, 1996).

Salaries and Wages

One of the major disadvantages and criticisms of service contracting is that displaced public employees who accept positions with contractors receive lower salaries and wages than they earned in their former government jobs. This is a concern frequently voiced by organized labor and particularly by the AFSCME (1983, 1987). Some studies have documented this phenomenon (Suggs, 1989). Other studies have found that salaries and wages frequently were held constant (Pendleton, 1997) and, in some cases, actually increased (Walsh & Davis, 1993). Much of the credible evidence suggests that a significant portion of public employees who accept positions with contractors do so at reduced salaries and wages, but that this is not a universal phenomenon.

More than a decade ago, researchers studying contracting for public sector services in the U.S. found that the ability of private sectors firms to reduce service delivery costs was related less to the lowering of salaries and wages and more to the differential use of labor. The differential use of labor includes such practices as the use of fewer workers, the use of more part-time workers, multitasking (i.e., employees performing more than one task), and the provision of fewer paid vacation and sick-leave days (Domberger et al., 2002; GAO, 2001b; Stevens, 1984). Studies of contracting for public sector services in the United Kingdom have reported similar findings. Contractors reduce costs through efficiency gains created by: using fewer total workers, using more part-time workers, making shift changes, and altering vacation schedules (Foster, 1993; Martin, 1997; Pendleton, 1997; Walsh & Davis, 1993). In a major study of contracting for public sector services in the United Kingdom, the researchers found that basic wages were not changed. However, reductions in staff hours worked occurred in 56% of cases; working hours were changed in 51% of cases; bonus systems were changed or abolished in 47% of cases; shift schedules were changed in 25% of cases; and holiday and sick-pay changes were instituted in 30% of cases (Walsh & Davis, 1993, pp. v-vi).

The Australian Industry Commission's study of contracting for public sector services cited above found that wages paid to former public employees working for contractors "are often lower," but also noted that "changes in wages and conditions may often reflect differences in private and public sector awards, as well as general labour market trends such as the greater use of part-time and casual labour" (Industry Commission, 1996, p. 15).

Competition

The *Dictionary of Purchasing Terms*, published by the National Institute of Governmental Purchasing (NIGP) (2002), defines competition as: "the effort of two or more vendors to secure the business of a purchaser by the offer of the most favorable terms as to price, quality, promptness of delivery, and/or service" (p. 17). Competition then involves at least two, but preferably more than two, responsive and responsible potential contractors. Little research on this topic exists because it is generally acknowledged that competition is absent for many, if not most, public sector service procurements (Kettl, 1993; Sclar, 2000). A few studies have documented the lack of competition. For example, a study in the United Kingdom over a three-year period found that governments actually received an average of only one bid per contract (Walsh & Davis, 1993, p. 67). Competition traditionally has been absent in contracts for human services in the U.S. (DeHoog, 1990). More recent research by Savas (2002), however, finds that the amount of competition is increasing.

Governments have struggled with various ways of promoting increased competition in public sector service contracting. Two approaches that have had positive results are public-private competition and the unbundling of public services. Unbundling refers to dividing a service into smaller portions. The idea is that by unbundling services and creating several smaller procurements, more small businesses and firms will be interested in and capable of competing to perform the work. Unbundling is frequently done on the basis of geography. A large service area, such as a city or county, is divided into geographical regions. Then, either concurrent or sequential procurements are conducted for the service in each of the regions. For example, the City of Phoenix, Arizona (Martin, 1999b) has conducted several *simultaneous* procurements for solid waste collection services, while the County of Arlington, Virginia (Martin, 1999a), has conducted multiple *sequential* procurements for park maintenance services. It should be noted that the competitive, or market model, is not the only approach to contracting for public sector services. There is at least some literature describing a "partnership" model of contracting that does not require the presence of competition (Lawther, 2002; Shetterly, 2000). The total quality management (TQM) literature also suggests that organizations should develop "partnership" relationships with their suppliers (Crosby, 1980; Gabor, 1990; Lawther, 2002; McRobb, 1989).

> *The total quality management (TQM) literature...suggests that organizations should develop "partnership" relationships with their suppliers.*

In summary, what does the majority of the credible research evidence suggest in terms of the purported advantages and disadvantages of contracting for public-sector services? As noted earlier, not all of the purported advantages and disadvantages have been subjected to empirical testing; for others, the research findings are mixed. However, for at least some of the purported advantages and disadvantages, clear and compelling research evidence does exist (see Figure 1).

Contracting for public-sector services usually results in:
• Lower service delivery costs;
• Equal or better service quality;.
• Fewer government employees;
• Transfer of most affected public employees to other government positions or to jobs with contractors;
• No disparate impact on minority public employees;
• Lower salaries and wages for public employees that accept employment with contractors, and
• The absence of competition for most public sector service procurements.

Figure 1. *What the Research Says about Contracting for Public Sector Services.*

Again, the caution is offered that not all examples of contracting for public sector services result in advantageous conditions. It should be noted that not all researchers are willing to accept the preponderance of the credible evidence as sufficient to support the noted conclusions; this is particularly true in cases involving issues of cost savings and service quality. For these researchers, only evidence "beyond a reasonable doubt" is sufficient to make such an assertion. For a representative sampling of this perspective, see Sclar (2000) and Boyne (1998).

Services Most Frequently Contracted

Two recent studies provide an overview of the services most frequently contracted for by U.S. state and local governments. The Council of State Governments (Chi & Jasper, 1998) conducted the state level study, which is based on interviews with 477 state officials. The data are presented by state (n=50) (Figure 2).

State Governments (No. of States)
27 states contracted out for Highway Maintenance
24 states contracted out for Correctional Medical Services
23 states contracted out for Custodial Services
23 states contracted out for Landscaping
21 states contracted out for Asbestos Removal
20 states contracted out for Pest Control
19 states contracted out for Moving Services
15 states contracted out for Facility Maintenance

Figure 2. *Contracting for Public Sector Services by States.*

Source: Adapted from Chi, K., & Jasper, C. (1998). *Privatization practices: A review of privatization in state government.* Lexington, KY: The Council of State Governments.

The International City/County Management Association (ICMA) (Martin, 1999a) conducted the local government study. The local government study is based on responses from 1,586 city and county governments nationwide (n=1,586) (Figure 3).

Local Governments (% of Cities/Counties)
Vehicle Towing & Storage (79%)
Solid Waste Collection (60%)
Legal services (51%)
Residential Solid Waste Collection (49%)
Child Day Care (48%)
Tree Trimming & Planting (36%)
Street Repair (34%)
Fleet Maintenance (33%)

Figure 3. *Contracting for Public Sector Services by Local Governments.*

Source: Adapted from Martin, L. L. (1999). *Contracting for service delivery: Local government choices.* Washington, DC: International City/County Management Association.

The differences in service contracting by state and local governments appear to be a function of particular service preferences rather than differences in governmental responsibilities. It appears that any of the services most frequently contracted by state departments and agencies could just as easily be contracted by local governments and vice versa. While these studies raise the question as to why there are so many differences, unfortunately neither of the two studies provides any answers. A series of studies conducted by the ICMA provide a broader view of the services most frequently contracted for by local governments.

ICMA (Moulder, 2003) has conducted five national surveys (1982, 1988, 1992, 1997, and 2003) of service contracting by U.S. local governments. In the series of tables presented as Appendix A, Tables 1 - 5, change and continuity in contracting for public sector services over time can be observed. These surveys were conducted using five ICMA service categories: (a) public works and transportation; (b) public safety; (c) health and human services; (d) parks, recreation, arts, and culture; and (e) support services. Not all services were included in all four surveys. An asterisk notes missing data in the tables. The 1997 and 2003 surveys collected data using four categories—intra-governmental contracts, for-profit, not-for-profit, and franchise/concessions. The 1982 and 1992 surveys collected data using two categories—contracts with for-profits and contracts with not-for-profits. The 1988 survey used only one category—contracts with private sector organizations.

Public Works and Transportation Services

Appendix A – Table 1 shows changes in local governments' use of contracting for public works and transportation services over the 21 years (1982-2003) covered by the five surveys. Three services that show significant increases are street repair (+12%), street/parking lot cleaning (+9%), and parking lot/garage operations (+ 9%). While the majority of the services in Appendix A – Table 1 show increases over the 21-year period, a few show little or no change, and some (bus system operations, para-transit system operations, and airport operations) show a slight decline. However, the most significant change in statistics shown in this table is the recent (1997-2003) declines in contracting for residential solid waste collection (-10%) and commercial solid waste collection (-17%). Solid waste collection, both residential and commercial, are two of the services that local governments first contracted out and which fostered and promoted much of the initial interest in contracting for services. The data suggest that contracting for solid waste collection may have lost some of its appeal in recent years.

The results of the surveys conducted in the Public Works and Transportation category, with the exception of bus system operations and para-transit system operations, indicate that local governments make more use of for-profit contractors for public works and transportation than they do of not-for-profit contractors. The other services identified in Table 1 of Appendix A remain relatively stable over the five studies.

Health and Human Services

Appendix A – Table 2 looks at the extent of local government contracting for health and human services across the five surveys. At first glance, the services appear to have remained fairly stable between 1982 and 2003. However, when focusing on the use of for-profits versus not-for-profits, a different and more interesting picture emerges. The use of for-profit contractors for child welfare (+6%) has doubled. Also, the use of for-profit contractors has significantly increased for both drug and alcohol treatment (+12%) as well as for the operation of mental health and mental retardation programs and facilities (+12%). These data suggest that local government attitudes may be changing when decisions are made regarding the use of for-profits to provide contracted health and human services traditionally provided by not-for-profits. Another interesting statistic shown in Table 2 of Appendix A is the finding that so many of the services demonstrate a decline between 1997 and 2003 (9 out of 12 categories declined in the last 5 years—five of which are in the range of 12-15%). Again, the data may be suggesting that contracting out for health and human services, like public works and transportation, has lost some of its appeal in recent years.

...the data may be suggesting that contracting out for health and human services...has lost some of its appeal in recent years.

Public Safety Services

Changes in local governments' use of contracting for public safety services between 1982 and 2003 are itemized in the table shown in Appendix A – Table 3. Most local government contracting in this area involves "ancillary" services (emergency medical, ambulance, and vehicle towing storage) as opposed to "core" services, such as crime prevention and patrol, police and fire communications, and fire prevention and suppression services. Contracting for ancillary services has remained relatively stable over the five studies. The area that utilizes contracting out the most is vehicle towing and storage; 80% of local governments reported contracting for this service in both 1982 and 2003.

Parks, Recreation, Arts, and Cultural Services

Appendix A – Table 4 presents the data covering local government use of contracting for parks, recreation, arts, and cultural services for the years 1982-2003. In reviewing the data of for-profits and not-for-profits, there are notable changes in three services: parks, landscaping, and maintenance (+9%); operation of convention centers and auditoriums (+17%); and operation of cultural and arts programs (+9%). Local governments make significant use of contracting for the operation of cultural and arts programs and the operation of museums. In both instances, contractors are predominately not-for-profits.

Support Services

Appendix A – Table 5 displays data dealing with local government use of contracting for support services over the 21-year period (1982-2003) covered by the five surveys. The first observation is that local governments do not often utilize not-for-profit contractors for support services. Upon observing the changes over time, the majority of services demonstrate increases between 1982 and 2003. The following increases are significant: building and grounds maintenance (+10); building security (+11); all three categories of fleet maintenance (+9%), heavy equipment (+5%) and all others (+7%); legal services (+7%); and delinquent tax collection (+8%). The steady decline in contracting for data processing services (-6%) during this same time period is also noteworthy. Finally, local governments make more use of contracting for "blue collar" types of services (e.g., building/grounds maintenance, building security, and fleet management) than "white collar" types of services (e.g., secretarial services, personnel services, public relations, and information services). An exception to this statement is legal services, which has been the most frequently contracted support service.

To summarize the trends in local governments' use of contracting for public sector services over the past two decades (1982-2003), it appears that their use of public sector service contracting is broad-based and involves all five of the ICMA service areas. The majority of services identified in Appendix A, Tables 1 – 5, demonstrate an increase over the last 21 years, albeit a modest increase in many instances. Certain historically popular services (e.g., commercial and residential solid waste collection) declined between 1997 and 2003, suggesting that local governments may be reevaluating their use of contracting in these areas. Local governments appear to be increasing their use of for-profit contractors for health and human services, an area traditionally dominated almost exclusively by not-for-profits. Regarding public safety services, local governments make more use of contracting for "ancillary" services than "core" services. Finally, local governments are more likely to use contracting for "blue collar" rather than "white collar" support services.

The Legal and Regulatory Context of Contracting for Public Sector Services

The widespread use of contracting for public sector services is still a relatively recent development compared to the procurement of supplies, materials, and construction. Consequently, legal and regulatory frameworks are not as well developed for public sector services. The constitution of a "public sector service" varies from government to government as do the circumstances under which various service contracting concepts and tools can be used, such as:

- Core services;
- Sealed competitive bidding;
- Competitive negotiation;
- Multi-step procurements;
- Best value analysis;
- Best and final offer;
- Public-private competition;
- Cost comparison approaches; and
- Contract types (cost reimbursement, fixed-fee, fixed price, performance-based, etc.).

Before attempting to implement any of the public sector service contracting concepts and tools discussed in this text, public procurement professionals should ensure that their legal and regulatory frameworks provide for their use.

The legal and regulatory context of contracting for public sector services is also constantly changing. New laws, statutes, ordinances and regulations are frequently issued, changed, and amended. Court decisions and decisions of boards of contract appeals also constantly alter the legal and regulatory framework of service contracting. Recent United States and state Supreme Court cases have altered the context of contracting for public sector services. These court cases touch on two areas of considerable importance: (a) government liability issues and (b) the legal right of governments to privatize or contract for public sector services.

U.S. Supreme Court Decisions

Richardson and Walker v. McKnight. Over the years, state, as well as some federal courts, have held that contractor employees working under government contracts are entitled to the same legal protection as regular public employees. The situation changed with *Richardson and Walker v. McKnight*. The 1997 case involved the legal liability of contractor employees working in a correctional facility. McKnight was an inmate serving time in a Tennessee prison operated by the Corrections Corporation of America (CCA). He alleged mistreatment by two CCA prison guards (Richardson and Walker). The major issue in this case involved whether contractors providing public services under government contractors are entitled to the same "qualified immunity" from legal actions that regular state employees have when carrying out their assigned duties. The court held that contract employees do not have qualified immunity (Associated Press, 1998).

This case has important implications when contracting for public sector services. Governments contract for a variety of public sector services (e.g., jails, prisons, nursing homes, and mental health facilities) that involve imposing involuntary restrictions on service recipients. The *Richardson and Walker v. McKnight* decision affords service recipients, and their advocates, additional legal protection. Governments face the possibility of being named as co-defendants in legal actions on the basis of failure to exercise due diligence in monitoring and supervising contractors.

Correctional Service Corporation v. Malesko. The rights of inmates to sue contractors were somewhat restricted by the U.S. Supreme Court decision handed down in 2001. In this case, an inmate (Malesko) sued a contractor (Correctional Services Corporation) operating a detention center under contract with the Federal Bureau of Prisons. Malesko's suit was based on alleged violations of his civil rights. The Court held that Federal prisoners being detained in contract facilities may not bring civil rights cases against either contractors or the Federal Government, but may bring actions against individual contractor employees (Segal, 2002).

O'Hare Truck Service, Inc. et al. v. City of Northlake. This 1996 decision involved the removal of a trucking company (O'Hare Truck Service) from the list of qualified approved bidders to provide vehicle towing and storage services in Northlake, Illinois. Like many governments, the City of Northlake used a rotational system for selecting contractors. The owner of O'Hare Truck Service had refused to contribute to the political campaign of the newly elected mayor of Northlake. In retaliation, O'Hare alleged, the mayor subsequently cancelled O'Hare's contract. O'Hare brought suit, which ultimately reached the U.S. Supreme Court. The court found for O'Hare. In the court's written opinion, Justice Kennedy, writing for the majority, reminds all U.S. governments, "We decline to draw the line excluding independent contractors from the same First Amendment safeguards of political association afforded to employees" (Hamilton, 1999, p. 57).

State Supreme Court Decisions

Professional Engineers in California Government et al. v. Department of Transportation. This California Supreme Court case, which had been in the courts since 1988, was finally decided in 1997. In the mid-1980s, the California Department of Transportation (CalTrans) adopted a policy of contracting for all professional engineering services. State engineers brought suit alleging that contracting violated constitutional provisions designed to protect the state's civil service system. The California Supreme Court found in favor of the state engineers stating that CalTrans had indeed violated provisions of the state's constitution. The court based its decision on the fact that CalTrans chose to privatize engineering services simply as a public policy preference. The court stated that privatization and contracting of public services is only permissible if such decisions are based on considerations of economy and efficiency (California Supreme Court, 1997). The Court's decision has been broadly interpreted as applying to all California governments. The decision also has implications for other governments. Public employee unions will undoubtedly be looking at what other state constitutions have to say about civil service protections vis-à-vis privatization and contracting out. Additionally, when courts look for guidance in deciding cases, they frequently turn to the decisions of other courts. The decision in *Professional Engineers in California Government et al. v. Department of Transportation* will probably receive a lot of attention in years to come.

Colorado Association of Public Employees v. Department of Highways. This case, decided by the Colorado Supreme Court in 1991, addressed the issue of the specific statutory authority for Colorado state departments and agencies to privatize and contract for public sector services. The Colorado Association of Public Employees alleged that the Colorado Department of Highways had no specific statutory authority to privatize or contract public sector services historically provided by state employees. The Colorado Supreme Court agreed. This decision forced the Colorado State Legislature to pass a series of statutes over a period of years (1991 to 1995) to provide a legal basis for Colorado state departments and agencies to engage in privatization and contracting (Colorado Commission on Privatization, 1997). The Colorado case, like the California case, has implications that transcend borders. Many governments have adopted privatization and contracting as a public policy preference. At least some of these governments may well have undiscovered constitutional or statutory provisions that preclude these practices.

Ethical Issues in Contracting for Public Sector Services

The ethical conduct of public procurement professionals is always important, but it becomes particularly important in the case of contracting for public sector services. Unlike contracting for goods and construction, service contracting is less structured and makes less use of competitive sealed bidding and fixed price contracts and more use of requests for proposals and various creative payment mechanisms such as performance-based contracts. In these situations, public procurement professionals are provided with, and are expected to use, *increased* professional *discretion*. With increased professional discretion comes increased professional responsibility to ensure that all activities associated with a public procurement, contract award, and subsequent contract administration and monitoring are conducted in accordance with the highest ethical standards.

With increased professional discretion comes increased professional responsibility...

In addition to the ethical prescriptions contained in NIGP's Code of Ethics as well as the ethics section of the American Bar Association's *2000 Model Procurement Code for State and Local Governments*, public procurement professionals should be particularly sensitive to the ethical issues involved in:

- Conducting a make-or-buy decision;
- Making cost comparisons between in-house and contract service delivery;
- Evaluating public sector service bids and proposals using subjective evaluation criteria such as occur in best value analysis; and
- Public-private competitions including: (a) the appropriateness of tax-supported

public units competing against the private sector, (b) level playing field considerations, (c) conflict of interest situations when evaluating in-house bids and proposals, and (d) the ethical treatment of displaced public employees.

References

American Bar Association (2000). *The 2000 model procurement code for state and local governments.* Chicago: American Bar Association.

American Federation of State, County and Municipal Employees (AFSCME). (n.d.). *Private profit, public risk: The contracting out of professional services.* Washington, DC: AFSCME.

American Federation of State, County and Municipal Employees (AFSCME). (1983). *Passing the bucks.* Washington, DC: AFSCME.

American Federation of State, County and Municipal Employees (AFSCME). (1987). *When public services go private.* Washington, DC: AFSCME.

Ammons, D., & Hill, D. (1995). The viability of public-private competition as a long-term service delivery strategy. *Public Productivity & Management Review, 19*(1), 12-24.

Associated Press. (1998). *Supreme Court rules on private prison guards.* Available from http://govnewsorg.mhonarc/gov/topic/admin/privatization/msg00011.html.

Bank of Canada. (1997, Summer). The fiscal impact of privatization in Canada. *Bank of Canada Review,* 25-40.

Boyne, G. (1998, November/December). Bureaucratic theory meets reality: Public choice and service contracting in U.S. local government. *Public Administration Review, 58,* 474-484.

California Supreme Court. (1997, May 15). *Opinion no. S042591.*

Chi, K., & Jasper, C. (1998). *Privatization practices: A review of privatization in state government.* Lexington, KY: The Council of State Governments.

City of Charlotte, North Carolina. (1995). *Competition process handbook.* Charlotte: City of Charlotte, North Carolina.

The Civic Federation. (1996). *From privatization to innovation: A study of 16 cities.* Chicago: The Civic Federation.

Colorado Commission on Privatization. (1997). *More competitive government: A report to the general assembly by the Commission on Privatization.* Denver: Colorado Commission on Privatization.

County of San Diego, California. (1998). *Managed competition guide.* San Diego: County of San Diego.

Crosby, P. (1980). *Quality is free.* New York: Mentor Books.

DeHoog, R. (1990). Competition, negotiation, or cooperation: Three models for service contracting. *Administration & Society, 22,* 317-340.

Dilger, R., Moffett, R., & Struyk, L. (1997, January/February). Privatization of municipal services in America's largest cities. *Public Administration Review, 57,* 21-26.

Dobel, J. (2001, March/April). Paradigms, traditions and keeping the faith. *Public Administration Review, 61,* 166-171.

Domberger, S., Jensen, P., & Stonecash, R. (2002). Examining the magnitude and sources of cost savings associated with outsourcing. *Public Performance & Management Review, 26*(2), 148-168.

Domberger, S., & Rimmer, S. (1994). Competitive tendering and contracting in the public sector: A survey. *International Journal of the Economics of Business, 1*(3), 439-453.

Donahue, J. (1989). *The privatization decision: Public ends, private means.* New York: Basic Books.

Drucker, P. (1969). *The age of discontinuity.* New York: Harper & Row.

Ewoh, A. (1999). An inquiry into the role of public employees and managers in privatization. *Review of Public Personnel Administration 19*(1), 8-27.

Fisk, D. (1982). Issues in contracting for public services from the private sector. *Management Information Service Report, 14*(5). Washington, DC: International City/County Management Association.

Fisk, D., Kiesling, H., & Muller, T. (1978). *Private provision of public services: An overview*. Washington, DC: The Urban Institute.

Foster, D. (1993). Industrial relations in local government: The impact of privatization. *The Political Quarterly, 64*(1), 49-58.

Gabor, A. (1990). *The man who discovered quality*. New York: Random House.

Gansler, J. (2002). *A vision of the government as a world-class buyer: Major procurement issues for the coming decade*. Arlington, VA: The IBM Center for the Business of Government. Retrieved March 10, 2003, from htttp://www.businessofgovernment.org.

Gore, A. (1993). *From red tape to results: Creating a government that works better and costs less*. Washington, DC: U.S. Government Printing Office.

Hamilton, D. (1999, January/February). The coming judicial assault on patronage. *Public Administration Review, 59*, 54-61.

Hatry, H. (1983). *A review of private approaches for the delivery of public services*. Washington, DC: The Urban Institute.

Henry. N. (1999). *Public administration and public affairs* (7th ed.). Upper Saddle River, NJ: Prentice Hall.

Hinke, J. (1993). *Cost savings from privatization: A study of study findings*. Los Angeles: The Reason Public Policy Institute.

Hodge, G. (1999). Competitive tendering and contracting out. *Public Productivity & Management Review, 22*(4), 455-469.

Hodge, G. (2000). *Privatization: An international review of performance*. Boulder, CO: Westview Press.

Industry Commission. (1996). *Competitive tendering and contracting by public sector agencies*. Report No. 48. Melbourne, Australia: Australian Government Printing Office.

Jensen, R. (n.d.). New wave privatization: or public-private competition and cooperation [Monograph].

Jensen, R. (1987). *The Phoenix approach to privatization*. Testimony in June before the Subcommittee on Small Business Anti-Trust Impact of Deregulation and Privatization, together with transcripts of various talk show interviews and newspaper articles from 1984 to 1988. Phoenix, AZ: City of Phoenix, Public Works Department.

Johnson, R., & Walzer, N. (1996). *Competition for city services: Has the time arrived?* Springfield, IL: Illinois Office of the Comptroller.

Kavanagh, I., & Parker, D. (2000). *Contracting out of local government services in the UK: A case study of transactions costs*. Retrieved August 27, 2002, from http://www.research.abs.aston.ac.uk/wpaper/wpmenu4.html.

Keene, W. (1998). Federal outsourcing: Part 1. *The Public Manager, 27*(1), 13-16.

Kettl, D. (1993). *Sharing power: Public governance and private markets*. Washington, DC: The Brookings Institution.

Kettner, P., & Martin, L. L. (1996). Purchase of service contracting versus government service delivery: The views of state human service administrators. *Journal of Sociology & Social Welfare, 23*(2), 107-119.

Lawther, W. (2002). *Contracting for the 21st century: A partnership model*. Arlington, VA: The IBM Center for the Business of Government. Retrieved March 10, 2003, from htttp://www.businessofgovernment.org.

Martin, L. L. (1997). Public-private competition in the United Kingdom: Lessons for U.S. local governments. *State & Local Government Review, 29*(2), 81-90.

Martin, L. L. (1998). Circular A-76: Privatization or public private competition. *The Public Manager, 27*(3), 51-53.

Martin, L. L. (1999a). *Contracting for service delivery: Local government choices*. Washington, DC: International City/County Management Association.

Martin, L. L. (1999b). Public-private competition: A public employee alternative to privatization. *Review of Public Personnel Administration, 6*(1), 59-70.

McDavid, J. (1996). Advantages and disadvantages of contracting out local government services. *Local Services Research Review, 1*(1), 1-5.

McDavid, J. (2001). Solid-waste contracting-out, competition, and bidding practices among Canadian local governments. *Canadian Public Administration, 44*(1), 1-25.

McRobb, M. (1989). *Purchasing and quality*. New York: Marcel-Dekker.

Moulder, E., Director of Survey Research and Information Management. (2003). *Contracting for service delivery: Local government choices*, Special Data Issue No. 4. Washington, DC: International City/County Management Association (ICMA).

National Commission for Employment Policy (NCEP) (1988). *Privatization and public employees: The impact of city and county contracting out on government workers.* Washington, DC: NCEP.

National Institute of Governmental Purchasing, Inc. (NIGP). (2002). *Dictionary of purchasing terms* (5th ed.). Herndon, VA: NIGP.

Osborne, D., & Gaebler, T. (1992). *Reinventing government.* Reading, MA: Addison-Wesley.

Pendleton, A. (1997). What impact has privatization had on pay and employment: A review of the UK experience. *Industrial Relations*, 52(3), 554-579.

Rao, N., & Young, K. (1995). *Competition, contracts and change: The local authority experience of CCT.* London: Joseph Rowntree Foundation.

Rendell, E. (1994). *Privatization: It can and does work.* New York: The Carnegie Council on Privatization.

Riccucci, N. (2001, March/April). The "old" public management versus the "new" public management: Where does public administration fit in? *Public Administration Review*, 61, 172-183.

Savas, E. S. (1971). Municipal Monopoly. *Harpers Magazine*, 55, 49.

Savas, E. S. (1977a). *Alternatives for delivering public services.* Boulder, CO: Westview Press.

Savas, E. S. (1977b). An empirical study of competition in municipal service delivery. *Public Administration Review*, 37, 717-724.

Savas, E. S. (2000). *Privatization and public-private partnership.* New York: Seven Bridges Press.

Savas. E. S. (2002). Competition and choice in New York City social services. *Public Administration Review*, 62(1), 82-91.

Sclar, E. (2000). *You don't always get what you pay for: The economics of privatization.* Ithaca, NY: Cornell University Press.

Segal, G. (2002). *Legal Brief: Supreme court rules on private prison liability.* Retrieved May 17, 2002, from http://www.rppi.org/pu15.html.

Shetterly, D. (2000). The influence of contract design on contractor performance: The case of residential refuse collection. *Public Performance & Management Review*, 24(1), 53-68.

Smith, G. (1996). The impact of privatization on public personnel administration: What happens to public employees. Unpublished doctoral dissertation, Auburn University, Alabama.

Stevens, B. (1984). *Delivering municipal services efficiently: A comparison of municipal and private service delivery.* Washington, DC: U.S. Department of Housing and Urban Development.

Stone, M. N., Bell, A. K., & Poole, J. B. (1997). *Perspectives of privatization by municipal governments.* Washington, DC: National League of Cities.

Suggs, R. (1989). *Minorities and privatization: Economic mobility at risk.* Washington, DC: Joint Center for Political Studies Press.

Treasury Board of Canada Secretariat (TBC). (n.d.). *1998 purchasing activity, revised.* Retrieved December 19, 2001, from http://www.tbs-sct.ge/.ca.pubs.

U.S. General Accounting Office (GAO). (1997). *Privatization: Lessons learned by state and local governments.* Report No. GAO/GGD-97-48. Washington, DC. GAO.

U.S. General Accounting Office (GAO). (2001a). Commercial Activities Panel, San Antonio Public Hearing. Retrieved December 6, 2001, from http://www.gao.gov.a76panel/index.html.

U.S. General Accounting Office (GAO). (2001b). Current condition of federal contracting. PowerPoint presentation to members of the Commercial Activities Panel. Retrieved December 10, 2003, from http://www.goa.gov/a76panel/powerpoint/ctcondition.

U.S. Office of Management and Budget (OMB). (2003). *Performance of commercial activities (Circular No. A-76, revised).* Washington, DC: OMB.

Walsh, K. (1995). Competition and public service delivery. In J. Stewart & Gerry Stoker (Eds.), *Local government in the*

1990s (pp. 28-48)). London: Macmillan.

Walsh, K., & Davis, H. (1993). *Competition and service: The impact of the Local Government Act of 1988*. London: Department of the Environment, HMSO.

Wilson, D., & Game, C. (1994). The impact of compulsory competitive tendering. In *Local government in the United Kingdom* (pp. 324-339). London: Macmillan.

Chapter 2

Deciding To Contract

A make-or-buy decision is a structured process for determining if a public sector service should be provided in-house by public employees or contracted out for delivery by a specific supplier. Conducting a make-or-buy decision requires an assessment of several factors. Price or cost is, of course, a major factor. However, other factors should also be considered: (a) service quality, (b) capabilities and capacities of potential contractors, (c) impact on public employees, (d) legal issues, and (e) political considerations. The nature of the service itself can also make it more or less amenable to contracting. How to conduct a make-or-buy decision and how to compute and compare the costs of in-house and contract service delivery, as well as the issues most frequently encountered carrying out these tasks will be discussed. A methodology for conducting a make-or-buy decision will be presented along with three approaches to comparing the costs of in-house versus contract service delivery.

Make-or-Buy Situations

The public sector must address some preparatory issues before moving to a make-or-buy decision: Is the issue a make-or-buy situation? Should the product or service be considered as an option? Is the issue an inherent governmental function? Is the issue a core or ancillary public sector service?

Not all decisions to contract for a public sector service involve a make-or-buy decision. Consider a public sector service that has a history of being contracted. Governments may use contracted services simply because elected officials or administrators prefer this form of service delivery. Funding source requirements, such as a federal grant, may also stipulate that a particular service or activity must be contracted. In these types of situations, no real make-or-buy decision is involved.

Inherently Governmental Functions

Some people, both inside as well as outside governments, believe that "inherently governmental functions" should not be contracted. The issue of inherently governmental functions is a controversial one. Not everyone agrees as to what constitutes an inherently governmental function, and some people argue that there is no such thing as an inherently governmental function. Regardless of whose position is correct on this issue, the decision to consider contracting for a public sector service that can be considered an "inherently governmental function" may never progress to the make-or-buy decision stage; it may, instead, generate into a debate about the appropriate roles of the public and private sectors. The U.S. Office of Federal Procurement Policy (OFPP) has studied the issue of inherently governmental functions and has provided guidance to federal departments and agencies. The OFPP (1992) defines inherently governmental functions as any function that

> . . . is so intimately related to the public interest as to mandate performance by Government employees. These functions include those activities that require either the exercise of discretion in applying Governmental authority or the making of value judgments in making decisions for the Government. (p. 2)

Figure 4 is a list of services and activities the OFPP considers inherently governmental functions. The list represents "guidance" and, as such, should not be considered binding on any federal department or agency or state or local government. To provide further clarification, Figure 5 is a list of functions that are not considered inherently governmental by OFPP but could be, depending upon how contractors perform the work or the manner in which contracts are administered.

1.	The direct conduct of criminal investigations.
2.	The control of prosecutions and performance of adjudicatory functions (other than those relating to arbitration or other methods of alternative dispute resolution).
3.	The command of military forces, especially the leadership of military personnel who are members of the combat, combat support or combat service support role.
4.	The conduct of foreign relations and the determination of foreign policy.
5.	The determination of agency policy, such as determining the content and application of regulations, among other things.
6.	The determination of Federal program priorities or budget requests.
7.	The direct control of Federal employees.
8.	The direction and control of intelligence and counter-intelligence operations.
9.	The selection or nonselection of individuals for Federal Government employment.
10.	The approval of position descriptions and performance standards for Federal employees.
11.	The determination of what Government property is to be disposed of, and on what terms.

12.	In Federal procurement activities with respect to prime contracts: determining what supplies or services are to be acquired by the government; participating as a voting member on any source selection boards; approval of any contractual documents, to include documents defining requirements, incentive plans, and evaluation criteria; awarding contracts; administering contracts; terminating contracts; determining whether contract costs are reasonable, allocable and allowable.*
13.	The approval of agency responses to Freedom of Information Act requests.*
14.	The conduct of administrative hearings to determine the eligibility of any person for a security clearance, or involving actions that affect matters of personal reputation or eligibility to participate in Government programs.
15.	The approval of federal licensing actions and inspections.
16.	The determination of budget policy, guidance, and strategy.
17.	The collection, control, and disbursement of fees, royalties, duties, fines, taxes and other public funds, unless authorized by statute.*
18.	The control of the treasury accounts.
19.	The administration of public trusts.

*Portions of text are deleted.

Figure 4. *Office of Federal Procurement Policy Guidance on Inherently Governmental Functions.*

Source: U.S. Office of Federal Procurement Policy (OFPP). (1992). Policy letter 92-1—Inherently governmental functions (pp. 7-9). Washington, DC: OFPP.

1.	Services that involve or relate to budget preparation, including workload modeling, fact-finding, efficiency studies, and cost analysis.
2.	Services that involve or relate to reorganization and planning activities.
3.	Services that involve or relate to analyses, feasibility studies and strategy options to be used by agency personnel in developing policy.
4.	Services that involve or relate to the development of regulations.
5.	Services that involve or relate to the evaluation of another contractor's performance.
6.	Services in support of acquisition planning.
7.	Contractors providing assistance in contract management. *
8.	Contractors providing technical evaluation of contract proposals.
9.	Contractors providing assistance in the development of statements of work.
10.	Contractors providing support in preparing responses to Freedom of Information Act requests.
11.	Contractors working in any situation that permits or might permit them to gain access to confidential information and/or any other sensitive information. *
12.	Contractors providing information regarding agency policies or regulations, such as attending conferences on behalf of agency, conducting community relations campaigns, or conducting agency training courses.
13.	Contractors participating in any situation where it might be assumed that they are agency employees or representatives.
14.	Contractors participating as technical advisors to a source selection board or participating as voting or nonvoting members of a source evaluation board.
15.	Contractors serving as arbitrators or providing alternative methods of dispute resolution.

16.	Contractors constructing building or structures intended to be secure from electronic eavesdropping or other penetration by foreign governments.
17.	Contractors providing inspection services.
18.	Contractors providing legal advice and interpretations of regulations and statutes to Government officials.
19.	Contractors providing special non-law enforcement security activities that do not directly involve crime investigations, such as prisoner detention or transport and non-military national security details.

*Portions of text are deleted.

Figure 5. *Office of Federal Procurement Policy Guidance on Non-Inherently Governmental Functions.*

Source: U.S. Office of Federal Procurement Policy (OFPP). (1992). Policy letter 92-1—Inherently governmental functions (pp. 9-10). Washington, DC: OFPP.

Core Versus Ancillary Services

An issue related to the "inherently governmental functions" debate is the subject of core versus ancillary services. Ancillary services, also referred to as "commercial-type services," can be operationally defined as support or housekeeping-type activities, such as printing, custodial, security, water billing, parks maintenance, and landscape maintenance, among others. No consensus exists as to what constitutes a "core" service, and different governments may identify different services as core. Services that local governments tend to consider core are police, fire, and land use planning (Martin, 1993a, p. 2). Studies suggest that public sector services that involve the regulatory or coercive power of governments, such as the operation of jails and prisons, are also generally considered to be core (Becker, 2001; Becker & Mackelprang, 1990; Thompson & Elling, 2000).

Elected officials, citizens, and other stakeholders tend to be more concerned about contracting for core services than ancillary services. A study in the State of Michigan provides insights into the views of citizens on the issue of core versus ancillary services (Thompson & Elling, 2000). The Michigan study demonstrates that, in general, citizens appear to support the contracting of ancillary services, but are less predisposed to the contracting of core services. As Figure 6 illustrates, an inverse relationship exists between services that involve the coercive and regulatory powers of government and support for the contracting of those services. The general public tends to believe that ancillary or "commercial-type" services (e.g., garbage collection, custodial services, street cleaning, etc.) are the most appropriate for private sector service delivery. For just this reason, the first services designated

Elected officials, citizens, and other stakeholders tend to be more concerned about contracting for core services than ancillary services.

for competitive tendering in the United Kingdom were ancillary services: refuse collection, building cleaning, street cleaning, catering, grounds maintenance, and vehicle maintenance (Audit Commission, 1993).

Citizen Support for Contracting	SERVICES	Government Coercive and Regulatory Power
LOW ↓ ↓ HIGH	Operation of Maximum Security Prisons	HIGH ↑ ↑ LOW
	Enforcement of Building Safety Regulations	
	Police Services	
	Operation of Minimum Security Prisons	
	Fire Services	
	Services to Mentally Ill	
	Operation of Schools	
	Street Cleaning	
	Snow Removal	
	Clerical Services	
	Emergency Medical Services	
	Custodial Services	
	Solid Waste Collection	

Figure 6. *Citizens Views on Government Services Considered Appropriate for Private Sector Delivery.*

Source: Thompson, L., & Elling, R. (2000, July/August). Mapping patterns of support for privatization in the mass public: The case of Michigan. *Public Administration Review*, 60, 341.

A 1998 Florida study found that state legislators hold views similar to citizens. Services that involve the coercive or regulatory powers of government are considered less suitable for contracting (Becker, 2001). The Florida study is a replication of an older study of state legislators in all 50 states that reported essentially the same findings (Becker & Mackelprang, 1990).

While the experiences of Michigan and Florida, as well as local governments in the United Kingdom, do shed light on the issue of contracting for core versus ancillary public sector services, the caution must be made that the debate is one that can have significant variation from government to government. For example, the city of Scottsdale, Arizona, has a long history of contracting for fire suppression services that is generally considered by most local governments to be a core service.

Conducting a Make-or-Buy Decision

When should consideration be given to contracting for a public sector service? What factors are important in making such a decision? How does one compare the costs of government delivery and contract service delivery?

No universally agreed-upon methodology exists that can be used to determine if, and under what circumstances, a public sector service should be considered for contracting. However, one methodology and set of criteria that have received considerable attention are contained in the *Privatization Assessment Workbook*, which was developed by the Colorado State Auditor's Office (1989, 1997). Although the term *privatization* appears in the title, the workbook is really a methodology and set of criteria for assessing the extent to which a public sector service is a good candidate for contracting. The International City/County Management Association (ICMA) (Martin, 1993a) has identified the Colorado approach as a best practice. Various state and local governments have adopted portions of the workbook; and, in at least four instances—State of Arizona (n.d.), State of Texas (1994); City of Charlotte, North Carolina (McGillicuddy, 1996), and the City of Portland, Oregon (1995)—the methodology and criteria have been adopted in total. The Colorado approach assumes that the service is either new or currently being provided by government and that public-private competition is not involved. Nine major factors comprise the Colorado approach: (a) market strength, (b) political resistance, (c) service quality, (d) impact on employees, (e) legal barriers, (f) risk, (g) resources, (h) control, and (i) cost. For each of the nine factors, the Colorado approach suggests several questions that should be asked and answered. As an aid in interpretation, responses can be identified as providing either support for contracting (+) or support for government delivery (-).

Market Strength

Market strength refers to the commercial characteristics of the public sector service that may make it more or less attractive to potential private sector providers.

Questions for Consideration:

- Do multiple potential service contractors exist? YES (+) NO (-)
- Are potential contractors interested in providing the service? YES (+) NO (-)
- Is the contract, or the nature of the financial commitment, so large that contractors may not be interested? YES (-) NO (+)
- Is the nature of the service highly complex? YES (-) NO (+)
- Will contracting result in a private sector monopoly for the service? YES (-) NO (+)

Political Resistance

Political resistance responds to and measures the amount of anticipated opposition to contracting for the service, as demonstrated by elected officials, citizens, public employees, unions, and other stakeholders. The debate over issues of "inherently governmental functions" and core versus ancillary services can be considered when assessing the degree of political resistance.

Questions for Consideration:

- Are stakeholders highly resistant to change? YES (-) NO (+)
- Does the service have high or low stakeholder support? HIGH (-) LOW (+)
- Do stakeholders have a clear preference for government service delivery? YES (-) NO (+)
- Is the service new or existing? NEW (+) EXISTING (-)
- Do problems exist with the current government delivery of the service? YES (+) NO (-)

Service Quality

Service quality questions derive anticipated changes in overall quality or in any particular dimension of service quality such as timeliness, reliability, access, if the service is contracted.

Questions for Consideration:

- Will quality increase, decrease or stay the same? INCREASE (+) DECREASE (-)
- Will the public trust, safety or welfare be put at risk? YES (-) NO (+)
- Will the confidentiality of clients, patients or other end-users be put at risk? YES (-) NO (+)
- Will accountability and responsiveness to the government be decreased? YES (-) NO (+)
- Can quality objectives be defined and included in the contract? YES (+) NO (-)

Impact on Public Employees

The impact on public employees refers to the numbers of public employees that will be displaced by contracting and what their ultimate disposition will be.

Questions for Consideration:

- Will large numbers of public employees be displaced? YES (-) NO (+)
- Will displaced public employees be offered other government jobs? YES (+) NO (-)

- Will contractors be required to hire displaced public employees? YES (+) NO (-)
- Will minority public employees be disproportionately affected? YES (+) NO (-)
- Will civil service policies be weakened as a result of contracting? YES (-) NO (+)

Legal Barriers

The legal barriers that need to be considered refer to the effect that existing laws, statutes, or ordinances may have on contracting decisions.

Questions for Consideration:

- Is the mode of service delivery publicly or privately mandated? PUBLICLY (-) PRIVATELY (+)
- Do laws, statutes or ordinances need to be changed to permit contracting? YES (-) NO (+)
- Is contracting compatible with the legislative council or commission intent that authorizes the service? YES (+) NO (-)

Risk

Risk factors measure the extent to which contracting may expose the government to greater hazards, such as legal or financial exposure, service disruption, corruption, or other risk factors.

Questions for Consideration:

- Does a significant probability exist for contractors' failure to complete the contracts? YES (-) NO (+)
- Will the consequences of any service disruptions be minor or major? MINOR (+) MAJOR (-)
- Will legal exposure be increased? YES (-) NO (+)
- Does an increased risk of corruption exist? YES (-) NO (+)
- Will contractors be responsible for cost overruns? YES (+) NO (-)
- Will risks be shared between the government and contractors? YES (-) NO (+)

Resources

Resource factors to be considered should address the efficient and effective use of government assets, including in-house or private sector expertise, facilities or equipment, time considerations, and revenue and expenditure restrictions.

Questions for Consideration:

- Does the private sector have expertise that the government does not?
  YES (+) NO (-)
- Does the private sector have equipment that the government does not?
  YES (+) NO (-)
- Does the private sector have other resources that the government does not?
  YES (+) NO (-)
- Will contracting reduce or extend required completion schedules?
  REDUCE (+) EXTEND (-)

Control

Control issues refer to the government's ability to exercise ultimate control over the service.

Questions for Consideration:

- Is direct control over the service important? YES (-) NO (+)
- Does the government have the ability to develop and administer the contract?
  YES (+) NO (-)
- Are the outputs (quantity) of the service easy to measure? YES (+) NO (-)
- Is the quality of the service easy to measure? YES (+) NO (-)
- Are the outcomes (results, accomplishments, or impacts) of the service easy to measure? YES (+) NO (-)

Cost

In the Colorado approach, the expected cost of contracting, assuming no change in service quantity, quality or outcomes and/or commensurate cost reductions for acceptable decreases in service quantity, quality or outcomes are addressed when discussing cost factors. As used here, the term cost includes price (cost + profit = price).

Questions for Consideration:

- Will service costs increase or decrease? INCREASE (-) DECREASE (+)
- Will increases in service costs be contained? YES (+) NO (-)
- Are quantity, quality or outcome reductions acceptable for commensurate cost reductions? YES (+) NO (-)

Figure 7 shows the "Privatization Profile Scoring Form" that is a part of the Colorado approach. Using the questions to be considered, the evaluator or evaluation team assigns a score (ranging from - 3 to + 3) for each of the criteria or major factors.

Privatization Profile Summary Form						
	Government Provision			Contract Provision		
Factor	Scoring					
Market Strength	-3	-2	-1	+1	+2	+3
Political Resistance	-3	-2	-1	+1	+2	+3
Service Quality	-3	-2	-1	+1	+2	+3
Impact on Employees	-3	-2	-1	+1	+2	+3
Legal Barriers	-3	-2	-1	+1	+2	+3
Risk	-3	-2	-1	+1	+2	+3
Resources	-3	-2	-1	+1	+2	+3
Control	-3	-2	-1	+1	+2	+3
Cost	-3	-2	-1	+1	+2	+3

Figure 7. *Privatization Profile Summary Form.*

Source: Adapted from Colorado State Auditor's Office. (1989, 1997). *Privatization assessment workbook*. Denver: Colorado State Auditor's Office.

Figure 8 shows what a completed Privatization Profile Summary Form might look like for custodial services. In analyzing a completed form, the emphasis is on the resulting visual profile that emerges rather than an attempt to summarize the scores. As Figure 8 clearly illustrates, the majority (6 of 9) of the scores are on the right side of the ledger, indicating that custodial services is a good candidate for contracting.

Privatization Profile Summary Form						
	Government Provision			Contract Provision		
Factor			Scoring			
Market Strength	-3	-2	-1	+1	[+2]	+3
Political Resistance	-3	-2	-1	[+1]	+2	+3
Service Quality	-3	-2	[-1]	+1	+2	+3
Impact on Employees	-3	-2	[-1]	+1	+2	+3
Legal Barriers	-3	-2	-1	[+1]	+2	+3
Risk	-3	-2	-1	[+1]	+2	+3
Resources	-3	-2	-1	+1	[+2]	+3
Control	-3	-2	[-1]	+1	+2	+3
Cost	-3	-2	-1	+1	[+2]	+3

Figure 8. *Completed Privatization Profile Summary Form for Custodial Services.*

Source: Adapted from Colorado State Auditor's Office. (1989, 1997). *Privatization assessment workbook.* Denver: Colorado State Auditor's Office.

A potential shortcoming of the Colorado approach is that each of the nine factors, is considered equally important and, thus, given equal weight. This assumption may not be valid in many make-or-buy decisions. For example, cost is generally one of the more important considerations in this type of decision as is political resistance and impact on public employees.

Figure 9 extends the Colorado approach to include: a weight for each factor, a weighted score for each factor, and a total weighted score. An advantage of adding weights to the Colorado approach is that a clearer and sometimes stronger case can frequently be made for contracting a service or maintaining it in-house. A disadvantage to adding weights is the problem of deciding upon the respective weights themselves. The assignment of weights to criteria or factors can be manipulated to influence the ultimate outcome of the decision. For this reason, the recommended practice is to decide upon the weights before the process begins (Michel, 2001, pp. 15-16). Copies of the Privatization Profile Summary Form, with and without weights, are included as Appendices B and C. These forms can be duplicated and used as tools in conducting a make-or-buy decision.

Privatization Profile Summary Form								
	Government Provision			Contract Provision			Weighted	
Factor			Scoring				Weight	Score
Market Strength	-3	-2	-1	+1	[+2]	+3	2	+4
Political Resistance	-3	-2	-1	[+1]	+2	+3	2	+2
Service Quality	-3	-2	[-1]	+1	+2	+3	1	-1
Impact on Employees	-3	-2	[-1]	+1	+2	+3	2	-2
Legal Barriers	-3	-2	-1	[+1]	+2	+3	1	+1
Risk	-3	-2	-1	[+1]	+2	+3	1	+1
Resources	-3	-2	-1	+1	[+2]	+3	2	+4
Control	-3	-2	[-1]	+1	+2	+3	1	-1
Cost	-3	-2	-1	+1	[+2]	+3	3	+6
							Total Weighted Score	+14

Figure 9. *Completed Privatization Profile Summary Form for Custodial Services with Weighted Scores.*

Source: Adapted from Colorado State Auditor's Office. (1989, 1997). *Privatization assessment workbook*. Denver: Colorado State Auditor's Office; and Martin, L. L. (1993). *Evaluating contracting out*. Washington, DC: International City/County Management Association.

Making Cost Comparisons Between In-House and Contract Service Delivery

While cost is only one factor involved in a make-or-buy decision, it is arguably one of the most important, if not *the* most important. As previously discussed, reducing the cost of service delivery is one of the most frequently cited reasons for governments' use of contracting. If there is little or no potential cost savings, there may be no incentive to contract. One might think that determining the cost of contract service delivery and the cost of in-house service delivery, and then comparing the two, would be a relatively simple and straightforward proposition. Unfortunately, this is not the case. No commonly accepted methodology exists. Considerable disagreement exists as to what costs should be included in determining the expense of in-house service delivery as well as what costs should be included in determining the expense of contract service delivery. Disagreement also exists as to how the costs of government and contract service delivery should be compared. The lack of cost accounting systems available in many governments and the lack of expertise on how to conduct a cost comparison have created additional issues. Further complicating these problem areas is the fact that many governments have formally adopted policy positions on how to conduct a cost comparison, which may or may not represent best practices.

> ...a cost comparison between in-house and contract service delivery is as much an art as it is a science.

At the outset of this discussion, the point should be made that making a cost comparison between in-house and contract service delivery is as much an art as it is a science. Searching for the perfect cost comparison methodology is akin to searching for the Holy Grail. If, in fact, it exists, no one knows where it is or how to find it. A case in point: the U.S. Office of Management and Budget (OMB) Circular A-76 (OMB, 2003). Circular A-76 sets forth a methodology for conducting a make-or-buy decision, including how to compute costs and how to make a cost comparison. The original intent of A-76 was to prescribe a simple, standardized process that could be used by federal departments and agencies. The result is a time-consuming and costly bureaucratic exercise that has been severely criticized by federal departments and agencies as well as the private sector. One notable A-76 review took five years to complete and cost approximately $8 million; the resulting contract saved the Federal Government only $480,000 (Kettl, 1993, p. 56). The desire of governments to be thorough in conducting decisions and cost comparisons should be tempered by the realities of time and cost. Governments can be comforted in the knowledge that the perfect cost comparison methodology does not exist and that one is not likely to be discovered anytime in the near future.

A complete and detailed discussion of how to conduct a cost comparison between in-house and contract service delivery, including an examination of all the major issues involved and the identification of all possible best practices, would take several chapters to accomplish and is, consequently, beyond the scope of this section. What can be done, however, is to identify the major issues involved, discuss what the research has to say about these issues, and provide references to other sources of information. This somewhat abbreviated discussion is divided into three parts: (a) determining the cost of contract service delivery; (b) determining the cost of in-house service delivery; and (c) comparing the costs of in-house and contract service delivery. As part of this discussion, special consideration is given to the two issues that generate the greatest amount of disagreement when making cost comparisons between in-house and contract service delivery: (a) how much to include for contract administration and monitoring costs when computing the cost of contract service delivery; and (b) what contract service delivery costs in comparison with what in-house service delivery costs.

Determining the Cost of Contract Service Delivery

The starting point for determining the cost of contract service delivery is with the contract price as identified in the contractor's bid or proposal. This is the easy part. The more difficult and uncertain part is to determine what other costs should be added to the contract price? Other costs frequently added to the contract price are: (a) contract administration and monitoring costs, (b) one-time conversion costs, and (c) a variety of other costs. Some governments also include various offsetting revenues.

CONTRACT ADMINISTRATION AND MONITORING COSTS

One cost comparison issue that is creating huge disagreement is exactly how much to include for contract administration and monitoring costs. Over the years, the Government Finance Officers Association (GFOA), the U.S. General Accounting Office (GAO), the International City/County Management Association (ICMA), the National League of Cities (NLC), and the Reason Foundation have all published studies and "how-to" guides suggesting that at least some costs should be added to the contract price to cover contract administration and monitoring costs (Kelly, 1984; Martin, 1992, 1993a, 1993b, 1993c; OMB, 1996).

Rehfuss (1989), a former city manager and long-time researcher in the area of contract service delivery, has estimated monitoring costs at between 5% and 10% of contract price. In his studies of solid waste collection services, Savas (1987) estimated contract-monitoring costs, exclusive of contract administration costs, at between 2% and 7% of the contract price. A major study of contracting for public sector services in the United Kingdom reported an overage monitoring cost of 6.2% of contract price across a range of services, including refuse collection, street cleaning, building cleaning, catering, vehicle maintenance, grounds maintenance, and leisure management services (Walsh & Davis, 1993, p. 148). The City of Phoenix, Arizona, has estimated contract administration costs of its solid waste collection contracts at 16% of the contract price (Rehfuss, 1990). Using these expert judgments, a cost range for contract administration and monitoring costs can be estimated at between 10% and 20% of the total contract price (Martin, 1992). Generally, the rule is to move to the higher side of the range for smaller dollar value contracts and to the lower side of the range for higher dollar value contracts.

OMB (2003) has suggested a formula that relates the number of full-time equivalent staff (FTEs) currently providing the service in-house to the number of FTEs that will be needed to administer and monitor the resulting contract. The OMB approach is illustrated in Figure 10.

Current In-House Staffing (FTE Positions)	Required Contract Administration Staff (FTE Positions)
10 or less	1/2
11 - 20	1
21 - 50	2
51 - 75	3
76 - 100	4
101 - 120	5
121 - 150	6
151 - 200	7
201 - 250	8
251 - 300	9
301 - 350	10
351 - 450	11
451 and above	2.5% of in-house FTE staffing

Figure 10. *Estimating Contract Administration and Monitoring Costs Using the U.S. Office of Management and Budget Approach.*

Source: U.S. Office of Management and Budget (OMB). (2003). *Performance of commercial activities (Circular No. A-76, revised)* (p. C23). Washington, DC: OMB.

While the OMB approach and the various expert opinions and research cited above provide guidance in terms of estimating contract administration and monitoring costs, caution should be exercised in relying too heavily on this guidance. Contract administration and monitoring requirements, and attendant costs, can vary considerably from government to government. What may be appropriate for federal departments and agencies may not be appropriate for state and local governments. The argument can also be made that service industries today are becoming less labor-intensive due to the increasing availability and use of information technologies (Mullins & Zorn, 1999). Additionally, as previously pointed out, one way in which contractors reduce service delivery costs is through the differential use of labor. Estimating contract administration and monitoring costs using a formula that relates service staff to contract administration staff may not be sensitive to contractor productivity increases due to the differential use of labor. As such, computing contract administration and monitoring costs primarily on the basis of FTE staffing levels may overstate actual costs.

Another consideration in estimating the cost of contract administration and monitoring is "risk assessment." In recent years, the assessment and management of risk has become increasingly important to organizations (McNamee & Selim, 1998). Applying the concept of risk management to contract administration and monitoring, governments would want to identify which public sector service contracts involve greater and lesser risk. More contract administration and monitoring resources would be devoted to those contracts that represent greater potential risk and less contract administration and monitoring resources to those contracts that represent less potential risk. Thus, the identification and use of contract administration and monitoring resources, as well as the costs involved, would be dependent upon the results of a risk assessment.

Figure 11 identifies the major contract administration and monitoring risk factors related to contracts for public sector services.

More Oversight	Less Oversight
• New Contractors	• Experienced Contractors
• Large Dollar Value Contracts	• Small Dollar Value Contracts
• Cost Reimbursement Contracts	• Fixed Fee, Fixed Price and Unit Cost Contracts
• Design-Based Statements of Work	• Performance-Based Statements of Work
• Soft Services	• Hard Services

Figure 11. *Contract Administration and Monitoring Risk Factors.*

As Figure 11 illustrates, some risk factors are associated with the need for more oversight and others with less oversight. Greater risk is associated with the use of new contractors, large dollar value contracts, cost reimbursement contracts, design-based statements of work, and soft services.

...identification and use of contract administration... would be dependent upon the results of a risk assessment.

New contractors pose greater risk than older, established contractors. New contractors are more likely to be unfamiliar with government contracts and government contracting policies, reporting requirements, etc. Clearly, governments would want to devote more human and financial resources to the administration and monitoring of large dollar value contracts compared to smaller dollar value contracts. Cost reimbursement contracts require more administration, monitoring, and auditing to ensure that costs are actually incurred and are reimbursable under the terms of the contract. Fixed-fee, fixed price, and unit cost contracts require less administration, monitoring, and auditing. Design-based statements of work require more verification than performance-based statements of work and, thus, more monitoring. "Soft services" refer to services done for or on behalf of people (e.g., patients, clients, etc.), while "hard" services refers to services done to things (e.g., streets, parks, buildings, etc.). Because soft services involve people, there is more monitoring than for hard services.

ONE-TIME CONVERSION COSTS

One-time conversion costs are costs incurred due to change in service delivery from in-house to contract. One-time conversion costs are usually either *personnel*-related or *material*-related. Personnel-related costs can include accrued annual and sick leave benefits owed public employees and any other severance-type costs. Material-related costs could include costs associated with the preparation and transfer of facilities or equipment to the contractor or penalties for terminating leases and the costs of maintaining underutilized facilities or equipment until they can be sold or leased. Little research exists on one-time conversion costs, and governments appear to be idiosyncratic in how they handle such costs.

OTHER COSTS/REVENUES

Different governments sometimes include other costs and revenues that are either added to or subtracted from the contract price. *Other costs* may include the cost of employees made redundant due to contracting, the cost of the disposal of assets no longer needed due to contracting, and the cost of unutilized or underutilized facilities or equipment made redundant by contracting. *Other revenues* may include new revenues that may be generated due to contracting and new taxes that will be paid by transitioning a service provided by government to a service provided by the private sector. *Other costs* represent add-ons to the contract price; *other revenues* represent subtractions to the contract price.

Determining the Cost of In-House Service Delivery

In this section, several costing terms are introduced and used repeatedly. The discussion can become somewhat complex. A mini-dictionary explaining costing terms utilized throughout the discussion is provided in Figure 12.

- *Contract Cost*—the contract price plus additional costs for contract administration and monitoring and one-time conversion costs plus or minus any other costs or revenues.
- *Direct Costs*—those government costs that benefit only the target service (the service to be contracted).
- *Indirect Costs*—those government shared or overhead costs that benefit the target service and at least one other service.
- *Fully Allocated Costs*—the total cost, or full cost, of a target service (direct costs plus a proportionate share of indirect costs).
- *Avoidable Costs*—those government costs (both direct and indirect) that will be avoided if a target service is contracted. Avoidable costs are sometimes referred to as "go-away costs" because they go away when a target service is contracted.
- *Unavoidable Costs*—those costs (usually some proportion of indirect costs) that will continue to be incurred by a government even though the target service is contracted.

Figure 12. *Mini-Dictionary of Costing Terms.*

The total cost, or fully allocated cost, of in-house service delivery of a target service is comprised of the direct costs and a proportionate share of indirect costs. A direct cost benefits only one cost objective; an indirect cost is one that benefits two or more cost objectives (Anthony & Young, 1999, p. 9). For purposes of making cost comparisons between in-house and contract service delivery, the term *cost objective* can be thought of as referring to the service being contracted, which will be called the "target service." If a cost (e.g., personnel, travel, supplies, etc.) benefits the target service 100%, and it benefits no other service, it is a direct cost. If public employees work 100% of their time on the target service this would be a direct cost. Conversely, an indirect cost is one that benefits two or more services. Indirect costs are also referred to as "overhead" costs and sometimes by their more descriptive name, "shared costs."

Governments use various approaches to allocate indirect costs to the in-house delivery of a target service. These approaches range from the simple to the complex, such as single step-down method, double step-down method, reciprocal method, multi-base method, and activity-based costing (Anthony & Young, 1997). Regardless of the allocation method used, some proportionate share of indirect costs is computed and added to the direct costs of the target service. Two major issues related to indirect costs and their allocation are the accuracy of the allocation method and determining which indirect costs are avoidable and which are not.

THE ACCURACY OF THE ALLOCATION METHOD

As service industries, including governments, become relatively less labor intensive through the use of information technologies, indirect costs become an increasingly larger part of the total cost, or fully allocated cost, of any government service. The more accurate the allocation methodology, the more appropriate are the indirect costs allocated to a target service.

DETERMINING WHICH INDIRECT COSTS ARE AVOIDABLE AND UNAVOIDABLE

Generally, the direct costs of a target service are avoided as a result of contracting. The staff, equipment, facilities, supplies, etc., are no longer needed to provide the service in-house. These costs will no longer be incurred if the public sector service is contracted. Not all indirect costs may be avoided when a target service is contracted, but at least some indirect costs will continue to be incurred. For example, a proportion of indirect costs charged to a target service will most likely include charges for maintaining such general government functions as the human resources department, the finance department, the facilities management department, and other support costs. These departments, and their costs, will continue after the target service has been contracted. The proportion of these costs charged to the target service, as indirect costs, will simply be reallocated to other government departments, agencies and programs, thus making these indirect costs unavoidable. What makes the distinction between avoidable and unavoidable costs so important is that it is the former that are used to pay the contractor. Thus, the greater the proportion of indirect costs that are unavoidable, the less attractive is the contracting option. Conversely, the greater the proportion of indirect costs that are considered avoidable, the more attractive the contracting option.

Comparing the Costs of In-House Versus Contract Service Delivery

There are three cost comparison approaches. The fully allocated costs approach and the avoidable costs approach are longstanding and generally accepted and recognized. The State of Texas approach is more recent and more experimental. In discussing these three approaches, a series of simple examples are used to illustrate how the cost comparison is made between in-house and contract service delivery.

THE FULLY ALLOCATED COSTS APPROACH

In this approach, the fully allocated costs (the total direct costs plus a proportionate share of indirect costs) are compared to the cost of contract service delivery (the contract price, plus contract administration and monitoring costs, *plus* any one-time conversion costs *plus* or *minus* other costs and revenues).

In the hypothetical example in Table 6, a government is considering contracting for a target service (custodial services) at a 150,000 square foot municipal building. The current in-house costs for a 12-month period consist of $157,000 in direct costs (comprised of $125,000 in salaries and employee-related expenses [ERE]), $10,000 in equipment, $20,000 in supplies, and $2,000 in the category of "other") and $23,550 in indirect costs (comprised of $15,700 in facilities management overhead and $7,850 in general government overhead). Following a common practice, indirect costs are expressed as a percentage of direct costs. Thus, the $15,700 in facilities management indirect costs represents 10% of the direct costs, and the $7,850 in general government overhead costs represents 5% of the direct costs. The total cost of in-house custodial service delivery at the municipal building is $180,550, which represents the fully allocated costs. Contract costs for a similar 12-month period include the contract price of $135,000 plus $13,500 in contract administration and monitoring costs (computed at 10% of the contract price). For purposes of simplicity, no other costs will be included in computing contract costs. Consequently, the total contract cost is computed at $148,500.

The cost comparison is made between the fully allocated costs of in-house service delivery at $180,550 and the total costs of contract service delivery at $148,500. In this instance, contracting should reduce custodial service delivery costs by $32,500 for one year. Table 6 also compares the unit costs between the two approaches. The unit cost (based on 150,000 square feet) for in-house service delivery is $1.20 per square foot, while the unit cost for contract service delivery is $.99 per square foot. Computing a cost per unit of service for both in-house service delivery and contract service delivery provides another perspective on the cost comparison.

TABLE 6

Cost Comparison Using the Fully Allocated Costs Approach

	Fully Allocated Costs	Contract Costs
1. Direct Costs - Salaries & ERE - Equipment - Supplies - Other	$125,000 10,000 20,000 2,000	
Total Direct Costs	$157,000	
2. Indirect Costs - Facilities Management @10% - General Government @5%	$15,700 $7,850	
	$23,550	
3. Contract Price		$135,000
4. Contract Administration & Monitoring Costs @10%		$13,500
5. One-Time Conversion Costs		
6. Other Costs/Revenues		
7. Total Costs	$180,550	$148,500
Cost per sq. ft	$1.20	$.99

The advantage most frequently claimed for the fully allocated costs approach is that it accounts for all in-house costs and, thus, comes the closest of the three approaches to representing the "true" cost of in-house service delivery. U.S. Federal Government departments and agencies are required to use the fully allocated costs approach under OMB's Circular A-76 (2003). At least two states (Colorado and Virginia) also use the fully allocated costs approach (Martin, 1999). The most frequently claimed disadvantage of the fully allocated costs approach is that it overstates the "true" cost of in-house service delivery (Martin, 1993b; 1999).

THE AVOIDABLE COSTS APPROACH

In this approach, only the avoidable costs (the costs the government will avoid if it contracts for the target service) are used in the cost comparison. The avoidable costs are compared to the contract cost. Continuing with the hypothetical example of custodial services, if the government contracts, it will avoid all the direct costs ($157,000) associated with in-house service delivery as well as the facility management department's operational overhead costs ($15,700). The general government overhead costs ($7,850) will not be avoided. These indirect costs or "shared costs" of operating the finance department, the human resource department, and other general government support functions will simply be reallocated to other government agencies and activities. The most frequently claimed advantage for using this approach is that the avoidable cost represents the actual funds that will be freed up to pay the contractor.

The longstanding decision rule is that contracting only makes economic sense when the avoided costs are greater than the contract costs (Kelly, 1984). In other words, if the existing costs the government will avoid are greater than the new costs the government will incur by contracting, contracting will reduce service delivery costs. In the example in Table 7, if the government contracts for custodial services, it will avoid $172,700 of the in-house costs and incur $148,500 in new contract costs. Thus, the costs to be avoided are greater than the new costs, and the cost of custodial services should be reduced by $16,350. Another perspective is provided by a comparison of the costs per square foot. If the government decides to contract, it will avoid $1.15 per square foot in costs and will only incur new costs of $.99 per square foot. Using the avoidable costs approach reduces (from $32,000 to $24,200) the estimated cost savings that can be achieved by contracting.

TABLE 7

Cost Comparison Using the Avoidable Costs Approach

	Fully Allocated Costs	Contract Costs
1. Direct Costs - Salaries & ERE - Equipment - Supplies - Other	$125,000 10,000 20,000 2,000	
Total Direct Costs	$157,000	
2. Indirect Costs - Facilities Management @10% - General Government @5%	$15,700 0	
	$15,700	
3. Contract Price		$135,000
4. Contract Administration & Monitoring Costs @10%		$13,500
5. One-Time Conversion Costs		
6. Other Costs/Revenues		
7. Total Costs	$172,700	$148,500
Cost per sq. ft	$1.15	$.99

The majority of state and local governments use the avoidable costs approach (e.g., State of Arizona; City of Phoenix, Arizona; City of Charlotte, North Carolina; San Diego County, California). The Treasury Board of Canada Secretariat (n.d.) also recommends using the avoidable costs approach. The avoidable costs approach has the added advantage of being recommended by many financial management texts (Anthony & Young, 1997, Garrison, 1991). Nevertheless, the avoidable costs approach can be criticized for possibly understating the cost savings attributable to contracting (Martin, 1993c). While the indirect costs may not be avoidable over the short term, they might well become avoidable over the long term.

THE STATE OF TEXAS APPROACH

Mindful of the arguments that the fully allocated cost approach may overstate and the avoidable costs approach may understate regarding the "true" cost of in-house service delivery, the State of Texas (1994) has devised yet a third approach. This approach has not received a lot of attention to date and even less usage. Nevertheless, it does appear to be an option worth considering because of its ability to overcome the objections to both the fully allocated costs approach and the avoidable costs approach. Under the State of Texas approach, the government determines the fully allocated cost of in-house service delivery and separates these costs into three categories: (a) direct costs, (b) avoidable indirect costs, and (c) unavoidable indirect costs. The fully allocated costs of in-house service delivery are then compared to the contract costs (contract price, contract administration and monitoring costs, one-time conversion costs, and any other relevant costs) plus the unavoidable indirect costs of in-house service delivery (see Table 8). This innovation–adding the unavoidable indirect costs of in-house service provision to the contract costs–makes considerable economic sense. If the unavoidable costs are those indirect costs that will not be avoided regardless of the mode of service delivery (in-house or contract), then it makes sense to add those costs to the costs of contract service delivery as well as in-house service delivery. In Table 8, the State of Texas approach is applied to the ongoing example of custodial services. When the unavoidable costs of in-house service provision ($7,850) are added to the contract costs, the adjusted contract costs are $156,350. Under this approach, the cost difference between in-house service delivery and contract service delivery is $24,200, and the costs per square foot are $1.20 for in-house service delivery and $1.04 for contract service delivery.

...adding the unavoidable indirect costs of in-house service provision to the contract costs– makes considerable economic sense.

TABLE 8

Cost Comparison Using the State of Texas Approach

	Fully Allocated Costs	Contract Costs

1. Direct Costs
  - Salaries & ERE
  - Equipment
  - Supplies
  - Other
	$125,000
	10,000
	20,000
	2,000	

Total Direct Costs	$157,000	
2. Avoidable Indirect Costs - Facilities Management @10%	$15,700	
3. Unavoidable Indirect Costs - General Government @5%	$7,850	
	$23,550	
4. Contract Price		$135,000
5. Contract Administration & Monitoring Costs @10%		$13,500
6. One-Time Conversion Costs		
7. Other Costs/Revenues		
8. Unavoidable Indirect Costs		$7,850
9. Total Costs	$180,550	$156,350
Cost per sq. ft	$1.20	$1.04

The three approaches to conducting a cost comparison arrive at different estimates of cost savings. While the three examples illustrated above all support contracting for the public sector service as the less expensive alternative, not all analyses will result in this finding. Changing from one cost comparison approach to another can result in contract service delivery being the more attractive alternative in one analysis and in-house service delivery in another. This realization points to the need for governments to adopt a formal cost comparison approach and consistently apply it. Without the adoption of a cost comparison approach and its consistent application, the analysis can be manipulated to favor contract service delivery over in-house service delivery or vice versa.

Other Cost Comparison Issues

Two other cost comparison issues that warrant specific mention are how long to carry out the analysis and minimum conversion differentials, or "hurdle rates."

- *Time Length of the Cost Comparison.* General agreement exists that the cost comparison should be carried out for more multiple time periods (regardless of the actual duration of the proposed contract) in order to spread out transition costs that would generally be incurred in the first year over a reasonable time period (Department of Finance and Administration, 1998; Martin, 1993). For example, the U.S. Federal Government recommends in OMB Circular A-76 that the cost comparison be carried out for three years (OMB, 2003). The Treasury Board of Canada Secretariat (n.d.) recommends that the analysis be carried out for five years. Because cost comparisons involve considerations of cash flow over time, the Treasury Board of Canada Secretariat also recommends that ". . . all cash flows be discounted to present value to permit costs to be compared without any bias for different timing" (p. 3).

- *Minimum Cost Differentials, or "Hurdle Rates."* A minimum cost differential (MCD), or "hurdle rate," refers to some predetermined amount of cost savings that must be achieved before a change in service delivery (e.g., government delivery to contract) is considered warranted. Little agreement exists on this subject. The national governments of Australia and the United Kingdom do not specify any MCD. OMB requires that the cost savings estimate be ". . . 10% of the MEO's (Most Efficient Organization) personnel related costs . . . or $10 million over the performance period stated in the solicitation (OMB, 2003, p. B16). The Canadian Department of National Defense (1997, p. 3) simply states that an MCD is in keeping with government policy but does not specify a rate.

References

Anthony, R., & Young, D. (1997). *Management control in non-profit organizations.* Boston: McGraw-Hill.

Audit Commission. (1993). *Realizing the benefits of competition: The client role for contracted services.* London: Her Majesty's Stationary Office.

Becker, F. (2001). *Problems in privatization theory and practice in state and local governments.* Lewiston, NY: The Edwin Mellen Press.

Becker, F., & Mackelprang, D. (1990). Attitudes of state legislators toward contracting for public services. *American Review of Public Administration, 20*(3), 175-189.

Canadian Department of National Defense. (1997). *Alternative service delivery costing guidelines.* Ottawa: Canadian Department of National Defense. Retrieved December 19, 2001, from http://www.dnd.ca.admfincs/financial_docs/alt_doc/toc.htm.

City of Portland, Oregon, Office of the City Auditor. (1995). *Competitive contracting: Opportunities to improve service delivery and save money.* Portland: Office of the City Auditor.

Colorado State Auditor's Office. (1989, 1997). *Privatization assessment workbook.* Denver: Colorado State Auditor's Office.

Department of Finance and Administration (DFA). (1998). *The performance improvement cycle: Guidance for managers.* Parkes, Australia: Department of Finance and Administration.

Garrison, R. (1991). *Managerial accounting* (6th ed.). Homewood, IL: Richard D. Irwin.

Kelly, J. (1984). *Costing government services: A Guide to decision making.* Washington, DC: Government Finance Officers Association.

Kettl, D. (1993). *Sharing power: Public governance and private markets.* Washington, DC: The Brookings Institution.

Martin, L. L. (1992). A proposed methodology for comparing the costs of government versus contract service delivery.

The municipal yearbook. Washington, DC: International City/County Management Association.

Martin, L. L. (1993a). *Evaluating contracting out.* Washington, DC: International City/County Management Association.

Martin, L. L. (1993b). *How to compare costs between in-house and contract service delivery.* Los Angeles: The Reason Public Policy Institute.

Martin, L. L. (1993c). *Bidding on service delivery: Public-private competition.* Washington, DC: International City/County Management Association.

Martin, L. L. (1999). *Developing a level playing field for public-private competition.* Arlington, VA: The IBM Center for the Business of Government. Retrieved March 10, 2003, from htttp://www.businessofgovernment.org.

McGillicuddy, J. (1996). A blueprint for privatization and competition. *Public Management,* 25(3), 8-13.

McNamee, D., & Selim, G. (1998). *Risk management: Changing the internal auditor's paradigm.* Altamont Springs, FL: The Institute of Internal Auditors.

Michel G. (2001). *Decision tools for budgetary analysis.* Chicago: Government Finance Officers Association.

Mullins, D., & Zorn, K. (1999, Summer). Is activity-based costing up to the challenge when it comes to privatization of local government services? *Public Budgeting & Finance,* 19, 37-58.

Rehfuss, J. (1989). *Contracting out in government.* San Francisco: Jossey-Bass.

Rehfuss, J. (1990, Winter). Contracting out and accountability in state and local government: The importance of contract monitoring. *State & Local Government Review,* 22, 44-48.

Savas, E. S. (1987). *Privatization: The key to better government.* Chatham, NJ: Chatham House.

State of Arizona. (n.d.). *Competitive government handbook.* Phoenix: State of Arizona..

State of Texas, Office of the State Auditor. (1994). *Guidelines and forms: Least cost review program.* Austin: Office of the State Auditor.

Thompson, L., & Elling, R. (2000, July/August). Mapping patterns of support for privatization in the mass public: The case of Michigan. *Public Administration Review,* 60, 338-348.

Treasury Board of Canada Secretariat (TBC). (n.d.). *Stretching the tax dollar—Make or buy.* Retrieved December 19, 2001, from http://www.tbs-sct.gc.ca/pubs.

U.S. Office of Federal Procurement Policy (OFPP). (1992). Policy letter 92-1—Inherently governmental functions. Washington, DC: OFPP. Retrieved November 14, 2003, from http://www.arnet.gov/Library/OFPP/PolicyLetters.

U.S. Office of Management and Budget (OMB). (1996). Circular A-76: *Revised Supplemental Handbook Performance of Commercial Activities.* Washington, DC: OMB.

U.S. Office of Management and Budget (OMB). (2003). *Performance of commercial activities* (Circular No. A-76, revised). Washington, DC: OMB.

Walsh, K., & Davis, H. (1993). *Competition and service: The impact of the Local Government Act of 1988.* London: Department of the Environment, HMSO.

CHAPTER 3

Public-Private Competition

Public-private competition is a special variant of contracting for public sector services because it allows in-house departments and public employees to compete with private sector businesses and firms to provide government services. In order to preclude confusion, public-private competition will be dealt with in this stand-alone chapter rather than attempting to integrate the material into the larger discussion of contracting for public sector services.

There are three major types of public-private competitions: ad hoc approach, informal bidding, and formal bidding. There are benefits of public-private competition, and data show how extensively in-house departments and public employees compete to win public-private competitions in Australia, the United Kingdom, and the United States.

The following is a Public-Private Competition Checklist consisting of 10 factors considered important in the selection of public-private competition:

- Core versus ancillary services and inherently governmental services;
- Hard versus soft services;
- Stand-alone versus interrelated services;
- Service segmentation,
- Service precedents,
- Private sector interest;
- Private sector competitiveness;
- In-house department interest;
- In-house department competitiveness; and
- Political opposition

The Public-Private Competition Checklist presented in this chapter differs significantly from the Privatization Profile Summary Form discussed in Chapter 2. The former involves both public and private sector competitors, while the latter involves only private sector competitors.

Level playing field issues will be presented and discussed. The idea behind the concept of a level playing field is that the process should not provide a competitive advantage to either the public sector or the private sector. A Level Playing Field Checklist will be presented. This checklist is based on 13 factors considered important in creating a level playing field:

- Type of competition;
- Public sector access to outside consultants;
- Independent review of public sector benchmarks;
- Bids and proposals;
- Separation of the purchaser and provider functions;
- Mandated private sector wage scales;
- Mandated private sector employee benefits;
- Minimum cost savings threshold;
- Cost comparison approach;
- Transition costs;
- Contract administration and monitoring costs;
- Public sector Memorandum of Understanding (MOU);
- Penalties for public sector failure to perform; and
- Provisions for monitoring.

Copies of the Public-Private Competition Checklist and the Level Playing Field Checklist are included as Appendices D and E, respectively. These forms can be duplicated and used to analyze and select services for public-private competition and to determine if an individual public-private competition or a government's overall public-private competition policy achieves a level playing field.

Public Employees as Competitors

Traditionally, contracting for public sector services has not involved the participation of in-house departments and public employees as competitors in the actual procurement process. One can argue that this "oversight" is directly attributable to the inherent private sector bias of privatization and contracting initiatives. By their very nature, the terms *privatization* and *contracting* imply that government functions, activities, and programs will flow from the public sector to the private sector. However, privatization and contracting initiatives are subject to major theoretical criticism: it is assumed *a priori* that private sector service delivery is always less costly and is always of equal or better quality. As previously noted, the majority of the credible evidence suggests that contracting does generally lead to lower service delivery costs and equal or better service quality, but not always. Additionally, the argument is made that it is not necessarily the nature of service delivery (public versus private) that leads to lower service delivery costs and improved service quality but, rather, the presence or absence of competition (Miller, 1996; Savas, 2000). Most service procurements involve little competition. One way that governments have found to increase competition in government service delivery is to allow in-house departments and public employees to compete against the private sector.

Beginning in the late 1970s and early 1980s, national and sub-national governments in Australia, Canada, the United Kingdom, and the United States began experimenting with what can be called "public private competition." Public-private competition is also referred to as "managed competition" in the United States, "alternative service delivery" in Canada, and "competitive tendering" in Australia and the United Kingdom. In the United Kingdom, the Conservative government of Prime Minister Margaret Thatcher made public-private competition compulsory for local governments under the provisions of The Local *Government Act of 1988* (Walsh & Davis, 1993). The Labor government and Prime Minister Tony Blair later dropped the compulsory aspects of what is now called simply "competitive tendering." Today, public-private competition, or competitive tendering, is authorized at all government levels in the United Kingdom. Public-private competition is also authorized at all government levels in the Commonwealth of Australia but occurs most frequently at the Commonwealth level, in select states such as Victoria and New South Wales, and in select local governments such as the City of Melbourne (Domberger & Hall, 1995; Industry Commission, 1996).

> *...some of the more notable public-private competition initiatives in the United States have occurred at the local government level.*

The U.S. Federal Government has had a public-private competition program in place since 1983. Under the provisions of the U.S. Office of Management and Budget (OMB) Circular A-76, federal departments and public employees can compete against the private sector to provide commercial-type government services (OMB, 2003). Outside of the Federal Government, some of the more notable public-private competition initiatives in the United States have occurred at the local government level. As noted earlier, the most famous example of public-private competition is probably the case of the City of Phoenix, Arizona, and solid waste collection services (Eggers, 1998; Jensen, 1987).

What is Public Private Competition?

Public-private competition can be defined as public procurement and quasi–procurement-type situations in which in-house departments and public sector employees compete against the private sector to provide government services (Martin, 1999a). Public-private competition usually takes one of three forms:

- *Ad hoc Approach.* An in-house service delivery is simply compared to private sector service delivery.

- *Informal Bidding.* In-house departments submit informal bids or proposals, sometimes referred to as "benchmarks," that are compared to formal bids and proposals submitted by private sector firms.
- *Formal Bidding.* In-house departments submit formal bids and proposals that are compared with formal bids and proposals submitted by the private sector (Martin, 1993a).

Because the ad hoc approach usually does not involve public procurement professionals, it is excluded from consideration here. The difference between informal bidding and formal bidding relates to differences in laws, regulations, and politics. Some governments have legal and/or regulatory restrictions against in-house departments competing with the private sector. For other governments, there may be a prevailing policy that in-house departments simply should not compete against the private sector. In such situations, the submission of an internal "benchmark" accomplishes the same objective as formal bidding. The City of Phoenix, Arizona, is a case in point. The City of Phoenix maintains that in-house departments and public employees do not actually compete against the private sector. When a city service is targeted for public-private competition, the in-house department prepares a service delivery plan and a cost proposal. The city then solicits formal bids or proposals from the private sector. If the in-house plan and cost proposal is the most advantageous to the city (price and other factors being considered), the city rejects all private sector bids or proposals and cancels the solicitation. This action equates to the city awarding the contract to the in-house department. If a private sector bid or proposal is the most advantageous to the city (price and other factors considered), then a formal contract is awarded. With formal bidding, the in-house department submits a formal bid or proposal that is treated exactly the same as private sector bids and proposals.

Advantages of Public-Private Competition

Public-private competition has several advantages that **may** make it an attractive alternative to simply contracting for a public sector service.

- The amount of competition in the delivery of public sector services can be increased. Allowing in-house departments and public employees to compete to provide public sector services ensures that there will be at least one more bid or proposal than would otherwise be the case.
- In-house bids and proposals can depress private sector costs. The simple fact that the private sector knows that the in-house department will also be competing can serve to constrain and even depress proposed private sector costs.
- Workplace relationships between managers and staff can be improved. In hearings before the U.S. General Accounting Office's (GAO) Commercial Activities Panel, the testimony repeatedly pointed out that public-private competitions under

OMB Circular A-76 brought federal managers and employees closer together and improved teamwork and mutual trust (GAO, 2001). The experiences of the cities of Philadelphia, PA; Phoenix, AZ; and Indianapolis, IN, with regard to public-private competition mirror the experiences of the Federal Government (City Club of Portland, 1999; The Civic Federation, 1996; Fantauzzo, 1996).

- Competition can have a positive impact on public employee morale. When in-house departments win a public-private competition, public employee morale soars.
- Competition shows elected officials the other picture. All too often, elected officials only hear how the private sector provides better- and lower-cost services. Public-private competition provides a way for in-house departments and public employees to demonstrate that they can be as creative, as entrepreneurial, and as cost conscious as the private sector.

Disadvantages of Public-Private Competition

Public-private competition also has at least two major disadvantages that may make it less attractive as an alternative to simply contracting for a public sector service.

- Having to compete for jobs can generate a high level of anxiety among government employees.
- The conduct of public-private competitions can lengthen the procurement process.

Are In-House Departments and Public Employees Competitive with the Private Sector?

One of the implicit assumptions of public-private competition is that in-house departments and public employees can successfully compete with private sector firms. What does the research evidence suggest? Data on public-private competitions, particularly win/lose data, are difficult to find. Data for comparable time periods is essentially nonexistent. Nevertheless, some data from the experiences of governments in the Commonwealth of Australia, the United Kingdom, and the United States do exist. This data provides insight into the question of the ability of in-house departments and public employees to compete against the private sector (see Table 9).

TABLE 9

Public-Private Competitions Won By In-House Departments and Public Employees

Governments	Number of Competitions	Percentages Won By In-House Departments and Public Employees
Commonwealth of Australia	1,515	1.5%
United Kingdom	3,500	75.0%
U.S. Department of Defense (1)	2,100	50.0%
U.S. Department of Defense (2)	314	60.0%
Charlotte, NC	34	70.5%
Indianapolis, IN	60+	72.0%
Philadelphia, PA	32	12.5%
Phoenix, AZ	56	39.3%

Source: Charlotte, NC, cumulative data from 1995 to 1997: Eggers, W. (1998). *Competitive neutrality: Ensuring a level playing field in managed competitions.* Los Angeles: The Reason Public Policy Institute.

Commonwealth of Australia, cumulative data for 1994 and 1995: Domberger, S., Hall, C., & Jeffries, M. (1996). *Competitive tendering and contracting in commonwealth government agencies: The 1995 survey findings.* Sydney, Australia: Graduate School of Business, The University of Sydney.

Indianapolis, IN, cumulative data from 1992 to 1995: Eggers, W. (1998). *Competitive neutrality: Ensuring a level playing field in managed competitions.* Los Angeles: The Reason Public Policy Institute; and The Civic Federation. (1996). *From privatization to innovation: A study of 16 cities.* Chicago: The Civic Federation.

Philadelphia, PA, cumulative data from inception of program to 1995: The Civic Federation. (1996). *From privatization to innovation: A study of 16 cities.* Chicago: The Civic Federation.

Phoenix, Arizona, cumulative data from 1979 to 1994: Flanagan, J., & Perkins, S. (1995). Public-private competition in the city of Phoenix, Arizona. Phoenix, AZ: City of Phoenix.

United Kingdom, cumulative data from 1989 to 1994: Cutler, T., & Waine, B. (1994). Competitive tendering: The case of the vanishing producers. In *Managing the welfare state: The politics of public sector management* (pp. 75-104). Oxford: Berg Press.

U.S. Department of Defense (1), cumulative data from 1978 to 1994: U.S. General Accounting Office (GAO). (1997). *Privatization: Lessons learned by state and local governments.* Report No. GAO/GGD-97-48. Washington, DC: GAO.

U.S. Department of Defense (2), cumulative data from 1997 to 2001: U.S. General Accounting Office (GAO). (2002). *Improving the sourcing decisions of the government.* Final Report of the Commercial Activities Panel. Washington, DC: GAO.

The data in Table 9 raises the question: Can in-house departments and public employees compete against the private sector? The answer appears to be a qualified "YES!" The answer must be qualified because in-house success rates vary considerably from government to government based on local contextual factors. For example, the high proportion of public-private competitions won by in-house departments and public employees in the United Kingdom (UK) can be explained by a combination of three contextual factors: (a) the historical preference of many UK local governments for direct service delivery (Rehfuss, 1991); (b) the lack of experience of the UK private sector in government procurement and in providing services under governments contracts (Rehfuss, 1991), and (c) the "unauthorized favoritism" shown to many in-house departments during the procurement process (Walsh & Davis, 1993). The small proportion of public-private competitions won by in-house departments and public employees in the Commonwealth of Australia can be attributed to the lack of in-house department experience in competing with the private sector. The small proportion of public-private competitions won by in-house departments and public employees in Philadelphia can be explained by the fact that the city's policy was initially one of privatization or contracting, which was subsequently changed to a policy of public-private competition (The Civic Federation, 1996; Rendell, 1994). Even after the change to public-private competition was made in Philadelphia, public managers and union workers still had to learn how to become more competitive and more entrepreneurial.

> ...managers and workers [can] learn how to become more competitive and more entrepreneureal.

The ability of in-house departments and public employees to successfully compete against the private sector and win public-private competitions is related to several contextual factors including:

- The existence of a government policy permitting, as well as encouraging, the practice;
- The extent to which public-private competitions are conducted on a level playing field (no advantage to either the public or private sectors);
- The familiarity of private sector businesses and firms with government procurement and contract service delivery; and
- The competitiveness of in-house departments and public-employees.

Selecting Services for Public-Private Competition

The decision to contract for a public sector service and a structured process for conducting a make-or-buy decision based on the methodology developed by the Colorado State Auditor's Office was previously discussed. The decision to use public-private competition, while similar to conducting a make-or-buy decision, is also substantively different. The International City/County Management Association (ICMA) has identified 10 major considerations that are believed to make a public sector service more or less appropriate for public-private competition (Martin, 1996). The 10 major considerations are grouped into four categories (see Figure 13).

Service Considerations

Service Considerations
1. Core versus ancillary and inherently governmental services
2. Hard versus soft services
3. Stand-alone versus interrelated services
4. Service segmentation
5. Service precedents
External Market Considerations
6. Private sector interest
7. Private sector competitiveness
Internal Market Considerations
8. In-house department interest
9. In-house department competitiveness
Other Considerations
10. Political opposition

Figure 13. *Major Considerations in Selecting Services for Public-Private Competition.*

Source: Adapted from Martin, L. L. (1996). *Selecting services for public-private competition.* Washington, DC: International City/County Management Association.

Core Versus Ancillary Services and Inherently Governmental Services

The concepts of core services, ancillary services, and inherently governmental services were previously addressed in regard to make-or-buy decisions. The point was made that citizens and elected officials tend to look more favorably on the contracting of ancillary services, less favorably on the contracting of core services, and even less favorably on the contracting of inherently governmental services. The same observations hold true for public-private competition. As was also mentioned earlier, a great deal of variation exists between governments in terms of what constitutes ancillary services, core services, and inherently governmental services. In general, ancillary services are preferred for public-private competitions over core services and inherently governmental services.

Hard Versus Soft Services

The distinction between hard and soft services when dealing with estimating contract administration and monitoring costs was previously considered. To briefly review, soft services are done for or on behalf of people (e.g., patients, clients. etc.), while hard services are done to things (e.g., streets, parks, buildings, etc.). The issue specifically relates to the relationship between design and performance specifications and hard and soft services. The research from the United Kingdom (Martin, 1996) suggests that in-house departments and public employees are more competitive when statements of work used in public-private competitions are based on performance specifications rather than design specifications. The rationale determined that the use of performance specifications gives in-house departments and public employees more discretion in redesigning and reengineering service delivery systems. In general, hard services are preferred for public-private competitions over soft services.

Stand-Alone Versus Interrelated Services

Stand-alone services are those that are essentially self-contained (e.g., food, custodial, reprographics, etc.). Interrelated services are those that are part of other services or other service delivery systems. For example, police communication services are an integral part of the public safety system. The issue here is that contract service delivery problems with interrelated services can also affect any and all "down stream" services, in-house departments, and public employees that rely on the work of the contractor in order to perform their own tasks and assignments. In general, stand-alone services are preferred for public-private competitions over interrelated services.

Service Segmentation

Service segmentation refers to the ability of a service to be subdivided. For contracting purposes, a public sector service can be segmented on the basis of geography or by simply dividing the amount of work to be accomplished between multiple procurements and multiple contract awards. Research suggests that service segmentation leads to more competition. Segmenting services on the basis of geography has resulted in more competition for solid waste collection services in Phoenix, AZ and more competition for parks maintenance services in Arlington County, VA (Martin, 1993, 1996). The antithesis of service segmentation is the "bundling" of services. Bundling refers to governments combining multiple services or multiple geographical areas into one large, winner-takes-all procurement. Bundling retards competition by driving out small businesses and firms that are not large enough to compete for a bundled services contract. For these reasons, the Audit Commission in the United Kingdom has identified the bundling of public sector services as "an anti-competitive practice" (Chartered Institute of Public Finance and Accountancy [CIPFA], 1995; Parker & Hartley, 1990). While anecdotal in nature, some evidence suggests that bundled service procurements, when combined with multi-year contracts, may lead to

...service segmentation leads to more competition.

more bid and proposal protests. In such situations, unsuccessful bidders and proposers have nothing to lose. They are effectively precluded from providing government services for several years (Thoma, 2001).

Yet another issue regarding service segmentation relates to the ability of governments to maintain a critical mass of in-house service delivery expertise. When an entire service is contracted, a significant proportion, if not all, of a government's in-house expertise can walk out the door. Little or no residual service delivery expertise may continue to reside within the government. The ability of the in-house department and public-employees to effectively engage in future public-private competitions for that service becomes highly problematic. When implementing public-private competition for solid waste collection services, the City of Phoenix requires that the in-house department and public employees serve at least one geographical area so that a critical mass of service expertise is maintained. In general, services that can be segmented are preferred for public-private competition over services that cannot.

Service Precedents

Nothing fosters success like success! Many governments like to select services for public-private competition that already have been successfully competed by other governments. The apprehensiveness of elected officials and citizens to adopt public-private competition is frequently assuaged by the knowledge that other governments have successfully gone before them. In general, services that have been used successfully in previous public-private competitions by other governments are preferred to services that have not.

Private Sector Interest

Nothing can derail a public-private competition faster than the absence of interest on the part of the private sector. In order for a public-private competition to take place, at least one private sector bid or proposal is required, although multiple bids or proposals are preferred. Determining the level of private sector interest in participating in a public-private competition is essential. Anecdotal evidence suggests several issues that are important to the private sector in deciding to participate in a public-private competition. First, the private sector wants to know up front that a particular procurement is going to be a public-private competition and not to have this information revealed to them during or at the close of the procurement. Second, the private sector generally wants to know up front if the public-private competition will actually result in a contract award to either the private sector or the in-house department, and that the real purpose of the competition is not simply to test the market (Department of Finance and Administration [DFA], 1998a). Third, the private sector wants to know up front that a level playing field will exist for the public-private competition

(Eggers, 1998). Finally, some limited research suggests that multi-year contracts generate more private sector interest than do single-year contracts (Kettner & Martin, 1998; Walker, 1993). One of the possible reasons for this finding is that multi-year contracts provide contractors with more time to recover start-up costs.

In general, services that are expected to generate high levels of private sector interest are preferred for public-private competition over services that are expected to generate lower levels of private sector interest. Services that result in multi-year contracts are preferred for public-private competitions over services that are restricted to single-year awards.

Private Sector Competitiveness

It may seem odd to include the issue of private sector competitiveness, but it actually is an important consideration in selecting services for public-private competition. Governments provide many services that the private sector has little or no expertise in or experience in providing. The City of Indianapolis popularized the idea of the "yellow pages" test. One can often determine the competitiveness of the private sector for a particular public sector service by simply looking in the yellow pages of the telephone directory. If the yellow pages contain numerous listings of providers for the service, then the private sector is probably highly competitive for that service.

As suggested earlier, research demonstrates that the competitiveness of the private sector is also related to structural characteristics of external service markets, such as salaries, wages, fringe benefits, vacation and sick leave policies, and the differential use of labor, including, in particular, the use of part-time employees (Foster, 1993; Martin, 1997; Stevens, 1984; Walsh & Davis, 1993)

In general, services in the private sector with a highly competitive market (in terms of number of firms, salaries, wages, fringe benefits, vacation and sick leave policies, and the use of part-time employees) are preferred for public-private competitions over services where the private sector is less competitive.

In-House Department Interest

It takes "two to tango." In order to conduct public-private competitions, in-house departments and public employees must be interested in competing. Not all in-house departments and public employees will demonstrate the same level of interest. Public employee unions can also affect the level of interest. Some unions oppose participating in public-private competitions; however, if the choice is privatization/contracting versus public-private competition, unions tend to demonstrate more flexibility.

In general, services that are expected to generate high levels of in-house department and public employee interests are preferred for public-private competitions over services that are expected to generate lower levels of interest.

In-House Department Competitiveness

Perhaps one of the most process-destructive actions that governments can take is to select services for public-private competition where in-house departments and public employees are not competitive. Conducting public-private competitions under such circumstances virtually ensures that the services will be contracted out and, therefore, destroys a sense of fairness on the part of in-house departments and public employees. Public-private competition also requires an entrepreneurial orientation on the part of in-house departments that is not universally shared in equal proportions by all government managers. Research on public-private competition in the United Kingdom suggests that in-house departments and public employees must abandon old bureaucratic attitudes and consider different ways of providing public sector services in order to be competitive with the private sector (Rao & Young, 1995). Public employee unions can also affect in-house department competitiveness. If public employees' unions are not willing to consider work rule and other types of changes, little opportunity may exist to redesign and reengineer service delivery systems and to reduce service delivery costs.

In determining if an in-house department and public employees are competitive in providing a particular public sector service, the following conditions are important:

- Salaries, wages and fringe benefits should be equal to or less generous than those of the private sector.
- Vacation and sick leave policies should be equal to or less generous than those of the private sector.
- In-house staffing levels should be equal to or lower than those of the private sector.
- In-house departments should already be using, or be willing to use, part-time employees. (Martin, 1996, p. 7)

In general, services provided by in-house departments whose management is more entrepreneurial are preferred for public-private competition over services whose management is less entrepreneurial. Services that are expected to generate higher levels of public sector union support for public-private competition are preferred to services that are expected to generate lower levels of public sector union support. Services for which in-house departments are highly competitive (in terms of salaries, wages, fringe benefits, vacation and sick leave policies, and the use of part-time employees) are preferred for public-private competition over services where the in-house departments are less competitive.

Political Opposition

Political opposition is an issue that is mentioned in virtually all proposed criteria for selecting services for privatization, contracting, and public-private competition. Political opposition can promote or undermine any attempt to use public-private competition for a particular public sector service.

Services that are expected to generate low levels of political opposition are preferred for public-private competition over services that are expected to generate high levels of political opposition.

Public-Private Competition Checklist

Based on the preceding discussion, a checklist, or protocol, can be developed for selecting services for public-private competition. The Public-Private Competition Checklist is shown in Figure 14. The checklist consists of 10 questions that should be asked and answered. There is no minimum number of "YES" answers that suggest a particular public sector service is a good candidate for public-private competition. Neither is there a maximum number of "NO" answers that indicate a particular public sector service is not a good candidate for public-private competition. The best that can be said, given the state of the research today, is that the more "YES" answers, the more appropriate the service is for public-private competition.

Service Considerations	Favors Public-Private Competition
1. Service is ancillary	X
2. Service is hard	X
3. Service is stand-alone	X
4. Service precedent exists	X
5. Multi-year contract can be awarded	X
External Market Considerations	
6. High private sector interest	X
7. High private sector competitiveness	X
Internal Market Considerations	
8. High in-house and public employee interest	X
9. High in-house and public employee competitiveness	X
Other Considerations	
10. Low political opposition	X

Figure 14 Public-Private Competition Checklist.

Source: Adapted from Martin, L. L. (1996). *Selecting services for public-private competition.* Washington, DC: International City/County Management Association.

A copy of the Public-Private Competition Checklist form is included as Appendix D. The checklist can be copied and used as a tool in determining if a public sector service is a good candidate for public-private competition.

Level Playing Field Issues in Public-Private Competition

Research suggests that private sector businesses and firms, public employees, and public employee unions are more willing to participate in public-private competitions when they perceive the process to be transparent (open) and fair (City Club of Portland, 1999; Martin, 1999a; 1999b; Walsh, 1995; Walsh & Davis, 1993). Transparency and fairness are related. The more transparent the public-private competition, the more likely it will be perceived as fair. When public-private competitions are perceived as not being transparent and fair, in-house departments, private sector businesses and firms, or both, may decline to participate. The experiences of national and sub-national governments in the Commonwealth of Australia, the United Kingdom, and the United States suggest that the best way of making public-private competition transparent and open is the creation of a "level playing field" (Eggers, 1998; Martin, 1999a).

A level playing field is a public-private competition that is structured in such a fashion as to be competitively neutral. In a situation of competitive neutrality, the process itself provides neither the in-house department nor the private sector with an inherent competitive advantage. Exactly when the term *level playing field* first appeared in the lexicon of public-private competition is unclear. What is clear, however, is that the terms *level playing field* and *competitive neutrality* (the Australian and United Kingdom equivalent) are heard today with increasing frequency. Competitive neutrality between the public and private sectors is an express national policy of the Commonwealth of Australia that affects not only the national government but state and local governments as well (DFA, 1998a, 1998b). When the Commercial Activities Panel of the GAO (2001) held hearings in 2001 on revising OMB's Circular A-76, a large number of those individuals and organizations testifying stated that creating a more level playing field should be a priority.

A level playing field is a ...competition that is... competitively neutral.

What does a level playing field look like? How can a government go about creating a level playing field? Although ideas and practices abound, the answers to these questions are virtually unknown. Public-private competition represents one of those interesting government phenomenon that arise from time to time where administrative practice has outpaced theory. Many of the early adopters of public-private competition in the United States (e.g., the cities of Phoenix, Indianapolis, and Philadelphia) essentially had to invent their processes. A few models of public-private competition did exist, such as competitive tendering in the United Kingdom and the U.S. Federal Government's OMB Circular A-76.

However, information about the United Kingdom's experience with competitive tendering has not been readily available outside of the country, and OMB Circular A-76 is generally considered to be overly complicated (Kettl, 1993).

When implementing public-private competition, a government is confronted with a number of level playing field issues. A study commissioned by the PricewaterhouseCoopers Endowment for the Business of Government (Martin, 1999a) identified 13 major level playing field issues that confront governments when implementing public-private competition. The 13 major issues are classified into three categories: (a) process issues, (b) costing issues, and (c) contract administration issues. Each issue usually has at least two possible government positions or responses. Each response or position can be classified as: (a) competitively neutral, (b) tends to favor in-house departments, or (c) tends to favor the private sector. Using the 13 major issues, a Level Playing Field Checklist (Figure 15) has been created that can be used by a government in determining the extent to which a particular public-private competition or a government's overall public-private competition policy achieves a level playing field.

Process Issues	Tends to Favor the Public Sector	Competitively Neutral	Tends to Favor the Private Sector
1. Type of Competition - Sequential Process - Parallel Process	X	X	
2. Public Sector Access to Outside Consultants - YES - NO		X	X
3. Independent Review of Public Benchmarks, Bids, and Proposals - YES - NO	X	X	
4. Separation of Purchaser and Provider Functions - YES - NO	X	X	

Costing Issues	Tends to Favor the Public Sector	Competitively Neutral	Tends to Favor the Private Sector

5. Mandated Private Sector Wage Scales
  - YES
  - NO
	X	X	

6. Mandated Private Sector Employee Benefits
  - YES
  - NO
	X	X	

7. Minimum Cost Savings Threshold
  - YES
  - NO
	X	X	

8. Cost Comparison Approach
  - Fully Allocated Costs Approach
  - Avoidable Cost Approach
  - State of Texas Approach
	X	X	X

9. Transition Costs
  - Private Sector Only
  - Public and Private Sectors
  - Excluded
	X	X
		X	

10. Contract Administration and Monitoring Costs
  - Included for Private Sector Only
  - Included for Both
  - Excluded
	X	X
		X	

Contract Administration Issues			

11. Public Sector Memorandum of Understanding
  - YES
  - NO
	X	X	

12. Penalties for Public Sector Failure to Perform
  - YES
  - NO
	X	X	

13. Provisions for Monitoring
  - Private Sector Only
  - Private Sector and Public Sector
	X	X	

Figure 15. *Level Playing Field Checklist.*

Source: Adapted from Martin, L. L. (1999). *Developing a level playing field for public-private competition.* Arlington, VA: The IBM Center for the Business of Government.

Process Issues

A number of level playing field issues deal with the treatment of in-house departments and private sector businesses and firms during the public-private competitions. Most governments have detailed procurement policies that apply to participating with private sector businesses and firms. These are usually carried over into public-private competitions. Consequently, the majority of process issues relate to the way in which governments treat and deal with in-house departments participating in public-private competitions.

Type of Competition—Sequential Versus Parallel Process. Public-private competitions use either a parallel or a sequential process. In a sequential process, an in-house department is usually allowed a period of time prior to the actual competition to restructure the organization and staffing patterns and reengineer service delivery systems to create the most efficient organization possible. In a parallel process, both the in-house department and private sector businesses and firms have the same period of time to develop their benchmarks, bids, or proposals and to implement any restructuring and reengineering. The usual justification for adoption of a sequential process is that an in-house department needs additional time to become competitive with the private sector. Regardless of the merits of this argument, a sequential process tends to tilt the playing field in favor of the in-house department. By contrast, a parallel process is a competitively neutral position that provides no advantage to either the in-house department or the private sector.

Access to Outside Consultants. Private sector businesses and firms sometimes retain the services of consultants to assist them during a public-private competition. An in-house department should be afforded an equal opportunity to retain outside consultants. An in-house department may be new to public-private competition, may lack experience in cost analysis and cost accounting, or may not be conversant with new technologies or state-of-the-art service delivery strategies. In such instances, an in-house department should be able to retain outside consultants in order to access needed technical assistance. The inability of an in-house department to access consultants tends to tilt the playing field in favor of the private sector. The ability of the in-house department to access consultants is a competitively neutral position because it provides neither side with a competitive advantage.

Independent Review of In-House Benchmarks, Bids, and Proposals. An in-house submission in a public-private competition usually takes one of three forms: (a) a benchmark, (b) a bid, or (c) a proposal. With a benchmark, an in-house department prepares a cost estimate that is sealed and subsequently compared against the lowest private sector bid or the most advantageous private sector proposal. With a bid or a proposal, an in-house department submits a formal bid or proposal in the same fashion as private sector bidders and proposers. The form of an in-house submission does not appear to have level playing field considerations, but the independent verification, or absence thereof, of an in-house submission does.

An in-house benchmark, bid or proposal that is not reviewed and verified by an independent party, e.g., internal audit department, citizens review committee, etc., provides no assurances that service delivery strategies, staffing requirements, and cost estimates are realistic and accurate. Additionally, when an in-house department knows that its benchmark, bid or proposal will not be subject to independent scrutiny, a temptation may exist to understate staffing needs, underestimate costs, or overestimate productivity increases due to new technologies or reengineering efforts. The requirement that an in-house submission be subjected to an independent review is a competitively neutral position; the absence of an independent review tends to tilt the playing field in favor of the in-house department.

Separation of the Purchaser & Provider Functions. This process issue is concerned with the ability of a government to act simultaneously as both a purchaser and a provider. The issue involves a government's ability to create a quasi-arms-length transaction between an in-house department involved in a public-private competition (the provider) and the departments, units or employees of the government that oversee the competition and will monitor service provision (the purchaser). In Australia and the United Kingdom, this issue is referred to as the "purchaser/provider split." To the extent that governments do not organizationally separate the purchaser and provider functions, no assurances exist that an in-house department will be treated the same as its private sector competitors, either during the conduct of a public-private competition or service delivery. For example, without a clear separation of the purchaser and provider functions, an in-house department can gain access to information during the procurement process that is not readily available to private sector businesses and firms. Likewise, during service delivery, an in-house department may be held to lower standards than a private sector business or firm. Separation of the purchaser and provider functions is a competitively neutral position because it attempts to ensure that the in-house department and private sector competitors are treated equally. The absence of a purchaser/provider separation tends to tilt the playing field in favor of the in-house department.

Costing Issues

Governments take a variety of positions on costing issues when implementing public-private competition. Many, if not most, of these costing issues have level playing field considerations. Since one of the major reasons for government use of such competition is to reduce service delivery costs, the government positions on costing issues take on an added dimension of importance. Several of these major issues were discussed at length in Chapter 2 under the subtitle of "Making Cost Comparisons Between In-house and Contract Service Delivery."

Mandated Private Sector Wage Scales. Many governments require that private sector businesses and firms pay employees who will be working under any resulting government contract according to prevailing or comparable wage scales (sometimes called "living wage" scales). Regardless of whether in-house wage scales are higher or lower than those of the private sector, in-house departments are artificially made more competitive by such requirements because the flexibility of private sector businesses and firms is reduced. Despite the social justice arguments in support of such mandates, requiring private sector businesses and firms to pay prevailing or comparable wage scales tends to give the advantage to the in-house department. The absence of prevailing and comparable wage scales is a competitively neutral position.

Mandated Private Sector Employee Benefits. Many governments also mandate that private sector businesses and firms provide specific benefits to employees who will be working under any government contracts. Mandated wage and salary scales and mandated employee benefits are treated as separate issues because governments have been known to mandate one, but not the other. Mandated employee benefits frequently mirror those provided to government employees. The result is that in-house departments are again given a competitive advantage by reducing the flexibility of private sector businesses and firms. Mandates that private sector competitors provide specific employee benefits tend to tilt the advantage in favor of the in-house department. The absence of mandated employee benefits provides a competitively neutral position.

The idea of services transitioning from the private sector to the public sector…was not envisioned.

Minimum Cost Savings Threshold. As previously discussed, many governments take the position that the cost of private sector service delivery must be lower than the in-house cost by some specified threshold (also referred to as a "minimum cost differential" or a "hurdle rate") for the private sector to win a public-private competition. While arguments can be made that a change in the service delivery mode for less than a 10% cost savings may be questionable, minimum cost savings thresholds give in-house departments a significant competitive advantage, particularly when large multi-million dollar public-private competitions are involved. Minimum cost saving thresholds of any kind tend to favor the in-house department. The absence of minimum cost savings thresholds is a competitively neutral position.

Cost Comparison Approach. How governments go about comparing the cost of in-house department service delivery versus private sector service delivery is perhaps the most important of all level playing field issues and plays a major part in the ultimate determination of who wins and who loses a public-private competition. A detailed explanation of the three major cost comparison approaches (fully allocated costs approach, avoidable costs approach, and the State of Texas approach) has been presented. In terms of level playing field considerations, the argument can be made that the avoidable costs approach tends to tilt the playing field in favor of the in-house department, while the fully allocated costs approach tends to tilt the playing field in favor of the private sector. The State of Texas approach is competitively neutral.

Transition Costs. Transition costs also have been discussed at length. Traditionally, privatization and contracting envisioned a one-way trip for services—from the public sector to the private sector. The idea of services transitioning from the private sector to the public sector as a result of a public-private competition was not envisioned. This level playing field issue concerns the consistent application of cost when the service is transferred from public sector delivery to private sector delivery and vice versa. The inclusion of transition costs in the cost of private sector service delivery occurs only when the service is transitioning from public sector to private sector and tends to tilt the playing field in favor of the in-house department. Including transition costs in the cost of contract service delivery when the service is currently in-house and including transition costs in the cost of in-house service delivery when the service is currently contracted is a competitively neutral position. Excluding the consideration of transition costs in both instances also would be a competitively neutral position, but it might understate the true cost of service provision.

Contract Administration and Monitoring Costs. Contract administration is a broad term used to cover all of the activities involved in managing, overseeing, and monitoring government service delivery. If governments incur costs in administering and monitoring contract service delivery, then at least some costs must also be incurred in administering and monitoring public sector service delivery. If including contract administration and monitoring costs when computing the cost of contract service delivery only, the playing field tends to tilt in favor of the in-house department. The inclusion of contract administration and monitoring costs when computing the cost of both in-house and contract service delivery is a competitively neutral position. Excluding contract administration and monitoring costs from both the cost of in-house and contract service delivery is also a competitively neutral position, but leads to understating the true cost of service provision.

Contract Administration Issues

Some contract administration issues, exclusive of costing issues, also have level playing field implications.

Public Sector Memorandum of Understanding (MOU). When a public-private competition is won by the private sector, a contract is subsequently entered into that specifies all the duties and obligations of the private sector business or firm. In order to hold an in-house department accountable, a quasi-contract, generally referred to as a "memorandum of understanding (MOU)," should exist between the in-house department and the department, unit or staff that will monitor service delivery. An MOU helps to ensure that the in-house department is held to the same standards of performance as private sector contractors. An MOU requirement for the in-house department is a competitively neutral position. The lack of an MOU requirement tends to tilt the playing field in favor the in-house department.

Penalties for Public Sector Failure to Perform. If no penalties exist when an in-house department fails to perform or exceeds the costs of its benchmark, bid or proposal, then the playing field tends to be tilted in favor of the same in-house department. The existence of penalties for public sector failure to perform and cost overruns is a competitively neutral position. Examples of penalties for failure to perform or cost overages can include exclusion of the in-house department from future public-private competitions for a specified period of time (e.g. six months or one year), the addition of any cost overage to the in-house department's next benchmark, bid or proposal, or some other agreed-upon penalty.

Provisions for Monitoring. The existence of monitoring procedures for contractors only, but not in-house departments, creates a double standard and tends to tilt the playing field in favor of the in-house department. The existence of monitoring procedures for in-house departments, as well as contractors, is a competitively neutral position.

Using and Interpreting the Level Playing Field Checklist

The idea behind the Level Playing Field Checklist is to provide governments with a structured, analytical tool that can be used to determine the extent to which an individual public-private competition, or a government's overall policy on public-private competitions, creates a level playing field. In using the Level Playing Field Checklist, some cautions are in order. First, the emphasis should not be on any single government response to or position on any single major issue but, rather, on the overall cumulative effect of a government's responses or positions on all 13 major issues. Second, it is not possible to identify with certainty any particular cut-off points because some of the major issues can be considered more important than others. Having made these disclaimers, some general guidelines for using the Level Playing Field Checklist are suggested in Figure 16.

- **If** all, or nearly all, of the responses to or positions taken on the checklist are competitively neutral, **then** an individual public-private competition or a government's overall public-private competition policy *has achieved a level playing field.*
- **If** a majority (8-10) of the responses to or positions taken on the checklist are competitively neutral, **then** an individual public-private competition or a government's overall public-private competition policy *approximates a level playing field.*
- **If** a significant number (6 or more) of the responses to or positions taken on the checklist are **not** competitively neutral, **then** an individual public-private competition or a government's overall public-private competition policy *neither achieves nor approximates a level playing field.*

Figure 16. *Using and Interpreting the Level Playing Field Checklist.*

Source: Adapted from Martin, L. L. (1999). *Developing a level playing field for public-private competition.* Arlington, VA: The IBM Center for the Business of Government.

A copy of the Level Playing Field Checklist is included as Appendix E. The checklist can be copied and used as a tool in determining if an individual public-private competition or government's overall public-private competition policy achieves a level playing field.

Separation of the Purchaser and Provider Functions

As stated earlier, the purchaser/provider split relates to a government's ability to create a quasi-arms-length transaction between an in-house department involved in a public-private competition (the provider) and the departments, units or employees of the government that oversee the competition and monitor subsequent service provision (the purchaser). The issue of the separation of purchaser and provider functions has not received much attention in the Canadian and United States literature on public-private competition. The best source of information on this topic is provided by the experiences of local governments in the United Kingdom. These local governments have conducted several thousand public-private competitions. As Figure 17 illustrates, local government researchers (Shaw, Fenwick, & Foreman, 1994, pp. 207-209; Wilson & Game, 1994, p. 332) have identified three primary ways to structure the purchaser function and three primary ways of structuring the provider function. In terms of structuring the purchasing function, the lead department model tends to predominate (p. 332), while the single department model is preferred for the provider function (Shaw et al., 1994, pp. 207-208). By mixing and matching these six different models, local governments in the United Kingdom attempt to ensure that a quasi-arms-length relationship exists between those organizational units and public employees providing the service and those organizational units and public employees performing the contract administration and monitoring functions.

Purchaser Function	Provider Function
1. The Lead Department Model - A different organizational unit is designated to perform contract administration and monitoring for each in-house provided service.	**1. The Single Department Model** - A separate stand-alone organizational unit houses and directly supervises the in-house staff that win a public-private competition.
2. The Interdepartmental Committee Model - A standing committee comprised of in-house user departments performs contract administration and monitoring for all in-house- provided services.	**2. The Interdepartmental Committee Model** - An interdepartmental standing committee directly supervises the in-house staff.
3. The Single Department Model - One organizational unit (frequently the Purchasing Department) performs all contract administration and monitoring for all in-house-provided services.	**3. The Board Model** - A standing board composed of elected officials and/or citizens directly supervises the in-house staff.

Figure 17. *Separating the Purchaser and Provider Functions.*

Ethical Issues in Public-Private Competition

Public-private competition is still a relatively new and developing form of public procurement and, because of that, many governments have few policies and procedures dealing with the conduct of public-private competitions; some governments may have none. Consequently, when conducting public-private competitions, public procurement professionals are called upon to use more discretion than in other types of public procurements. The absence of policies and procedures and the exercise of increased individual discretion mean that public procurement professionals must be constantly on guard to identify and avoid ethical problems. Some of the major "red flag" areas that can give rise to ethical issues and problems include: (a) the basic concept of the public-private competition; (b) market testing; (c) after-the-fact notification; (d) conflicts with open records statutes; (e) separation of the purchaser/provider functions; and (f) level playing field issues versus the best interests of the government (Martin, 2002, p. 3).

...the public sector competing with the private sector raises ethical issues.

The Basic Concept of Public-Private Competition

The basic idea of the public sector competing with the private sector raises ethical issues. Because in-house departments are supported by tax dollars, the question arises: Is it ethical for tax-supported, governmental units to compete with private sector businesses and firms that must pay taxes? This is an ethical question inherent in every public-private competition. While there are no generally accepted rules, current governmental practice suggests that the public sector competing with the private sector is: (a) less of an issue when the service would otherwise be privatized; (b) more of an issue when the service is currently provided by the private sector; and (c) still more of an issue when in-house departments reach out into the marketplace in an attempt to provide services to other non-governmental organizations. This last approach not only generates considerable ethical debate but is actually illegal under the statutes of many states.

Market Testing

Market testing refers to the use of public-private competitions to compare or benchmark in-house service delivery approaches and costs against the private sector. The ethical issue here is that private sector businesses and firms are competing in good faith and incurring costs in the process when there is no real intention on the part of the government to award a contract.

After-the-Fact Notification

After-the-fact notification refers to the practice of governments not informing private sector businesses and firms up front that an in-house department will also be competing. The ethical issue here is one of making full disclosure to private sector competitors. Some anecdotal evidence exists that not only have in-house departments been invited to submit bids and proposals after the fact, but also some have even been given access to the competing private sector bids and proposals. The latter practice clearly represents an ethical transgression.

Conflicts with Open Records, Statutes, and Ordinances

Situations have arisen where private sector competitors have used open records, statutes, and ordinances to gain access to in-house bids and proposals. Since public administrators cannot control the ethical behavior of private sector individuals, the solution is to preclude this type of situation from arising. Public-private competitions can require that all bids and proposals (including those of in-house departments) remain sealed until bid/proposal opening or in-house departments can retain the services of an outside organization or individual (not subject to government open records, statutes, and ordinances) to prepare and submit their bids and proposals.

Separation of the Purchaser/Provider Functions

As noted earlier, governments in the United States have not given as much attention as they probably should to the issue of separating the purchaser and provider functions in a public-private competition. This ethical issue involves the ability of a government to create a quasi-arms-length transaction between the in-house department and public employees involved in a public-private competition (the provider) and the governmental units and public employees that oversee the competition, evaluate the bids and proposals, and monitor subsequent service provision (the purchaser). In Australia and the United Kingdom, this issue is referred to as the "purchaser/provider split." Failure to organizationally separate the purchaser and provider functions can give rise to serious ethical issues. For example, the Comptroller General of the United States (1999) issued a decision specifically prohibiting federal employees actively engaged in preparing in-house bids and proposals for public-private competitions from also serving as the government evaluators of competing private sector bids and proposals. It should seem obvious to many that serving as both a competitor and as your competitor's evaluator is a conflict of interest.

Level Playing Field Issues Versus Best Interests of the Government

During recent hearings before the GAO Commercial Activities Panel, private sector individuals and organizations repeatedly stressed the need for OMB Circular A-76 public-private competitions to be conducted on a more level playing field. While only a speculation at the present time, the possibility exists that, at some point, the desire to create an increasingly more level playing field may eventually come to conflict with the best interests of governments in providing contractual services. The potential ethical issue lies in which public policy objective should take precedence—level playing field considerations or ensuring that the best interests of governments are fostered and promoted when providing public services through contractual arrangements.

References

Chartered Institute of Public Finance and Accountancy (CIPFA). (1995). *Code of practice for compulsory competition.* London: CIPFA.

City Club of Portland, Oregon. (1999). *Privatization of government services.* Portland: City Club of Portland, Oregon.

The Civic Federation. (1996). *From privatization to innovation: A study of 16 cities.* Chicago: The Civic Federation.

Comptroller General of the United States. (1999). *Comptroller General Decision in DXS/Baker LLC; Morrison Knudsen Corporation, B-281224-B-281224.6.* Retrieved August 26, 1999, from http://www.access.gpo.gov/su_dics/aces/aces170.shtml.

Department of Finance and Administration (DFA). (1998a). *Competitive tendering and contracting: Guidance for managers.* Parkes, Australia: Department of Finance and Administration.

Department of Finance and Administration (DFA). (1998b). *The performance improvement cycle: Guidance for managers.* Parkes, Australia: Department of Finance and Administration.

Domberger, S., & Hall, C. (1995). *The contracting casebook.* Canberra, Australia: Australian Government Publishing Service.

Eggers, W. (1998). *Competitive neutrality: Ensuring a level playing field in managed competitions.* Los Angeles: The Reason Public Policy Institute.

Fantauzzo, S. (1996). Interview with Stephen Fantauzzo. *Michigan Privatization Report,* 10-11.

Foster, D. (1993). Industrial relations in local government: The impact of privatization. *The Political Quarterly,* 64(1), 49-58.

Industry Commission. (1996). *Competitive tendering and contracting by public sector agencies.* Report No. 48. Melbourne, Australia: Australian Government Printing Office.

Jensen, R. (1987). *The Phoenix approach to privatization.* Testimony in June before the Subcommittee on Small Business Anti-Trust Impact of Deregulation and Privatization, together with transcripts of various talk show interviews and newspaper articles from 1984 to 1988. Phoenix, AZ: City of Phoenix, Public Works Department.

Kettl, D. (1993). *Sharing power: Public governance and private markets.* Washington, DC: The Brookings Institution.

Kettner, P., & Martin, L. L. (1998). Factors affecting competition in state contracting for human services. *Journal of Sociology & Social Welfare,* 16(2), 181-194.

Martin, L. L. (1993a). *How to compare costs between in-house and contract service delivery.* Los Angeles: The Reason Foundation.

Martin, L. L. (1993b). *Bidding on service delivery: Public-private competition.* Washington. DC: International City/County Management Association.

Martin, L. L. (1996). *Selecting services for public-private competition.* Washington, DC: International City/County Management Association.

Martin, L. L. (1997). Public-private competition in the United Kingdom: Lessons for U.S. local governments. *State & Local Government Review, 29*(2), 81-90.

Martin, L. L. (1999a). Developing a level playing field for public-private competition. Arlington, VA: The IBM Center for the Business of Government. Retrieved March 10, 2003, from htttp://www.businessofgovernment.org.

Martin, L. L. (1999b). *Contracting for service delivery: Local government choices.* Washington, DC: International City/County Management Association.

Martin, L. L. (2002). Ethical issues in conducting public-private competitions. *The Public Administration Times, 25*(4), 3.

Miller, S. (1996). *Public private competition: The case of Phoenix.* Unpublished dissertation, University of Chicago.

Parker, D., & Hartley, K. (1990). Competitive tendering: Issues and evidence. *Public Money and Management, 10*(3), 9-16.

Rao, N., & Young, K. (1995). *Competition, contracts and change: The local authority experience of CCT.* London: Joseph Rowntree Foundation.

Rehfuss, J. (1991). The competitive agency: Thoughts from contracting out in Great Britain and the United States. *International Review of Administrative Sciences, 57,* 465-482.

Rendell, E. (1994). *Privatization: It can and does work.* New York: The Carnegie Council on Privatization.

Savas, E. S. (2000). *Privatization and public-private partnership.* New York: Seven Bridges Press.

Shaw, K., Fenwick, J., & Foreman, A. (1994, Summer). Compulsory competitive tendering for local government services: The experiences of local authorities in the north of England 1988-1992. *Public Administration, 72,* 201-217.

Stevens, B. (1984). *Delivering municipal services efficiently: A comparison of municipal and private service delivery.* Washington, DC: U.S. Department of Housing and Urban Development.

Thoma, T. (2001). *Developing model performance contracts.* Presentation at the conference on "Performance-Based Contracting in the Public Sector." Ottawa, Canada, September 5 and 6.

U.S. General Accounting Office (GAO). (2001). Commercial Activities Panel, San Antonio Public Hearing. Retrieved December 6, 2001, from http://www.gao.gov.a76panel/index.html.

U.S. Office of Management and Budget (OMB). (2003). *Performance of commercial activities (Circular No. A-76, revised).* Washington, DC: OMB.

Walker, B. (1993). *Competing for building maintenance: Direct labor organizations and compulsory competitive tendering.* London: Her Majesty's Stationary Office.

Walsh, K. (1995). Competition and public service delivery. In J. Stewart & Gerry Stoker (Eds.), *Local government in the 1990s* (pp. 28-48)). London: Macmillan.

Walsh, K., & Davis, H. (1993). *Competition and service: The impact of the Local Government Act of 1988.* London: Department of the Environment, HMSO.

Wilson, D., & Game, C. (1994). The impact of compulsory competitive tendering. In *Local government in the United Kingdom* (pp. 324-339). London: Macmillan.

Chapter 4

The Request for Proposal Document

The Request for Proposal (RFP) is a formal solicitation issued by a government agency to a contractor/supplier inviting them to submit an offer. Generally, the contractor's experience, qualifications, financial strength, and other defined criteria will take precedence over price. The RFP will consist of multiple parts including the Statement of Work (SOW). (Note: Scope/Statement of Work are used interchangeably and are abbreviated as SOW throughout this text.) A statement of work is the written description of the contractual requirements for materials and services. The National Institute of Governmental Purchasing, Inc.'s (NIGP) *Dictionary of Purchasing Terms* defines the statement of work as the "detailed description of the work that the purchasing jurisdiction wants the contractor to perform" (NIGP, 2002). It can be compared to the specifications contained within an Invitation for Bids (IFB). It is an integral part of the RFP process, and its importance cannot be overstated. A poorly designed SOW will result in misunderstanding, negative outcomes and, in some cases, a failed project. A well-conceived and clearly written SOW serves four main purposes:

- To establish a clear understanding of what is needed by articulating performance standards;
- To encourage competition in the marketplace and promote economic stimulus;
- To satisfy a critical need of government; and
- To obtain the best value for the taxpayer.

The SOW is the heart and soul of the contracting for services process. A weak SOW can be manipulated to support biases either for or against the contracting-out process. In some cases, the SOW may become a political football and subject to much criticism. Purchasing officials must become skilled in the intricacies of SOW writing and must add this to their skill repertoire.

Following the completion of the SOW, the next phase consists of multiple decision points that result in a packaged RFP. Decisions such as what type of contract will be the most appropriate, what boilerplate language should be included, and how to structure the evaluation process must be agreed upon.

The relationship that will eventually ensue between the government and the contractor will rest upon the correct strategic decisions made during this phase. The evaluation and selection of the contractor, one of many steps in a complex process, can be the most difficult and controversial phase of procurement.

Each contract for service is unique, and it is impossible to exercise a cookie-cutter approach to contract development. Procurement must align individual contracts with the mission, goals, and strategic plan of the particular government agency.

Request for Proposal (RFP) and Invitation for Bids (IFB)/ Invitation to Tender (ITT) (CN)

The SOW for a competitive sealed proposal is considered more difficult to prepare than specifications for competitive sealed bids. A quick review of the process, which is applied to either, is in order (NIGP, 2001, p. 55).

There are several differences as well as similarities between competitive sealed bidding and competitive sealed proposals/competitive negotiations. Competitive sealed bidding is formal, rigid, and always inflexible. Competitive sealed proposals are flexible, much less formal, and contain a degree of subjectivity that must be addressed.

Competitive sealed bidding requires that bids be evaluated and awarded solely on information contained in the IFB at the time of bid opening. No substantive changes, or any changes that would affect the determination of award, are permitted in either the content of the bid or the price. Competitive sealed proposals, on the other hand, allow an offeror to modify both content and price after offers are submitted and throughout the evaluation process.

There are similarities between the two methods. Many procedural aspects of competitive sealed bidding are applicable to competitive sealed proposals. Both require issuing a solicitation, with a public notice establishing the time and place where the solicitation is to be received. Although both methods require the opening to be public, a competitive sealed proposal solicitation usually requires that only the names of the offerors be revealed. In some jurisdictions, the prices and other information provided in a competitive sealed proposal are not disclosed until a Notice of Intent to Award is publicly posted. Not disclosing the contents of a proposal strengthens the negotiating power of a jurisdiction. An exception to this non-disclosure rule is the State of Florida, where state statutes, often referred to as sunshine laws, prohibit the withholding of information.

There are several advantages to competitive sealed proposals. The scoring, interview, and negotiation process permits in-depth analysis of every offeror's qualifications and capabilities. Competitive sealed bidding requires that only the lowest responsible and responsive bidder can be considered for award, regardless of the qualifications of the remaining bidders.

The SOW or specifications and price may be negotiated to meet the jurisdiction's needs. If the original prices are too high, the jurisdiction can use negotiation tactics to reduce the amount. In a competitive sealed bidding situation, if the prices are unacceptably high, the only remedy is to cancel the solicitation. It is then re-bid with revised specifications in an effort to lower the price.

Finally, in a limited market, there is little incentive to reduce prices. The entity's ability to negotiate terms and conditions so as to reduce prices is an effective technique when there is little or no competition. Options may be to negotiate a longer term agreement or unloading assistance may be considered.

Competitive sealed proposal disadvantages can be significant. The evaluation and award process can be lengthy, sometimes lasting up to three months, depending on the complexity of the solicitation. Meticulous record keeping is necessary, and complex scoring methods must be used that require specific knowledge and application. If protests are received, the jurisdiction may be required to defend subjective decisions made during the selection process.

There are several advantages to competitive sealed proposals.

The entire process must be carefully managed to ensure that evaluations and final recommendations for award are objective and ensures that every offeror receives fair and impartial treatment. Inexperienced staff can be at a disadvantage in such negotiations, particularly when the private sector offeror has a trained negotiator taking part in the process.

Generally, those outside the professional procurement arena who may be involved in the procurement of services, have difficulty appreciating the difference between the two principal methods: (a) competitive sealed bid/tender (IFB/ITT) and competitive sealed proposal (RFP) and (b) the use of corresponding documents employed for solicitation.

The American Bar Association's (ABA) *2000 Model Procurement Code for State and Local Governments* explains the difference in its Commentary on Section 3-203:

> Under *competitive sealed bidding*, judgmental factors may be used only to determine if the supply, service, or construction item bid meets the purchase description. Under *competitive sealed proposals*, judgmental factors may be used to determine not only if the items being offered meet the purchase description, but may also be used to evaluate competing proposals. The effect of this different use of judgmental evaluation is that under competitive sealed bidding, once the

judgmental evaluation is completed, award is made on a purely objective basis to the lowest responsive and responsible bidder.

Under *competitive sealed proposals*, the quality of competing products or services may be compared and trade-offs made between price and quality of the products or services offered (all set forth in the solicitation). Award under competitive sealed proposals is then made to the responsible offeror whose proposal is most advantageous to the jurisdiction.

Competitive sealed bidding does not allow for any change in the bids once it has been opened, except for the correction of errors in limited circumstances. On the other hand, the competitive sealed proposal method permits discussion after opening proposals to allow clarification and changes in proposals, providing that adequate precautions are taken to ensure fair treatment of each offeror and that information gleaned from competing proposals is not disclosed to other offerors. Figure 18 briefly summarizes the differences between the IFB and RFP processes.

Invitation for Bids (IFB) Versus Request for Proposal (RFP)		
	IFB	RFP
Sealed bids (IFB) or offers (RFP) are always opened at a public meeting; response becomes a binding contract; usually award is made after bids or offers are agreed to without further dialogue.	Yes	No
Candidates may be eliminated on quality grounds.	Yes	Yes
Among qualified candidates, preference is given to more qualified candidate even though price is higher.	No	Possibly
Pricing is the main basis of award.	Yes	No
Commonly, a follow-up conference is conducted for negotiation after bids or offers are received and before award is made.	No	Yes
Most commonly used for purchase of commodities.	Yes	No
Most commonly used for purchase of professional services.	No	Yes
Competition a factor; federal antitrust laws apply.	Yes	Yes

Figure 18. *IFB Versus RFP.*

Source: Rehfuss, J. (1993, February). *Designing an effective bidding and monitoring system to minimize problems in competitive contracting: How-to guide no. 3* (p. 7). Los Angeles: The Reason Public Policy Institute.

Opening the Bid/Tender/Proposal

The term bid/tender/proposal opening in the traditional procurement environment is typically associated with procurement of goods and commodities via sealed competitive bids/tenders. Depending on the procurement method selected, the term might not be applicable. NIGP's (2002) *Dictionary of Purchasing Terms* defines bid opening as:

> The formal process in which sealed bids are opened, usually in the presence of one or more witnesses, at the time and place specified in the Invitation for Bids. The amount of each bid is recorded and bids are made available for public inspection.

The National Association of State Procurement Officials' (NASPO) purchasing guide defines public bid openings as: "The process of opening and reading bids, conducted at the time and place specified in the Invitation to Bid and/or the advertisement, and in the presence of anyone who wishes to attend." If the method of service procurement is competitive negotiation, competitive sealed proposal, or multi-step competitive sealed proposal, the term *proposal opening* is more appropriate.

Unlike the IFB, few jurisdictions open proposals in public. The ABA's Model Procurement Code (2000) speaks to the differences between opening of sealed bids and the receipt of proposals. The Code states in Section 3-203(4):

> Proposals shall be opened so as to avoid disclosure of contents to competing offerors during the process of negotiation. A Register of Proposals shall be prepared in accordance with regulations promulgated by the (Policy Office) and shall be open for public inspection after contract award.

The Request for Proposal Team

The RFP planning process begins with the designation of a team that is charged with preparing the RFP for solicitation. The procurement manager is usually the designated chairperson and will assemble the team in collaboration with those who will be impacted by the service targeted for contracting. Normally, the team is an uneven number between three and seven members, with the chairperson voting only to break a tie vote. The intended service targeted for contracting will dictate the size of the team, with flexibility being a key to the success of the solicitation. If a small service has been targeted, such as mowing the lawn at several playgrounds, a simple RFP could be prepared by only one member of the procurement staff. The team will expand accordingly if the targeted service is technically complex and will require large amounts of monetary expenditures. The RFP team should be composed of cross-functional, subject-matter experts (SMEs) selected from various government agencies that will be most affected by the implementation of the service contract. Quite often, the team will include a representative from law, finance, or budget in addition to the agency representatives.

Harney (1992), in his book *Service Contracting: A Local Government Guide* states:

> For more complex service contracts, the core of the team consists of the field manager, who monitors the delivery of the service; a member of the purchasing staff, who is experienced in service contracting; and the contract manager, who is in charge of administering the contract. Other team members may be added, but they function primarily as resources, providing assistance as required. They may

be drawn from the legal department, from the department currently providing the service, or from any other department of the local government; consultants may also be used. Ordinarily, only the field manager, a member of the purchasing staff, the contract manager, and a representative of the department providing the service meet regularly and function as a working committee. The other team members are called on as the need arises.

He states that while most contract staffing positions can be filled from existing positions within the jurisdiction, candidates for the team may require training in the basics of contract administration. Team designations, as described below, have been taken/adapted from Harney's book.

Project Manager

The duties of the project manager relate primarily to oversight of the program as a whole...

The project manager is often selected from the jurisdiction's staff and should have the authority to act independently on most contracting issues, obtaining program direction from a jurisdiction's senior manager as necessary. The duties of the project manager relate primarily to oversight of the program as a whole and do not normally require an extensive knowledge of the finer details of the contracted service.

Contract Manager

The contract manager's responsibilities include: determining the priority of service requests from citizens or the jurisdiction; reviewing and resolving contract disputes; negotiating contract amendments; evaluating contractor performance; approving contractor request for payment; preparing performance records with information from field managers, clients, personal observations, and other sources; and training field managers in contract administration and monitoring techniques. In addition, the contract manager plans for future contracts by updating the original contract and SOW to reflect innovation in service delivery and identifies new areas of possible contracting efforts.

As a mediator of contract disputes, the contract manager must be able to understand contract issues from the contractor's and the jurisdiction's points of view. Finally, the contract manager must have a demonstrated ability to work effectively with all levels of jurisdiction employees and with contractors ranging from small entrepreneurs to global corporations.

The Procurement Office as Contract Manager

If the jurisdiction's end-user agency does not have a management staff member qualified to perform the duties of a contract manager, the agency should receive guidance from the procurement office. The procurement office has experience in contracting for goods and services, is accustomed to mediating disputes between the jurisdiction and sources of services and supplies, and should have a close working relationship with staff throughout the jurisdiction.

The Consultant as Contract Manager

Some consulting firms offer contract management services. If funds are available, consideration should be given to training internal staff in contract management. If there is no viable internal candidate for contract management, consideration could be given for hiring a consultant. If a consultant is engaged, the jurisdiction should consider the training of in-house staff in contract management by the consultant. This would allow the jurisdiction to have a qualified contract manager during the start-up of the service and, as in-house employees become proficient in contract management, phase out the consultant.

The Circuit-Riding Contract Manager

A jurisdiction that cannot afford a full-time contract manager may be able to hire a qualified contract manager who is on the staff of a nearby jurisdiction. This particular approach is effective when several geographically connected jurisdictions have service contracts that require a high level of contract management expertise. It allows the jurisdictions with limited funds to engage the necessary expertise of a contract manager.

Contract Administrator

A contract administrator is usually located with the end-user agency responsible for the service under contract. The duties of a contract administrator are not full-time and are usually assumed by staff members who have other administrative functions, such as managing the procurement, budget, or accounts payable process within the agency. Training in the theory and practice of contract administration is needed to properly carry out the contract administrator's duties.

Field Manager

A field manager, the first and most important contact with the contractor, is responsible for overseeing and objectively evaluating a contractor's performance and addressing minor issues before they become major issues. A field manager may oversee four to 10 contracts or more, depending on the complexity and size, and may have additional supervisory duties with the end-user agency.

Hands-on service experience is invaluable in performing assigned duties, and field managers are usually recruited from line supervisors who have been involved in the delivery of the service prior to it being contracted out. The contract administrator or even the contract manager sometimes performs the duties of the field manager. The difference between the performance monitoring and evaluation functions of field and contract managers is one of perspective. Field managers monitor and evaluate on a one-on-one basis and report their personal observations to their supervisors. Contract managers monitor and evaluate from a broader perspective, using information collected from various sources, including the field managers, and weighing the objectivity and level of competence of the sources.

When selecting a field manager from within the jurisdiction, be certain that the candidate can handle the additional responsibilities. To be effective, new field managers require specialized training in contract monitoring and administration. Reports to management and the governing body of the jurisdiction rely on data compiled by field managers. It is essential for field managers to understand how management will use this data to assess the performance and effectiveness of the contractor.

Consultants

The RFP team is usually composed of all in-house members. Occasionally, the size, scope, and complexity of a targeted service will require the use of an independent consultant to assist the team in preparing the RFP and the SOW. The independent consultant should be selected through competitive proposals and be prohibited from submitting a bid or offer on the intended service, which preserves the integrity of the process. Contractors, manufacturers, and potential service providers also should be prohibited from serving in a consulting capacity. Many jurisdictions have regulations that prohibit consultants from bidding on contracts that they have helped to develop.

A consultant may serve as a valuable resource to the team, but the team is ultimately responsible for the content of the RFP. Working drafts of the RFP should be submitted on a predetermined schedule, such as 25%, 50%, 75%, and completion of the draft. The consultant also may be retained during the solicitation process and at the time of response evaluation.

The RFP Draft

Once an RFP outline has been finalized and agreed upon, the team will use the outline to develop the RFP draft. All impacted stakeholders should review the draft and make corrections, suggestions, and critical comments. Many jurisdictions use a sign-off sheet that is signed by each reviewer to indicate that they reviewed the draft and, where appropriate, have commented on its content. Senior management officials, elected officials, the finance and budget office, and legal counsel may also review the draft. The final document usually emerges stronger if a comprehensive draft review is conducted. This review also creates a feeling of ownership and support by those who have placed their signatures on the draft.

If the draft review is too extensive, it is possible that certain negatives might occur. For example, the larger the group, the slower the review process. Radical changes may be suggested in terms of scope, intent, or content that can dilute the original requirements of the RFP. A professional procurement manager will be able to successfully balance the positive and negative aspects of a draft review.

RFP Outline

The RFP outline should include four main parts by organizing all of the pertinent elements into appropriate areas of information that will be included in the final document. This outline might be constructed in the following order:

Part I. General Information
    A. Introduction/Overview
    B. Purpose/Objective
    C. Background/History
    D. Contact with Jurisdictional Staff
    E. Pre-Proposal Conference
    F. Contract Writing/Contract Negotiations
        (1) Contractor Qualifications
        (2) Terms/Conditions/Boilerplate
        (3) Contract Extension and/or Renewal
    G. Outcomes
    H. Applicable Documents
        (1) Calendar of Events
        (2) Task Description
        (3) Trade References and Standards
    I. Evaluation Process/Methodologies
        (1) Constraints
        (2) Work-site Conditions

(3) Jurisdictional Responsibilities

Part II. Statement/Scope of Work
   A. Statement of Work Checklist
   B. Statutes/Ordinances
   C. Unambiguous SOW
   D. Security Controls
   E. Technical Requirements
      (1) Writing Specifications
         (a) Design-Based versus Performance-Based
   F. Deliverables
   G. Quality Control Program
   H. Work Schedule

Part III. Supporting Information
   A. Personnel Qualifications
      (1) Employee Identification
      (2) Additional Personnel Requirements
   B. Place and Evaluation of Performance
   C. Performance Standards
      (1) Service Complaints
      (2) Emergency Assistance
   D. Period of Performance
   E. Liquidated Damages
   F. Evaluation of Non-Quantitative Service Areas
   G. Special Considerations
      (1) Payment Procedures
      (2) Insurance
      (3) Bonds
      (4) Alternative Surety
      (5) Considerations: Legal, Fiscal, Price, and Timing
   H. Format for Technical/Price Proposals
      (1) Special Instructions
      (2) Price Ranking of Offerors
      (3) Technical Exhibits
   I. Affidavit and Signature Page

Part IV. Supporting Documents
   A. Appendices
   B. Charts, Graphs, and Drawings
   C. Exhibits

Separating the outline into four major categories ensures that the RFP and the SOW are written in a coherent fashion. By formatting the outline, it will be easier to write and, more importantly, easier for potential offerors to understand.

The items that follow may or may not apply to every RFP/SOW but are listed in order to provide a general overview of what may be included in the outline and, in turn, a completed document. The following was taken/adapted from Harney (1992, pp. 47-74).

General Information

INTRODUCTION/OVERVIEW

The introduction states what the jurisdiction expects to accomplish from the contract and may include a history or background of the service. It gives a brief overview of the work required and defines the extent of the service to be provided and the contract terms. Generally included in the introduction are the names of the jurisdiction's contact persons from whom additional information can be obtained, the time and place of any pre-proposal conferences, and a general statement of the minimum experience and qualifications required of the contractor.

PURPOSE/OBJECTIVE

The Statement of Purpose expands the brief overview of the service included in the introduction by identifying the rules that apply to its use and the jurisdiction whose service is being contracted out. It also states if the jurisdiction's end-user agency or a central contract monitoring and administration team will monitor the contract. The Statement of Purpose also provides the start and end dates of the contract and the location of where the work is to be performed; the goals and objectives of the service that may include the relationship of the service to the overall jurisdiction's operation; and the frequency of service.

The size of the contract should be expressed in terms of the annual expenditure by the jurisdiction for the services, using information such as the number of clients to be served; pieces of equipment to be maintained; acres of grass to be mowed or curb miles swept; the level of effort expected of the contractor; and any other information helpful to the offeror in identifying the jurisdiction's needs.

BACKGROUND/HISTORY

The inclusion of background or history will help the offerors to better understand the service to be provided. This section could provide the offerors with a better understanding of how the jurisdiction delivered the service previously and might also explain why a private contractor is offering it for delivery.

Contact with Jurisdictional Staff

During the RFP process, many jurisdictions prohibit an offeror from directly contacting any of the jurisdictions' employees except the procurement staff. This policy can be effective when applied to the procurement of goods; but, when applied to the procurement of services, it can generate unnecessary issues. No matter how well written the SOW, it cannot provide an offeror the same grasp of service delivery as one-to-one contacts with knowledgeable jurisdictional end-users.

If circumstances dictate, it is possible to limit contact with jurisdictional employees and still provide an offeror access to the information necessary to be intelligently responsive. Offeror contacts can be limited to a *technical source* (an end-user representative who is familiar with the service) that is responsible for addressing service delivery questions and a *contract source* (a procurement staff representative) that is responsible for addressing solicitation questions. The RFP solicitation must clearly state that any responses by a jurisdiction representative that appear to change the SOW or any other part of the solicitation document cannot be relied on unless a formal amendment to the solicitation is issued by the jurisdiction.

If possible, any contact between offerors and the jurisdiction should be prohibited for the last seven to 10 calendar days before the date set for receiving the responses. This is done to curtail offerors from trying to contact a jurisdiction representative to ask questions, which could result in the need to issue an amendment and delay the acceptance and opening of responses.

If the offeror's questions and comments are within the cutoff date and are judged to be material to the solicitation, such as omitted information, then an amendment is necessary.

Pre-Proposal Conference

When using the RFP process, a pre-proposal conference rather than a pre-bid conference, is utilized. If a pre-proposal conference is scheduled, the time, date, and location of the conference are included in the solicitation advertisement and in the introduction section of the solicitation. It should also be indicated if the pre-proposal conference is optional or mandatory for the offerors. This information should be included on the cover page of the solicitation document.

The pre-proposal conference should be held at the service delivery site. The conference provides offerors with an opportunity to ask questions about the solicitation in a public setting and afterwards tour the service delivery site in order to note apparent service constraints or visible areas of concern. Some pre-proposal conferences are held in two parts: a guided tour of the service site followed by a conference with those who attended the tour. If attendance at the pre-proposal is mandatory, the solicitation must state *mandatory attendance* at both the tour and the conference in order for offerors to qualify for participation.

Contractor Qualifications

The required experience, qualifications, and evidence of financial stability must be described completely in the qualifications section. The description of experience may include the number of years of service experience, level of technical knowledge, and degrees and certifications required. The financial stability of an offeror can be determined by requesting the most recent financial statements, bonding capacity and capability, and evidence of the ability to obtain the necessary insurance. Recent references should be required, providing the name and telephone number of the referenced contact person. This is done to ensure that the offeror has performed satisfactorily on contracts of similar size and scope.

If, by law, any special trade, professional, or business licenses are required of offeror employees, those requirements must be listed in the qualifications section of the solicitation. If the jurisdiction deems it necessary that other special experience or qualifications are needed, these should be listed in the qualifications section.

Boilerplate

The NIGP (2002) *Dictionary of Purchasing Terms* defines boilerplate as "a colloquialism used in purchasing to identify standard terms and conditions incorporated in solicitations, contracts, and purchase orders, which are often preprinted or incorporated by reference." The boilerplate is a critical component of a solicitation document. It will be incorporated into the contract along with other applicable standard clauses, special conditions, the governing rules for the submission of a response, and the stipulations applicable to most contracts.

Many procurement offices will use the same boilerplate for the procurement of both goods and services. This is a practice that should be avoided because it will ultimately weaken the final contract. An IFB/ITT document for services must have its own boilerplate. Many standard clauses applicable to supplies and equipment do not apply to services. Generally, the preprinted forms that are used for goods and equipment will cause confusion with a service solicitation. The use of a preprinted boilerplate that includes an irrelevant or contradictory clause is not good practice. The development of an effective boilerplate should be a collaborative effort between the procurement office and legal counsel and should be frequently updated in order to include current legislation as well as any federal or state laws that impact the jurisdiction. Special clauses required by policy, ordinance, or executive order should also be included and updated as needed. The jurisdiction's legal counsel must approve the final boilerplate document.

Figure 19 summarizes the standard clauses included in the RFP boilerplate. (See Appendix G for a description of these clauses.)

Standard Clauses Included in the RFP Boilerplate	
Acknowledgement of Amendments	Expenses Incurred in Bid/Proposal Preparation
Alternative Bids	Failure to Enforce
Antitrust	Force Majeure
Applicable Law	General Terms and Conditions
Assignment	Indemnification
Bid/Proposal Acceptance Period	Informalities and Irregularities
Bid/Proposal Form Submission	Instructions to Bidders/Proposers
Bid Withdrawal	Late Submissions
Bidder Classification	Non-conforming Terms and Conditions
Bidder Investigation	Non-substitution
Certificates and Licenses	Oral Statement
Certification of Independent Price Determination	Patents, Copyrights, Royalties
Changes in the Statement of Work	Procurement Regulations
Collusion among Bidders/Offerors	Qualifications of Bidders/Proposers
Cost Reimbursement	Recovery of Money
Debarment	Rights to Audit
Economic Price Adjustment	Termination
Employee Discrimination	Traffic Control
Estimate of Requirements	Unnecessarily Elaborate Responses
Ethics in Public Contracting	Vehicle/Equipment Buy-Back

Figure 19. *Standard Boilerplate Clauses for RFPs.*

Source: Harney, D. (1992). *Service contracting: A local government guide.* Washington, DC: International City/County Management Association.

APPLICABLE DOCUMENTS

Calendar of Events. Include a calendar of key events that reflects the estimated date of occurrence for each event in the solicitation and award process. It should be mentioned that stated dates are estimated and could change. The calendar usually includes time of distribution of the solicitation document, the pre-proposal conference and site tour, the solicitation opening, interviews, selection of the successful offeror, the contract award date, and the notice to proceed date for the contract.

Task Description. The task description sets forth the duties of the contractor. The jurisdiction's end-user agency prepares a draft task description that narrowly focuses on the service delivery as it is understood and defined by the agency. Although the end-user agency might have a good understanding of the delivery from a practical operations perspective, it may have difficulty defining the service on paper.

The end-user agency must also identify aspects of the service that can be evaluated when determining if the service is being effectively delivered. This requires a *quality oriented* assessment that specifies how may units of work should be delivered in a given period of time (curb miles swept, clients served, acres mowed, etc.) and how it will be determined if the units of work meet the contract requirements (height of grass, degree of cleanliness, client satisfaction levels, complaints received, etc.). Although this information is not directly related to the task description, it is necessary to develop the performance section of the SOW.

While the jurisdiction's end-user staff prepares a draft of tasks, the team should also contact other geographically close jurisdictions and professional organizations to obtain SOW samples. Such resources may be obtained from NIGP, NASPO, Service Corps of Retired Executives (SCORE), and the Institute for Supply Management (ISM). The team should also collect information on how the private sector delivers the service through such organizations as the National Association of Purchasing Management (NAPM), and ISM. It is important to collect more than one SOW sample in order to establish a broad frame of reference on descriptions of the service, evaluation methods used, and any issues unexpectedly encountered during delivery.

Based on the information gathered, the team prepares a draft task description. This draft should represent a sound, composite view of the service and may include details and address issues associated with the service beyond the draft prepared by the end-user agency.

> *...a quality oriented assessment...is intrinsic for developing the performance section of the SOW.*

Upon completion, both drafts should be merged. This may require a face-to-face meeting of both parties to ensure clarity and agreement. The final task description should reflect the end-user's service needs, incorporate the best features of the task descriptions collected from the other sources, and provide a sound basis for a quality solicitation. Before incorporating the task description into the solicitation, a final review should be made by the first-line supervisors or key employees who are responsible for delivering the service. This final review can help eliminate many serious questions that may arise after the solicitation document is published.

Trade References and Standards. If statutes, ordinances, regulations, trade standards, or other materials are used to establish requirements in the solicitation, a copy of these references must be available on demand for review by the offerors. If the jurisdiction cannot produce a copy of a referenced material within a reasonable time after an offeror's request, the offeror may be successful in challenging the inclusion of the material in the solicitation.

Evaluation Process/Methodologies

Constraints. Any conditions that could affect efficient service delivery, hamper effective performance, or increase costs to the offeror must be detailed in the solicitation document. Typical constraints might be work-site conditions, unique ordinances, or administrative requirements imposed by the jurisdiction.

Work-Site Conditions. All known conditions at the work site that could adversely affect the offeror must be identified in the solicitation document to avoid disputes after the award. The RFP should describe any unusual conditions that exist at the work site. Such conditions can have service delivery implications. For example, defective floor coverings can affect the cost of maintenance. Limited or extended hours of operation of a jurisdiction's facility can affect the cost of service delivery to that facility.

Jurisdictional Responsibilities. The jurisdiction has its own contractual obligations. Its principal obligations are to ensure that the contract service delivery is being provided and to make payment for acceptable service. Some lesser obligations might include the coordination of a contractor for general public activities such as open-air concerts and art exhibits in public parks.

The jurisdiction's... principal obligations are to ensure that the contract service delivery is being provided and to make payment...

The team must assess the financial impact of any additional contractual function. If the jurisdiction requires support services for an offeror in conjunction with the assumed contractual function, a higher fee will be charged by the offeror to provide these services. The SOW team must realize that if additional contractual functions with offeror support are performed, the cost will not represent the offeror's actual cost. If the jurisdiction can provide existing facilities, equipment, and amenities to the offeror without any additional expense, the provision of support services can contribute to overall contract savings.

The jurisdiction may choose to assume certain obligations because of a desire to retain a measure of control in functions performed better or more securely by the jurisdiction itself. Jurisdictions often maintain control of functions such as daily revenue deposits received by a concessionaire, the retention of facility access keys, or providing repairs and maintenance to jurisdiction facilities. The jurisdiction may also want to purchase and retain ownership of specialized equipment needed for the performance of tasks required in the solicitation. The team would then have to decide if the equipment is to be provided at no cost or leased to the offeror. This stipulation should be noted in the solicitation.

Statement of Work/Scope of Work

PLANNING THE STATEMENT/SCOPE OF WORK

An SOW is a document intended to detail a strategy for a contractor and the jurisdiction to accomplish the objectives of a particular service requirement. The planning phase of the SOW preparation is focused on a thorough investigation of the why and what of the service requirement. The team should prepare a checklist that will assist in developing the SOW strategy (see Figure 20) that may include the following:

- Identify the resource, schedule, and compensation constraints for the project.
- Identify all jurisdiction and service contractor participation needed for the project and define the extent and nature of their responsibilities. Jurisdictional support such as equipment, materials, facilities, and personnel should be specifically stated.
- Determine the minimum service requirement.
- Challenge the tasks identified in the Needs Statement, including sequencing interrelationships of the required tasks. For example, a Needs Statement for school custodial services might require that the chalkboards must be completely washed every evening. Is this task really necessary on a daily basis? Why not just erase the chalkboards every evening and wash only once a week?
- Identify specific technical data requirements such as plans, specifications, reports, etc.
- Develop a task list of all the activities that will be included in the targeted service. The task list can be formatted according to *input* (personnel and material resources needed to accomplish the service); *process* (the work element that transforms the resources into the output); and *output* (which defines the specific services).
- Identify who does *what* and *when* it should be done. This activity will help the team develop performance specifications.
- Performance levels can be determined by asking: How much? How often? At what skill level?
- Determine where the service is to be performed and who should pay for it.
- Identify specific mandates or directives that may influence the contract (OSHA; OMB, Circular A-102, etc.). Special attention should be given to requirements for licenses or registration. (Dobler, Burt, & Lee, 1990, p. 345)

Is the Statement/Scope of Work (SOW) appropriate?
The following questions may be used as tests for the appropriateness of the SOW: • Does the Statement tell the offeror what is required to be done? • Is the information necessary to assist the offeror in understanding what is required? • Will the offeror and the jurisdiction be able to negotiate reasonable pricing parameters for tasks, services, etc.? • Will the tasks, when accomplished, produce results consistent with project objectives?
Are the objectives clear?
Do they provide a method for the procurement officer to keep salient features of the procurement's objectives foremost while preparing and reviewing the SOW? • Is the SOW sufficiently specific to permit the offeror to identify and the jurisdiction to evaluate the manpower and resources needed to accomplish it? • Are the specific duties of the offeror stated in such a way that it is known what is required and permit the jurisdiction to determine if the requirements have been met prior to signing the acceptance document? • Are sentences written so that there is no question of whether the offeror is to be obligated, such as: *The successful offeror shall do the work*, **not**, *This work will be required*. • Are the proper reference documents provided? Are they pertinent to the SOW? Are they properly cited in the solicitation? • Are the specifications or exhibits applicable, i.e., latest revisions of each document? If so, are they properly cited in the solicitation? • Are the specifications restrictive? Are only the necessities specified? • Are there dates for the key tasks to be accomplished by the offeror in the solicitation document? Is the time reflected in working or calendar days? • Are proper quantities shown?
Some do's and don'ts
• Avoid misunderstandings and eliminate possible doubts. • Describe the *what, where*, and *when*, and avoid loopholes. • Avoid over-specifying and clarify the contractual obligations of the jurisdiction

Figure 20. *Statement of Work Checklist.*

STATUTES/ORDINANCES

Any state law, jurisdictional ordinances, regulations, and policies that may affect the offeror's level of service, workweek, or the time of day that performance is permitted to occur must be identified in the SOW. Some jurisdictional ordinances may require refuse collection and disposal to be more complex than standard industry refuse collection practices. The use of heavy construction equipment or other machinery may be restricted by noise abatement ordinances that limit the hours of operation. Consider the following case: The offeror's normal workday is from 6:00 a.m. to 3:00 p.m. (typical in the construction industry), and the jurisdiction's noise abatement ordinance is in effect until 8:00 a.m. The offeror must schedule shifts for later in the workday. This could require the contractor to pay higher hourly wages, resulting in a higher contract cost. Contract costs may also increase if the offeror must schedule work on weekends and holidays.

THE UNAMBIGUOUS SOW

Cross-functional team members should compose the SOW in a language plainly understandable to the selected or potential consultant(s). Clear and exact language is essential, as courts generally rule against vague service contracts. When developing the SOW, team members should:

- State activity or work requirements plainly, logically, and in chronological order.
- Include graphics (e.g., illustrations, diagrams, tables, and charts) to assist in describing the activity or work and the related requirements.
- Avoid words that allow for multiple interpretations (e.g., "include," "average," "adequate," and "or equal").
- Employ plain words and phrases (no esoteric technical jargon).
- Use "shall" to express a mandatory condition; use "will" to state a declaration of purpose or intent.
- Emphasize the active rather than the passive voice.
- Select verbs that identify activity or work specifications (e.g., "analyze," "attend," and "audit") and those that answer explicit questions.
- Avoid "and/or," "any," and "either: because these words imply that the consultant may make a choice, which could conflict with the intent of the SOW.
- Replace pronouns and repeat nouns to preclude any misinterpretation.
- Use the same phrase or word, especially when referring to technical terms or items.
- Avoid "catch-all" phrases (i.e., "to the extent necessary," "as required," or "as applicable") because they confuse the scope of the issue/problem.
- Spell out acronyms and abbreviations the first time they are used and put the abbreviated version in parentheses after the spelled-out phrase. (Adapted from ISM, 2000)

In addition, team members should be sensitive to any loopholes in the SOW because a consultant, and possibly contract auditors, will adhere to the letter of the SOW in potential future disputes. The team should ensure that the SOW is reviewed for technical content; editorial structure (i.e., grammar, syntax, and diction) and style; and management concurrence. Clearly defining an SOW through the collaborative effort of a strong cross-functional team ultimately will result in better performance from the selected contractor.

Security Controls

A jurisdiction's building and security regulations must be described clearly in the solicitation document to alert offerors of possible entry constraints. Access to some jurisdictional facilities may require the offeror's employees to obtain security clearances. For example, if a key to a parking meter collection system is lost, it must be the responsibility of the successful offeror to re-key every affected parking meter. Appropriate damages must be noted in the solicitation document.

Technical Requirements

Design-Based Versus Performance-Based. Like design or performance specifications used in purchasing materials and commodities, the SOW for a service contract can be design- or performance-based. During the planning of the SOW, the team should consider a *performance*-based rather than *design*-based SOW. A performance-based SOW describes the duty, method, and the frequency that allows the contractor maximum flexibility in the selection of specific methodologies for accomplishing the service outcomes as required. An example of a performance standard is, *Floors shall show no dust or dirt streaks after cleaning*. Performance-based SOWs describe the nature and scope of the issue/problem as well as the preferred results from exercise of the performance criteria, quality assurance requirements, delivery schedule, and other variables.

> ...for a service contract ...the team should consider a performance-based rather than design-based SOW.

A design-based SOW is specific as to the desired results and how the task will be accomplished. An example of a design-based SOW for a custodial contract is, *Wax floors once a week using Johnson's floor wax and a Tennant floor scrubber with #2 buffing pads*. A design-based SOW specifically states what is required and exactly how the requirements will be fulfilled. An organization uses this type of SOW when it desires strict control of the specific methodology applied in the performance of the activity or work. This control can contribute to greater direct costs, restrictive competition and higher indirect costs associated with compliance monitoring (NIGP, 2001, p. 53).

Understanding Deliverables

An important element of the work requirement section is a description of contract deliverables. It is necessary to separate work requirements from delivery requirements. Work requirements must be detailed in the technical requirements section. The outputs of the work requirements and their scheduled delivery over the life of the contract, within specified time lines, are described in the deliverables section. Figure 21 lists the most common types of deliverables.

A deliverable may be the completion of a milestone or the accomplishment of a task and is used to measure successful performance. Frequently, the completion of a deliverable will trigger a payment, which may be referred to as a progress payment.

The most common types of deliverables are:	
Computer Software	Prototypes
Design	Reports
Drawings	Service
Education	Studies
Findings	Test Results
Labor	Training
Products	

Figure 21. *Common Types of Deliverables.*

QUALITY CONTROL PROGRAM

Service delivery contracts that require complex or highly visible services must have a quality control program in place to ensure that the service being provided reflects the services specified. The SOW should require offerors to submit an outline with their proposal that itemizes their existing quality control program. If the proposer does not have such a program, the company should be required to draft a quality control program that can be submitted with the proposal. If the contract is awarded to the offeror who submitted a draft quality control program, a fully developed program should be required within a specified period of time after award.

A service provider quality control program should include, minimally, the following points:

- An inspection system that covers all of the performance requirements in the SOW, specifying the areas to be inspected on a scheduled or unscheduled basis and the individuals responsible for the inspections;
- A method of identifying unacceptable service quality; and
- A description of the corrective action to be taken if the service quality is unacceptable.

WORK SCHEDULE

It is essential to effective contract administration to know where any work crews may be located at any time. The SOW minimally requires the submission of a biweekly schedule that is approved in advance by the jurisdiction's contract administrator. This schedule should reflect the status of all work crews.

Supporting Information

PERSONNEL QUALIFICATIONS

Few issues affect the quality of a service delivery as much as the use of unqualified personnel. The solicitation document must clearly request that offerors submit, with the sealed proposal, detailed information on the experience and qualifications of first-line personnel assigned to the service delivery.

The solicitation document must require that resumés of the offeror's field supervisor, team leader, or project manager be submitted with the sealed proposal. Minimum experience and qualification requirements must be outlined in the RFP. Do not expect that only qualified employees will be reflected in the offeror's list of key personnel. The jurisdiction has the unilateral right to request replacement of key personnel if the originally assigned key personnel fail to perform to the standards of the resumés submitted with the sealed proposal.

Employee Identification. For some service delivery contracts, such as day janitorial work, refuse collection, food concessions, or any other service delivery requiring the offeror's employees to be in contact with the public, it may be desirable to require that those employees be provided a full work uniform. Contract employees can be easily identified for complaints received about discourtesy or poor performance, and the successful offeror's reputation and image are on public display.

Many service providers, such as refuse collection, landscaping, and janitorial services routinely provide their employees with uniforms. It is in the interest of the jurisdiction to require, in the SOW, a specific description of any required uniform. The standard for a service provider might be to furnish a minimum uniform of a T-shirt, jacket, coveralls, or smock with the service provider's name prominently displayed. A means of enforcing a uniform requirement also should be included in the SOW.

The need for a full- or partial-uniform requirement must be determined before the solicitation is ready to be published. A full uniform could add considerable cost to the contract.

Additional Personnel Requirements. Requirements that are included in the SOW should be monitored and enforced throughout the contract. Consider the following list of possible inclusions:

- A policy of employing only those who possess the required skills and experience for the service delivery;
- Maintenance of a workforce sufficient in size to perform the contract, including reserve personnel to fill vacancies during absences due to illness, vacations, and holidays;
- Written personnel policies that govern behavior, substance abuse, and relations with customers and the public; and

- A Table of Organization reflecting the number of personnel assigned to the service delivery, vacancies, and weekly work schedules.

Evaluation of Performance

The jurisdiction's end-user agency should identify the areas of performance to be evaluated and the quality and quantity for each area. These identifiers may be used in the SOW to establish performance standards. If liquidated damages are included in the solicitation, these standards will be the gauge to measure unacceptable performance. The description of the performance standard evaluation method does not need to be lengthy. It should, however, be detailed enough to identify the areas of evaluation with a definition of deficient service delivery performance when compared to the performance standards. A performance evaluation system should be structured so that it does not interfere with service delivery. It should also encourage cooperation with all contractual parties to ensure that an acceptable level of service is provided throughout the term of the contract.

Performance Standards

A zero-fault performance standard is unrealistic. A single point, where acceptable performance stops and unacceptable performance begins, is also unrealistic. The team must consider establishing performance standards that reflect reality. To be realistic, the performance evaluation system should be established several levels below the acceptable performance level. One such striated plan may offer the first level, defining a specific range of up to three faults within a month. Performance within this range is acceptable. The second level would be four to seven faults within a month, which reflects marginal performance. The third level, more than seven faults a month, is considered unacceptable performance.

Performance at the second level would generate a warning notice by the contract administrator. Performance at the third level would signify serious issues surrounding service delivery and would require a written notice to the service provider to cure the delivery lapses.

Service Complaints. Communicate to the offerors that they are responsible for and must respond to any service complaints. Indicate the need for a response time, the resolution of complaints, and payment for the costs of the resolution if the fault lies with the offeror. If the jurisdiction requires the offeror to respond directly to service requests, it must specify the records to be maintained and the frequency of review by the jurisdiction.

Emergency Assistance. For the situations that may arise as a result of an emergency, the jurisdiction should describe the possible types of emergencies and the minimum needs to be furnished by the offeror.

Liquidated Damages

A provision for liquidated damages should be a part of the solicitation when the jurisdiction reasonably expects to suffer a loss (damage) for unacceptable performance. The RFP must describe the method of liquidated damages to be used in the event of unacceptable service delivery.

Liquidated damages may cause an offeror to not submit a response if the provisions are too harsh. To protect themselves against being assessed liquidated damages, offerors may increase the proposed pricing schedule.

The term *penalty clause* is often used incorrectly when addressing liquidated damages. Never consider or refer to liquidated damages as a penalty for unacceptable performance. The exact amount of damage is usually difficult to establish. The key to establishing liquidated damages is *reasonableness*. When establishing a monetary amount for liquidated damages, the jurisdiction request must not be excessive. Courts have dismissed liquidated damages because the amount was excessive or beyond reasonable cost and was, in fact, a penalty against the service provider.

Evaluation of Non-Quantitative Service Areas

Quantitative measures can be used to evaluate aspects of service that appear not to apply. For example, the cleanliness of a street or facility, the impact of a service on a client, and the effectiveness of a training program can be measured quantitatively.

First, an analysis of the deliverables of the service must be made. If the evaluation is to be based on cleanliness, assign a scale of point values to a written or photographic description of cleanliness. When assessing end-user satisfaction, the most likely types of complaints and the number of complaints that represent unacceptable performance should be listed. To evaluate quality of workmanship, photographic or published trade standards can be used to establish standards of workmanship. Point values can be assigned to varying levels of workmanship. If the goal of the solicitation is to improve the recipient's skills or mental or physical well-being, designing a matrix that defines levels of accomplishment or progress and assigning point values to those levels is appropriate.

> *The key to establishing liquidated damages is reasonableness.*

Questionnaires designed to assess service quality directly from clients is another approach. Although a subjective evaluation received from an end-user may not be ideal for use in all service solicitations, it can be an effective performance indicator. It may also be the only reasonable or cost-effective method for measuring the qualitative aspects of performance.

Special Conditions

Special Conditions are usually solicitation-specific. This section should address payment procedures, insurance, bonds, and any extension or renewal requirements. Requirements that are specifically tailored for the solicitation should be included in this category.

Payment Procedures. Details of the manner and methods to be used for submission of request for payment of invoices should be identified in this section. Such inclusions may be procedures for separate billings, special invoice formatting, and invoice attachments. The jurisdiction's financial staff can offer information to the team on required time frames to meet internal processing deadlines. The time needed for the jurisdiction to process payment must be clearly identified in the solicitation (e.g., 20 or 30 days after receipt of a correct invoice).

Speed of payment is of prime importance to a service provider. If the jurisdiction can guarantee that payment will be made no later than 10 days after receipt of invoice, it will probably attract more potential service providers. Small service providers, the foundation of most service contracting programs, have difficulty waiting more than 20 or 30 days for payment, especially if labor costs are a major portion of the contract. If payment terms are more than 30 days, small service providers may not be able to respond to the solicitation or may be forced to submit higher pricing that would offset the lack of immediate cash flow.

Insurance. The RFP team does not establish the appropriate insurance requirements. This is a function of the jurisdiction's risk manager or legal counsel. Every service delivery solicitation should require insurance coverage sufficient to protect the jurisdiction. Such insurance requirements verify that the service provider is financially capable of obtaining liability and medical coverage that will compensate the public and jurisdiction for service provider negligence in addition to protecting the assets of the jurisdiction from damage claims that may result from such negligence.

To develop the correct insurance requirements, all risks inherent in the service delivery should be analyzed. For example, if the service solicited includes the temporary or semi-permanent garaging of jurisdiction vehicles at the provider's facility, then Bailor/Bailee insurance coverage should be required. Service deliveries that may deal with the transportation of fuel or hazardous materials or underground excavations require special insurance coverage to protect the jurisdiction.

Bonds. The most common method of transferring the risk of nonperformance is the requirement of a Bid, Performance, or Payment Bond issued in the interest of the jurisdiction. Even though the prospect of transferring risk to a third party (a bonding surety) may seem appealing, the SOW team must be cautious about requiring bonds. A bonding surety is an insurance company. The team must understand that payment against the bond could take many months. First, the jurisdiction has to declare the service provider in default. Normally, this cannot be done until the service provider has had an opportunity to cure the reason for default. The surety must agree with the jurisdiction's claim. Even though the jurisdiction might have good cause to file against the bond, a surety could delay any action while an investigation is conducted. Litigation is often the only way to force the surety to perform.

On the other hand, a service provider's bonding capacity is thought to be a good indicator of financial stability. This may not always be the case because a surety's investigation of the service provider's financial stability may have occurred years ago. Relying on a surety company to establish the financial responsibility of a service provider is often a poor substitute for independent investigation by the jurisdiction.

In many instances, bonds are not necessary if a service provider has been selected after a thorough review of references, qualifications, and financial stability. A formal guarantee is of little consolation to a jurisdiction that is faced with an under-performing, but not defaulting, service provider. Finally, the SOW team should be aware that both bonds and any other guarantee could eliminate many small, disadvantaged, or minority business enterprises from successfully competing for the jurisdiction's business.

The three types of bonds most commonly used in service delivery are the Performance Bond, the Payment Bond, and the Bid Bond. The Bid Bond guarantees that the offeror will enter into a contract. The Performance Bond guarantees that the service provider will perform the contract. The Payment Bond guarantees the service provider will pay all suppliers and sub-service providers who assist in the performance of the contract. In each case, a surety issues the guarantee to the jurisdiction. A fourth type of bond is the *Fidelity Bond*, which is an insurance policy that guarantees the reimbursement to the jurisdiction for losses resulting from proven acts of dishonesty by the service provider's employees who handle cash or other revenue generators.

Alternative Surety. Many service providers who are otherwise qualified to perform a service may not be able to obtain the necessary bonding from a surety as a result of size or financial condition. Some service providers may choose not to obtain a bond because it is considered expensive or unnecessary. It is a fact, however, that service providers include the cost of bonds and insurance in the solicitation response to negate the expense.

If the RFP team determines that a Performance Bond is necessary and does not want to eliminate those firms that cannot obtain a Performance Bond because of financial reasons, the team can decide to accept alternative guarantees.

Alternative sureties include a certified or cashier's check, personal bond, property bond, cash escrow deposit, or an irrevocable letter of credit from a bank or a savings and loan institution. These types of guarantees may be more appropriate and easier to enforce for low-risk service delivery contracts than a Performance Bond. When a default causes disruption in a critical service delivery and rapid response is imperative, alternative guarantees can provide immediate cash to be used to replace the defaulting provider. When considering the use of alternative surety, either the jurisdiction's risk manager or legal counsel must approve it. Some state statutes may prohibit its use. (A description of alternative sureties is included as Appendix F.)

Contract Extension and Renewal. A contract extension differs from a contract renewal. An extension is generally unplanned and is seldom forecast in the solicitation or contract document. The term *renewal* refers to a planned additional period of contract performance after the expiration of the original period of time, whether it is for one year, five years, or more. A renewal is a planned event that must be identified by a clause in the solicitation. Contracts may be providing and installing a computer system, completing an architectural design, or completing a construction project on or before a specific date. When the work cannot be completed on time, it is appropriate for a contract extension to be granted. Even with this distinct definitional difference, procurement and contract administrators use the term *extension* commonly, but incorrectly, to refer to a renewal. There are legal, fiscal, pricing, and timing considerations associated with any contract renewal. More detailed issues concerning contract extension and renewal are addressed in a later chapter.

Legal Considerations. Failure to include a specific renewal period with terms in the original solicitation document may prevent the jurisdiction from legally granting a renewal, even if the renewal is in the best interest of the jurisdiction. If no renewal provisions are included in the original solicitation document, any attempt to renew the contract after the original contract period should be legally viewed as a new contract, not a renewal. The RFP team should ensure that the solicitation document contains a method of determining prices, terms, and conditions for any renewal period.

A renewal provision in a solicitation document often stipulates that the renewal is offered at the discretion of the jurisdiction. This provision usually states that the jurisdiction is not required to offer the option of renewal to the service provider, and the provider has the option to accept or decline any renewal offered. If the solicitation document contains a unilateral clause allowing for the jurisdiction to automatically renew under the same conditions as the original contract, and the service provider accepts such a clause, the contract can be automatically renewed by the jurisdiction.

Fiscal Considerations—Non-Appropriations Clause. A non-appropriations clause may be included in the solicitation document to protect the jurisdiction in the event the contract must be cancelled due to funding restrictions. This clause gives the jurisdiction the right to cancel the contract if funds for the contract are not appropriated.

A non-appropriations clause must be reviewed and approved by the jurisdiction's legal counsel before insertion in a solicitation document. The clause should be a part of every solicitation that may begin in one fiscal year and conclude in another.

The three types of bonds most commonly used in service delivery are the Performance Bond, the Payment Bond, and the Bid Bond.

Price Considerations. There are options available for addressing price increases in multiple-year contracts. The jurisdiction may request a firm price for the succeeding years of the contract in the original solicitation. This approach can be costly because the service provider may propose higher prices for the succeeding years that address possible inflation factors. Conversely, modest cost projections can easily lead to performance issues if the actual cost of subsequent years is higher than those projected. The provider may cut back on the quality or the quantity of the service if a potential loss is incurred.

The safer approach is to obtain a firm price for the first year of the contract and link succeeding year price increases to a recognized index or escalator. To reduce the amount of increase for any succeeding year, the RFP team can consider using the Consumer Price Index for the jurisdiction's geographical area and the Producer's Price Index. By adding the two indices and calculating the average, the percentage of increase usually will be lower than if only the Consumer Price Index is applied. Both of these indices are available on the Internet (www.bls.gov/cpi). Contract pricing can be adjusted annually, quarterly or monthly, depending on the volatility of the marketplace.

A third option allows for *renewal* of the contract, upon mutual agreement between the service provider and the jurisdiction, at the same prices, terms, and conditions. This option assumes that the conditions of performance will not change substantially for one or more years. This approach is especially appropriate when the service provider receives a percentage of the revenues, possibly for food concessions, day-care services, or if the service provider is being paid a fixed fee in addition to reimbursement for the cost of professional or similar services. This option is also used when the jurisdiction is not sure if it wants to renew for additional years at the time of contract award.

Timing Considerations. It is important to allow enough time in the original solicitation to decide if a renewal may be desired. Adequate time must be established to give the jurisdiction time to re-solicit if the incumbent service provider declines to renew. The time established should equal the number of days required to assemble the original solicitation, publicize the requirements, conduct a pre-proposal conference, evaluate the responses, award the contract, and for the contracted service to commence. Because renewals are usually incorporated into contracts that do not require extensive lead times for establishment, the total time required to decide on re-solicitation may be three to four months.

Consideration must be given for a solicitation that involves the service provider's investment in capital equipment. If the provider requires longer than five years to amortize the equipment needed to perform the contract, the RFP team might consider a five-year base contract period with options for contract renewal in five-year increments. This clause would require language asserting and affirming that the renewals would be granted on satisfactory performance.

Format for Technical/Price Proposals

Special Instructions. The Special Instructions section of the solicitation document often contains information not appropriate to be included in the SOW but is important to both the jurisdiction and the offeror. This section may include the method of response evaluation, the formula for ranking the offeror by technical and pricing points, how to format the response, and the procedures to follow when the non-consideration of an offer is protested.

Price Ranking of Offerors. The price ranking of offerors differs with the type of solicitation document. If the solicitation is an IFB/ITT, award will be made to the lowest responsive and responsible bidder. If the solicitation is an RFP, price is a consideration but is addressed separately after the technical part of the responses are evaluated and scored. It is a responsibility of the SOW team to select the most appropriate method of price ranking of responses and include this information in the solicitation document.

Technical Exhibits. Technical Exhibits, if any, follow the SOW in the solicitation document. They may include a map of the area of operation; reports or studies pertinent to the SOW; specifications from trade or professional associations used to prepare the SOW; manufacturers' product descriptions, sketches, or photographs; tables and charts; and applicable statutes, ordinances, or regulations. If the Technical Exhibits cannot be bound within the solicitation document, the team may insert a page after the SOW identifying and summarizing each exhibit.

References

American Bar Association (2000). *The 2000 model procurement code for state and local governments.* Chicago: American Bar Association.

Dobler, D., Burt, D., & Lee, L. (1990). *Purchasing and materials management* (5th ed.). New York: McGraw-Hill.

Harney, D. (1992). *Service contracting: A local government guide.* Washington, DC: International City/County Management Association.

Institute for Supply Management (ISM) (formerly known as National Association of Purchasing Management [NAPM]). (2000). *Consulting services guide.* Tempe, AZ: ISM.

National Association of State Procurement Officials (NASPO). (1997). *State and local government purchasing: Principles and practices.* Lexington, KY: NASPO.

National Institute of Governmental Purchasing, Inc. (NIGP). (2001). *Contracting for services.* Herndon, VA: NIGP.

National Institute of Governmental Purchasing, Inc. (NIGP). (2002). *Dictionary of purchasing terms* (5th ed.). Herndon, VA: NIGP.

Chapter 5

Performance-Based Contracting

Performance-based contracting for public sector services is one of the key trends in public procurement today. The Federal Government established a goal of making 50% of all service contracts performance-based by fiscal year 2005 (U.S. General Accounting Office [GAO], 2001). State and local governments are also making increased use of performance-based contracting (Gordon, 2001; Martin, 2002b). At least part of the current interest in performance-based contracting can be attributed to principal/agent theory and the government performance accountability movement. Principal/agent theory provides useful insights into the management of relationships between governments and contractors, while the government performance accountability movement establishes a larger context in which performance-based contracting takes place.

Principal/Agent Theory

One of the frameworks most frequently employed to understand government contracting and, in particular, contracting for public sector services is called principal/agent theory. In applying principal/agent theory to contracting for public sector services, the government is the principal and the contractor is the agent. Some of the major insights provided by principal/agent theory include the issues of: (a) agent opportunism, (b) information asymmetry, (c) the use of *ex ante* incentives and penalties, and (d) *ex post* monitoring (Organisation for Economic Co-operation and Development [OECD], 1999).

Agent opportunism refers to the phenomenon that contractors sometimes pursue their own interests rather than the interests of governments. Agent opportunism may occur if contractors provide lower quality service than called for in the contract, thereby increasing their own profits. Agent opportunism is also the reason that "cost plus a percentage of cost" types of contracts are unallowable under U.S. Federal Procurement Policy and in most U.S. state and local governments. It is also the least preferred contract type in Canada. These types of contracts create perverse economic incentives; contractors can increase their profits by increasing their costs. One of the reasons that contractors can operate in these opportunistic ways is due to information asymmetry.

Information asymmetry refers to the imbalance of information that always exists between principals and agents. For example, contractors always know more about their day-to-day service delivery operations than the government knows. The ability of governments to acquire detailed information about day-to-day service delivery activities of contractors is largely a factor of what contractors are willing to voluntarily divulge and what governments can discover through contract monitoring. Governments, however, have little economic incentive to monitor contractors because monitoring increases transaction costs, which leads to increased service contracting costs. This presents a challenge to the government to devise relatively inexpensive, yet valid, approaches to contract monitoring.

Because of the problems created by agent opportunism and information asymmetry, principal/agent theory suggests that governments should attempt to constrain the actions of contractors through a combination of contractual *ex ante* (before the event) incentives and penalties tied to *ex post* (after the event) monitoring.

Ex ante incentives and penalties are ways in which agent opportunism can be reduced by directly linking the interests of contractors to the interests of governments. When the interests of governments and contractors are aligned, contractors have few, if any, economic reasons for engaging in agent opportunism. *Ex ante* incentives are used to reward contractors for meeting the needs of governments (relative to service delivery considerations, such as quality, timeliness, efficiency, effectiveness, etc.). *Ex ante* penalties are used to correct and discipline contractors for failing to meet the needs of governments. *Ex ante* incentives and penalties most often take the form of additional compensation awarded to contractors for superior performance or compensation denied contractors for sub-standard performance. Incentives can take the form of contract extensions and renewals or the award of additional work and exclusivity arrangements.

> ...governments should attempt to constrain the actions of the contractors through...contractual ex ante *incentives and penalties tied to* ex post *monitoring.*

Ex post monitoring is the way in which governments attempt to mitigate the problems of information asymmetry during service. Principal/agent theory suggests that if a government identifies the most important aspects of contract service delivery and attaches *ex ante* incentives and penalties, then *ex post* monitoring will be primarily concerned with determining and validating the extent to which contractors achieve the desired performance.

According to principal/agent theory, the linkage of *ex post* monitoring to *ex ante* incentives and penalties should also help to reduce monitoring costs.

The Public Management Committee of the OECD identifies several guiding concepts that it believes should be followed in structuring principal/agent relationships (see Figure 22).

- The duties and responsibilities of both the government and the contractor should be clearly spelled out in the contract.
- The *ex ante* incentives and penalties should be aligned with the needs of the government.
- The contractor should understand the consequences of superior and inferior performance.
- The *ex ante* incentives and penalties should provide the basis for *ex post* monitoring.
- The contractor should be given increased discretion over inputs, while being held accountable for outputs, quality, and outcomes.

Figure 22. *Guiding Concepts in Structuring Principal/Agent Relations Service Contracting.*

Source: Organisation for Economic Co-operation and Development (OECD). (1999). *Performance contracting lessons from performance contracting case studies: A framework for public sector performance contracting* (pp. 57-58) Paris: OECD.

The duties and responsibilities of both the government and the contractor should be clearly delineated in the contract, with a focus on performance. *Ex ante* incentives and penalties should be used to constrain agent opportunism by linking the contractor's interests directly to the interests of the government. The contract should clearly identify the *ex ante* incentives and penalties so that the contractor can understand the implications of superior and inferior performance. The *ex ante* incentives and penalties should be the primary focus of contract monitoring. Finally, the contractor should be given increased control over inputs while being held accountable for outputs, quality, and outcomes.

The Context of Government Performance Accountability

Performance-based contracting does not take place in a vacuum. The current interest in performance-based contracting is directly related to the ongoing interest and concern of governments with performance accountability. In the United States, interest in performance accountability is largely due to two major initiatives, **The Government Performance and Results Act of 1993** (GPRA) and the "service efforts and accomplishments" reporting initiative of the Governmental Accounting Standards Board (GASB).

The Government Performance and Results Act of 1993

GPRA (Public Law 103-62) requires that all programs in all federal departments and agencies report annually to the U.S. Congress on their performance. Section 1115(4) of this Act states that each federal department and agency shall "establish performance indicators to be used in measuring or assessing the relevant outputs, service levels and outcomes of each program activity." Outputs are defined as measures of "activity or effort." Applied to services, an output can be conceptualized as a measure of service volume or how much service a program provides. Outcomes are defined as "the results of a program compared to its intended purposes." As used in the Act, the terms *output* and *outcome* are sufficiently broad so that they also encompass issues of quality.

The Governmental Accounting Standards Board

GASB is the organization that establishes generally accepted accounting principles for state and local governments. In 1994, GASB released an exposure draft of its proposed rules governing "service efforts and accomplishment" (SEA) reporting (GASB, 1994). The purpose of SEA reporting is essentially the same as GPRA—the promotion of performance accountability in government. SEA reporting has not been formally mandated by GASB, but state and local governments have been strongly encouraged to prepare for its inevitable implementation. SEA reporting identifies two major types of performance measures—outputs and outcomes. As defined, outputs include quality. GASB SEA reporting defines outputs as measures of the "quantity of service provided" and quality as measures of the "quantity of a service that meets a quality requirement." Outcome is defined as a measure of "the results that occur (at least partially) because of services provided" (GASB, 1994, p. 22).

GPRA, GASB SEA Reporting and Contracting for Public Sector Services

GPRA and GASB SEA reporting are highly complementary. Although approaching the issue from slightly different perspectives, both GPRA and GASB SEA reporting identify three dimensions of performance—outputs, quality and outcomes. Outputs, quality, and outcomes can be thought of as the "three musketeers" of government performance (Wimmer, 2003, p. 15). The measurement, assessment and the provision of feedback on outputs, quality and outcomes can be thought of as an "expanded systems model" (see Figure 23). This expanded systems model is self-evaluating. Feedback on the production of outputs compared to the consumption of inputs provides a measure of efficiency. Feedback on quality relative to the consumption of inputs provides a measure of quality. Feedback on the production of outcomes relative to the consumption of inputs provides a measure of effectiveness. All three perspectives are considered important to the evaluation of government programs (Martin, 2002; Martin & Kettner, 1996).

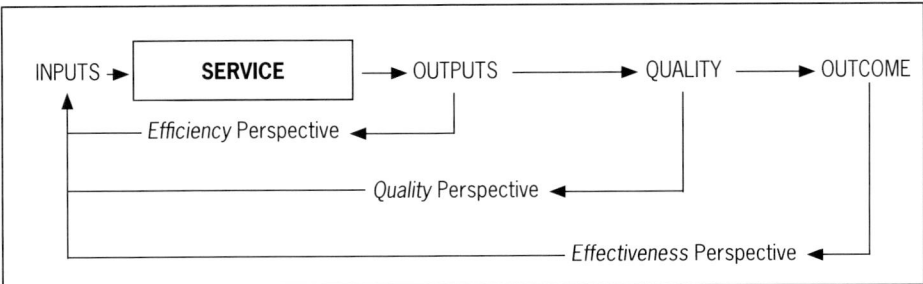

Figure 23. *The Expanded Systems Model.*

GPRA and GASB SEA reporting define the context in which federal, state, and local government performance accountability and performance-based contracting take place. While the relationship is seldom made explicit, it is not overstating the case to suggest that GPRA and GASB SEA reporting are two major drivers promoting the increased use of performance-based contracting. Because of the influence of GPRA and GASB SEA reporting along with the widespread use of contracting for public sector services, the only way in which many federal, state, and local government departments and agencies can meet the data and reporting demands of performance accountability is to pass along these requirements to their contractors.

Defining Performance-Based Contracting

No commonly agreed-upon definition of performance-based contracting exists (GAO, 2002). However, several working definitions have been proposed. For example, the U.S. Office of Federal Procurement Policy (OFPP) defines performance-based contracting as an approach where the statement of work is based on "objective, measurable performance standards outputs" (OFPP, 1998a, p. 5). In a related policy memorandum, the OFPP further states that a performance-based contract contains "performance standards (i.e., quality, quantity, timeliness)" (OFPP, 1997, p. 2). The U.S. Department of Defense (DOD), which contracts for more services than any other federal department or agency, defines a performance-based contract as one that "describes the requirements in terms of measurable outcomes rather than by means of prescriptive methods" (DOD, 2000, p. 1). The *Federal Acquisition Regulation* (FAR) Part 2.101 states:

> Performance-based contracting means structuring all aspects of an acquisition around the purpose of the work to be performed with contract requirements set forth in clear, specific, and measurable outcomes as opposed to either the manner by which the work is to be performed or broad and imprecise statements of work.

The National Association of State Procurement Officials (NASPO) states that performance-based contracting is characterized by "specification of the outcome expectations of the contract and the requirement that any renewals or extensions be based on the achievement of the identified outcomes" (NASPO, 1997, p. 120). While not made explicit in these various definitions, the implicit assumption in each case is that contractor compensation (in part or in total), as well as contract extensions and renewals, may also be tied to performance. For example, the FAR Part 37.601 states: "Performance-based contracting methods are intended to ensure that required performance quality levels are achieved and that total payment is related to the degree that services performed meet contract standards."

The various working definitions of performance-based contracting identified above all address performance accountability, albeit with different emphases on output, quality, and outcome. As Figure 24 illustrates, all the proposed definitions shift the emphasis of public sector service contracting away from its historical reliance on input and process *design* specifications (telling contractors how to perform the work) in favor of output, quality, and outcome *performance* specifications (telling contractors what is expected) and leaving the how-to up to them. By permitting contractors to determine how best to accomplish the work, performance-based contracting seeks to control and reduce service delivery costs by fostering and promoting increased contractor creativity and innovation.

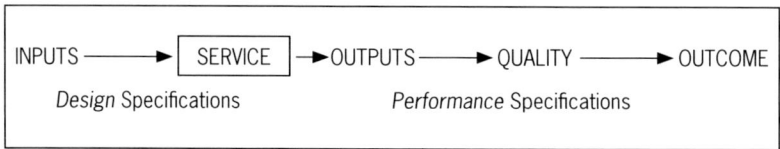

Figure 24. *The Expanded Systems Model and Design and Performance Specifications.*

Building upon the preceding discussion, it is possible to derive a consensus definition of performance-based contracting. A performance-based contract can be defined as one that "focuses on the outputs, quality, and outcomes of service provision and may tie at least a portion of a contractor's payment, as well as any contract extension or renewal, to their achievement" (Martin, 1999, pp. 1, 8). This consensus definition has several advantages. It is expansive, rather than restrictive, by suggesting that performance-based contracting can involve outputs, quality, outcomes, or any combination thereof. It is also compatible with the output, quality, and outcome foci of both the GPRA and the SEA reporting initiative of the GASB. Because this consensus definition is compatible with GASB's SEA reporting, it is also compatible with most state government performance measurement and performance budgeting systems (Melkers & Willoughby, 1998).

Does Performance-Based Contracting Work?

Performance-based contracting is still a relatively new concept; and, consequently, research in the area is somewhat limited. OFPP (1998b) has conducted the largest study of performance-based contracting to date. Some studies of performance-based contracting for human services have also been conducted and will be discussed in this chapter.

Office of Federal Procurement Policy Study

OFPP evaluated an experiment in transforming traditional service contracts into performance-based contracts. The experiment involved 26 contracts in 15 federal departments and agencies with a combined total value of some $585 million. The contracts ranged in price from $100,000 to $325 million (OFPP, 1998b, p. 3). The major study findings are shown in Figure 25.

Evaluation:	26 performance-based contracts in 15 Federal departments and agencies totaling $585 million.
Results:	Overall costs decreased 15%. Overall customer satisfaction increased 18%. Average number of bids or proposals increased from 5.3% to 7.3%.

Figure 25. *Office of Federal Procurement Policy Study of Performance-Based Contracting.*

Source: U.S. Office of Federal Procurement Policy (OFPP). (1998). *A report on the performance-based service contracting pilot project* (pp. 2-5). Washington, DC: OFPP.

As Figure 25 demonstrates, the OFPP experiment produced some remarkable results. In addition to reducing costs and increasing customer satisfaction, the number of bids and proposals received also increased. The study found that the greatest cost savings were achieved when previous cost reimbursement contracts were changed to performance-based, fixed-price contracts (OFPP, 1998b, p. 11).

Performance-Based Contracting for Human Services

Some of the most interesting examples of performance-based contracting have involved the human services. Figure 26 presents the results from Illinois and Minnesota. Illinois used performance-based contracting for adoption services, while Minnesota used it for job placement services. Both studies achieved dramatic results. If performance-based contracting can be used for services like adoptions and job placement (so called "soft" services), then it most likely can be used for some, if not all, public sector services.

Illinois Department of Children and Families			
	Fiscal Year 1997	Fiscal Year 1998	Fiscal Year 1999
Number of Adoptions	2,229	4,293	7,315
Minnesota Department of Human Services			
	Fiscal Year 1995	Fiscal Year 1998	Fiscal Year 1999
Number of Job Placements	591	1,136	1,423

Figure 26. *Performance-Based Contracting for Human Services.*

Source: Illinois Department of Children & Families (Illinois DCF). (2000). Application for the Harvard University/John F. Kennedy School of Government "Innovations in American Government" award. Springfield, IL: Illinois DCF; Minnesota Department of Human Services (Minnesota DHS). (2000). *Request for proposals to provide social services to refugees in the State of Minnesota.* St. Paul: Minnesota DHS; and Vinson, E. (1999). *Performance contracting in six state human service agencies.* Washington, DC: The Urban Institute.

The U.S. Department of the Treasury (Rogin, n.d., p. 3) summarizes the benefits of performance-based contracting as shown below:

- Better performance is achieved.
- Costs are reduced.
- Governments do not have to develop detailed design specifications.
- Contractors have more flexibility.
- Less day-to-day contract monitoring is required.
- Contractors are motivated to be innovative and save money.

Performance-Based Statements of Work

In developing statements of work for public sector service contracts, governments can choose between design specifications, performance specifications or a combination of the two. Historically, design specifications were used in statements of work for the procurement of supplies and equipment. Consequently, when governments first began to contract for public sector services, it was perhaps only natural that design specifications were also used. Over time, the use of design specifications became the norm in service contract statements of work. However, when defining statements of work for performance-based contracting, it is necessary to think about public sector services more in terms of performance specifications and then to expand on this by placing "performance" into its relationship to the expanded systems model.

Performance Specifications

The National Institute of Governmental Purchasing, Inc.'s (NIGP) (2002) *Dictionary of Purchasing Terms* defines a performance specification as one that sets forth the capabilities and performance characteristics the service must satisfy. NASPO (1997, p. 153) states that a performance specification is a purchase description that emphasizes performance over design. The use of performance specifications, as well as the ability to mix and match performance specifications and design specifications, provides public procurement professionals with more options when developing statements of work for performance-based contracts.

Expanded Systems Model

By conceptualizing a public sector service in terms of its system components (inputs, process, outputs, quality, and outcomes), public procurement professionals are provided with a more detailed approach to thinking about and drafting statements of work for performance-based contracts. By conceptualizing public sector services in terms of their system elements, public procurement professionals are also adopting what is rapidly becoming the language of government performance accountability. The mastery of this language should lead, in turn, to greater clarity when public procurement professionals attempt to translate the needs of government-user departments into statements of work for performance-based contracts.

Using custodial services as an example, input design specifications address such issues as the number of custodial workers and supervisors, along with their qualifications, the contractor is to make available (see Figure 27). Input design specifications address the types of equipment (e.g., vacuum cleaners, floor buffers/polishers, carpet cleaners, etc.) and cleaning supplies (e.g., soaps, detergents, etc.) the contractor is to provide and use. Input design specifications also address the types of facilities to be maintained, their locations and square footage. Process design specifications address such issues as the tasks (e.g., emptying wastebaskets, mopping and buffing floors, etc.) to be performed by the contractor, the frequency of task performance (e.g., daily, weekly, or monthly), and the days and hours of service provision (e.g., after 6:00 p.m. and before 7:00 a.m.).

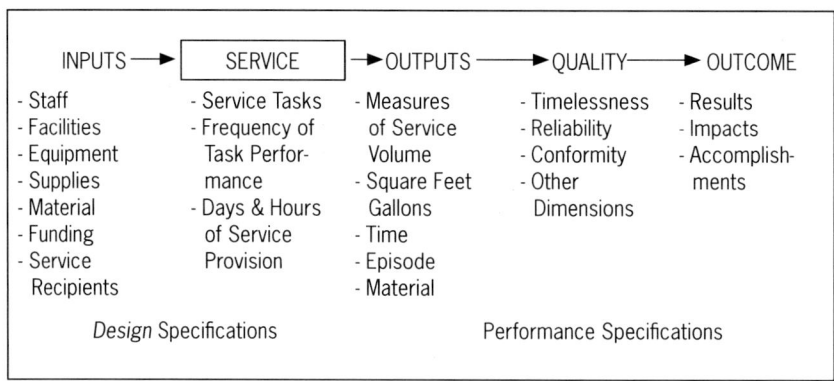

Figure 27. *The Expanded Systems Model and Statements of Work.*

Continuing with the example of custodial services, output performance specifications address the volume of service provision or how much service the contractor is to provide. Measures that might be used include: square feet of office space maintained, number of hours of service provision, number of days of service provision, or some other such metric. Quality performance specifications address the service quality standards (timeliness, reliability, conformity, etc.) that the contractor is to satisfy. Quality might be measured by a customer satisfaction survey administered to a random sample of facility occupants once each fiscal quarter. Outcome performance specifications address the service results the contractor is to achieve, e.g., a clean facility. Government contract service monitors, using specific custodial service criteria, may evaluate the service outcome.

Performance-based contracts for most public sector services will probably consist of a combination of both design and performance specifications. Some types of public sector services may require significant use of design specifications in order to ensure that the interests of governments are protected. However, most contracts for public sector services should be able to make at least some use of performance specifications. In the case of performance-based contracting, performance specifications should predominate.

The Elements of a Performance-Based Statement of Work

There is no single, generally accepted approach to the development of a performance-based statement of work. The whole idea of performance-based contracting is to get public procurement professionals to try different approaches to contracting for public sector services—*to think creatively (to think outside the box)*. Performance-based statements of work are constrained only by laws and regulations, the imagination and creativity of public procurement professionals, and to what extent contractors are willing to agree. The approach to performance-based statements of work presented here (see Figure 28) generally follows the model developed by OFPP (1997, 1998a) as further refined by DOD (2000).

• Service Definition
• Specification of Tasks/Statement of Objectives
• Performance Measures/Performance Requirements
• Performance Standards/Acceptable Quality Level (AQL)
• Incentives and Penalties
• Monitoring/Quality Assurance Plan
• Contract Types

Figure 28. *The Elements of Performance-Based Statement of Work.*

The elements identified in Figure 28 are sufficiently comprehensive so that any statement of work that might include all seven would generally be considered "performance-based" by most governments. While these seven elements are discussed here as part of a single document called a "performance-based statement of work," it is recognized that some elements may appear in other parts of a performance-based contract (e.g., compensation and method of payment clause, special provisions, attachments, etc.). The element that makes a contract performance-based is not its *format*, but its *content*.

Performance-based statements of work are constrained only by laws and regulations...

The case example of "elevator maintenance and repair" services can be used to demonstrate how these seven elements are addressed when developing a performance-based statement of work. This example is presented as Figure 29. A blank template is included as Appendix H, which can be duplicated for use in developing a performance-based statement of work.

Service: Elevator Maintenance and Repair

Service Definition: This service involves maintaining in good working order the three elevators located in the General Government Building, 200 Rue Royal, Nullepart, Quebec, Canada, including responding to emergency service calls, making emergency repairs in a timely manner and submitting all required maintenance and repair reports.

Specifications of Tasks/ Statement of Objectives	Performance Measures/ Performance Requirements	Performance Standards/ Acceptable Quality Level	Incentives/ Penalties	Monitoring/ Quality Assurance Plan
To maintain elevators in working order (outcome)	All three elevators are functioning at all times	95%	Standard = None Above Standard = Incentive Below Standard = Penalty	Periodic Inspection (Government) Customer Input
To perform preventive maintenance (output)	All preventive maintenance conducted as scheduled	95%	Standard = None Above Standard = Incentive Below Standard = Penalty	Periodic Inspection (Government)
To respond to emergency calls (process)	All emergency calls responded to within 2 hours	95%	Standard = None Above Standard = Incentive Below Standard = Penalty	100% Inspection (Government)
To complete emergency service repairs (output)	All emergency repairs completed within 8 hours	92%	Standard = None Above Standard = Incentive Below Standard = Penalty	Periodic Inspection (Government)
To satisfy building employees (quality)	All government employees satisfied with elevator operations	85%	None	Customer Input
To submit maintenance and repair reports (process)	All reports submitted on time	95%	Standard = None Above Standard = None Below Standard = Penalty	Third-party Certification (City Department of Business Regulation)

Figure 29. *Performance-Based Statement of Work.*

Service Definition

A service definition is the description of the public sector service to be provided. The length of the service definition will vary, depending upon the nature and complexity of the service. The idea behind the service definition is to succinctly tell the contractor what the government intends to purchase. Figure 30 illustrates some examples of service definitions used in public sector service contracts by the State of Arizona (Arizona Department of Economic Security, 2003). Arizona state departments and agencies add detail to these basic generic service definitions in order to ensure that contractors understand what is wanted. The service definition for elevator maintenance and repair services is short, focused, and identifies the number and location of the elevators to be maintained.

Program Evaluation. This service systematically assesses the impact and/or efficiency of programs.
Program Development. This service researches and/or establishes a new service or improves, expands, or integrates an existing service.
Public Health Services. This service provides for the enforcement of public health statutes, codes, and regulations as they pertain to the design and function of sewage collection systems, waste treatment works, water supplies, water distribution systems, land subdivisions, public and semipublic swimming pools, and trailer parks.

Figure 30. *State of Arizona Examples of Service Definitions.*

Source: Arizona Department of Economic Security (Arizona DES). (2003). *Arizona dictionary and taxonomy of human services* (pp. 48-50). Retrieved December 10, 2003, from http://www.de.state.az.us/taxonomy.

Specification of Tasks/Statement of Objectives

In developing performance-based statements of work, some governments prefer to use the "specification of tasks" approach; others prefer to use the "statement of objectives" approach (e.g., DOD, 2000). The choice of which approach should be used appears to be left up to individual preferences. The specification of tasks approach reflects the more traditional public procurement flow (i.e., the use of design specifications). Consequently, many public procurement professionals may find this approach more familiar and, thus, easier to implement. The statement of objectives approach reflects the basic idea of performance-based contracting (Thoma, 2001).

The elevator maintenance and repair case example, illustrated in Figure 29, uses the statement of objectives approach. There are six objective statements. For example, the first objective statement is "to maintain elevators in working order." As an aid in maintaining a focus on performance, the systems element (input, process, output, quality, or outcome) to which the objective statement relates can be included in the analysis. In keeping with the basic notion of performance-based contracting and with reference to the expanded systems model, statements of objectives should focus primarily on outputs, quality and outcomes, but may include inputs and process.

Performance Measures/Performance Requirements

Performance measures/performance requirements refer to the criteria by which contractor performance will be evaluated. Some governments use the term *performance measures*, while others prefer the term *performance requirements*. The terms mean the same thing substantively. Each task specification/statement of objective has a corresponding performance measure/performance requirement. In the elevator maintenance and repair case example (Figure 29), the performance measure/performance requirement for the objective statement "to maintain elevators in working order" is "all three elevators are functioning at all times." A performance measure/performance requirement is essentially an operational definition of its related task specification/statement of objective.

Performance Standards/Acceptable Quality Levels (AQLs)

A performance standard is the allowable deviation from a performance measure/performance requirement. In U.S. Federal Government performance-based contracting language (OFPP, 1998a), this deviation is called the Acceptable Quality Level. As a general rule of government contract law, governments are entitled to *strict compliance* with their design specifications, but only *substantial compliance* with their performance specifications (Federal Acquisition Institute, 1979). The doctrine of substantial compliance is operationalized in performance-based contracting by the fact that a government establishes a performance measure/performance requirement and then determines how much deviation from the measure/standard is acceptable. In the elevator maintenance and repair case example (Figure 29), all performance measures/performance requirements have related performance standards or AQLs. For example, for the performance measure/performance requirement for the objective statement "all three elevators are functioning at all times," the performance standard, or AQL, is 95%. The interpretation is that performance will be considered acceptable if the contractor meets this performance standard 95% of the time. With the use of performance specifications, contractor performance is expected to be high but is not generally expected to be perfect. The types of performance standards most frequently employed in performance-based statements of work are shown in Figure 31.

> *...governments are entitled to* strict compliance *with their* design specifications, *but only* substantial compliance *with their* performance specifications...

• Response Times: Timeliness, responsiveness in meeting prescribed due dates and deadlines
• Errors Rates: Number of mistakes/errors allowable (usually expressed as whole numbers, e.g., not more than 5 per 100 cases)
• Accuracy Rates: Reverse of error rates. Degree of accuracy expected (usually expressed as a percentage, e.g., 95%)
• Milestone Rates: Completion rates at various milestones. Used with project-oriented, performance-based contracts (e.g., 85% of trainees will complete the training program; 80% will score 75% or better on the final examination

Figure 31. *Types of Performance Standards/AQLs.*

Source: U.S. Department of Defense. (2000). *Guidebook for performance-based services acquisition (PBSA) in the Department of Defense* (p. 10). Washington, DC: U.S. Department of Defense.

Incentives/Penalties

Incentives usually take the form of additional compensation that contractors can earn for superior performance (performance above the performance standard or AQL). Penalties usually take the form of compensation that is denied contractors for inferior performance (performance below the performance standard or AQL). Contractor performance that exactly matches the performance standard or AQL usually does not warrant either an incentive or a penalty. Most performance-based contracts usually contain a combination of both incentives and penalties. An incentive that is sometimes used for superior performance may be to offer contractors extensions of their existing contracts or awards of new contracts. This type of incentive also addresses the issue of "past performance" and provides a mechanism by which past performance considerations can be included in performance-based contracting.

The appropriate mix of incentives/penalties can and does vary from contract to contract, depending upon the public sector service, the preferences of individual governments, and the extent to which contractors are willing to agree. Figure 32 identifies several questions that the DOD (2000) believes should be asked and answered when considering the use of incentives and penalties.

- Will the incentive/penalty enhance contractor performance?
- Which tasks or objectives will benefit most from enhanced performance?
- Which tasks or objectives do not need incentives or penalties?
- How much is the government willing to pay for enhanced performance?
- Do funds exist to cover additional compensation incentives?
- Does the contractor value non-monetary incentives (contract extension, new contract)?

Figure 32. *Considerations in the Adoption of Incentives and Penalties.*
Source: U.S. Department of Defense. (2000). *Guidebook for performance-based services acquisition (PBSA) in the Department of Defense.* Washington, DC: U.S. Department of Defense.

Incentives and penalties can be overused. Every task specification or statement of objective does not need, nor would it necessarily benefit from, an incentive or penalty. If a proposed incentive or penalty has little probability of affecting the behavior of a contractor, then it probably should not be used. In the case example of elevator maintenance and repair services (Figure 29), incentives/penalties are proposed for only five of the six objective statements. No incentive or penalty is proposed for the objective statement, "to satisfy building employees," which is considered too subjective to warrant the attachment of an incentive or penalty.

Incentives and penalties are frequently constructed in such a way that they step up and step down from the performance standard or AQL. Continuing with the case example of elevator maintenance and repair, similar monetary incentives and penalties are proposed for both superior performance (performance above the standard or AQL) and inferior performance

(performance below the standard or AQL). Figure 33 demonstrates how step-up and step-down incentives and penalties can be operationalized for the objective statement, "to complete emergency service repairs." The related performance measure/performance requirement states, "all emergency repairs completed within 8 hours," and the performance standard or AQL is 92%. As the figure indicates, the contractor can earn incentive payments for achieving a performance level greater than the base line: 1% of monthly billing for a performance level between 93% and 95% and 2% of monthly billing for a performance level of 96% or greater. Conversely, the contractor can be assessed a penalty for performance below the base line: 1% of monthly billing for a performance level between 91% and 89% and 2% of monthly billing for a performance level between 88% and 85%. If the contractor's performance falls below the level of 85% for a given month, it will not be entitled to a contract renewal or extension. Instead, the contract will be re-bid at the end of the contract term.

Performance Standard: All emergency repairs completed within 8 hours.		
		(Incentives)
	96% & Above	+ 2% of Monthly Billing
	93% - 95%	+ 1% of Monthly Billing
92% Base Line		
- 1% of Monthly Billing	89% - 91%	
- 2% of Monthly Billing	85% - 88%	
- No Contract Renewal or Extension	Below 85%	
(Penalties)		

Figure 33. *Objective Statement, Performance Standard and Step-Up/Step-Down Incentives and Penalties.*

In addition to the method illustrated in Figure 33, other methods exist to structure monetary incentives and penalties, including:

- Additional compensation (over and above the base figure) may be tied to overall contract performance (e.g., performance that exceeds the performance standards/AQLs on some specific number or proportion of all performance standards/AQLs);

- "Hold-back" compensation (a portion of the contractor's base compensation retained by the government) that is tied to overall contract performance (e.g., performance that exceeds the performance standards/AQLs on some specific number or proportion of all performance standards/AQLs);

- Using progress payments tied to milestones (refer to "Milestone Contracting" section presented later in this chapter); and

- The timing of incentive payments or the release of hold-back compensation. Money has a time value. Additional compensation and hold-back compensation can be paid/released on a monthly, quarterly, semi-annually, or end-of-contract-term basis.

Non-financial incentives also can be used in performance-based contracts to reward contractors for superior performance. Two common types of non-financial incentives are "term extensions" (where the contractor receives an extension of its existing contract) and "exclusivity arrangements" (where the contractor is awarded all future work for the same service).

The Ontario Realty Corporation (ORC) has adopted a unique and quite promising approach to structuring incentives and penalties in a large and complex performance-based contract (see Figure 34).

> The Ontario Realty Corporation (ORC) is a public corporation of the Ontario, Canada Provincial Government. In 1999, ORC awarded a large performance-based contract for management services covering some 9,000 government properties. In addition to its massive scale, what is perhaps most interesting about this performance-based contract is that the statement of work contains 112 performance measures/performance requirements that relate to five overall performance objectives.
>
> A question that ORC had to resolve in developing the performance-based statement of work was: Which of the 112 performance measures/performance requirements should have associated incentives and penalties? Given the size and complexity of the contract, ORC believed that all 112 performance measures/performance requirements were important. But ORC also knew that it would be difficult to administer and monitor a contract with 112 incentives and penalties.
>
> The solution that ORC devised was to create a system of "floating" incentives and penalties. The performance-based statement of work contains incentives and penalties tied to a dozen performance measures. But, ORC reserves the right to change the mix of performance measures with 30 days' notice to the contractor.
>
> Through the use of floating incentives and penalties, ORC hopes to address the problems associated with agent opportunism and *ex post* monitoring. Because ORC can change the mix of performance measures/performance requirements with only 30 days' notice, the contractor is discouraged from acting opportunistically and paying close attention to only those performance measures/performance requirements with related incentives and penalties. Because only a dozen performance measures/performance requirements have related incentives and penalties at any one time, the work and costs associated with contract monitoring are greatly reduced.

Figure 34. *Ontario (Canada) Realty Corporation Performance-Based Contracting for Property Management Services Case Example.*

Source: Adapted from Kessel, C. (2001). *Performance-based contracts case study: Ontario Reality Corporation land management contract with Del Management Solutions, Inc.* Presentation at the Conference "Performance-Based Contracting in the Public Sector," Ottawa, Ontario, Canada, November 5 & 6, 2001. Sponsored by The Canadian Institute; and Martin, L. L. (2002). *Making performance-based contracting perform: What the federal government can learn from state and local governments.* Arlington, VA: The IBM Center for the Business of Government

Monitoring/Quality Assurance Plan

Basic compensation as well as incentives and penalties are tied to performance; and, therefore, objective methods are needed to determine and document contractor performance. The process of determining and documenting contractor performance may be called "quality assurance," "surveillance," or "contract monitoring." OFPP (1998a) uses the term "quality assurance." DOD (2000) prefers the term "monitoring" and takes exception to the term "quality assurance," which it believes is the responsibility of the contractor. Regardless of which philosophical approach the government adopts, methods need to be in place, and included in the contract, that will document the actual performance of contractors and compare performance against the actual contract performance standards or AQLs. For purposes here, the term *monitoring* will be used. Governments are said to have six major ways of monitoring performance-based contracts (see Figure 35): (a) 100% inspection, (b) random sampling, (c) periodic inspection, (d) trend analysis, (e) customer input, and (f) third-party certification (DOD, 2000; OFPP, 1998a).

Percent Inspection. Either the contractor or the government compares all service inputs, process, outputs, quality, and outcomes against performance measures/performance requirements and performance standards/AQLs.

Random Sampling. Either the contractor or the government randomly compares service inputs, process, outputs, quality, and outcomes against performance measures/ performance requirements and performance standards/AQL.

Periodic Inspection. Either the contractor or the government inspects all service inputs, process, outputs, quality and outcomes against performance measures/performance requirements and performance standards/AQL using a system other than 100% inspection or random sampling (e.g., periodic site visits).

Trend Analysis. Either the contractor or the government regularly analyzes data trends. The U.S. Department of Defense recommends that the database used for trend analysis be maintained by the government.

Customer Input. Either the contractor or the government relies on customer satisfaction surveys or customer complaints to compare service inputs, process, outputs, quality, and outcomes against performance measures/performance requirements and performance standards/AQL.

Third-Party Certification. Someone or some organization, other than the government and the contractor, inspects (e.g., certification, licensure. ISO 9000, accreditation, etc.) service inputs, process, outputs, quality, and outcomes against generally recognized standards.

Figure 35. *Major Approaches to Monitoring/Quality Assurance.*

Source: Adapted from U.S. Department of Defense. (2000). *Guidebook for performance-based services acquisition (PBSA) in the Department of Defense* (pp. 16-17). Washington, DC: U.S. Department of Defense; and U.S. Office of Federal Procurement Policy (OFPP). (1998). *A guide to best practices for performance-based service contracting* (p. 16). Washington, DC: OFPP

Percent Inspections. Defects, poor performance, and failure to meet contract standards or benchmarks can be uncovered by percent inspections. For large, technically complex contracts, it is impossible to perform 100% inspection. It is possible, however, to perform percent inspections where a service delivery area is targeted and a certain inspection percentage is stipulated. For example, in a food service contract at a major state university, produce deliveries are made 20 times a month. The contract stipulates that there will be a 25% inspection requirement for produce. In this example, produce is inspected on four different occasions within a 30-day period.

Random Sampling. Generally, random sampling can occur at any time and in any place. Random sampling can take the form of a very sophisticated statistical model or can be very basic and simple. An example applicable to the produce inspection could be for the produce to be randomly sampled during the month. It may be sampled four times in one month and eight times the following month.

Periodic Inspection. Defects can be uncovered during an on-site inspection. The same rationale that applies to percent inspections applies to periodic inspections; 100% inspection is too costly. Periodic inspections are generally unannounced in order to provide more effective monitoring. A contract for fleet maintenance could include the statement, "Preventive maintenance records may be inspected periodically." Such an inclusion would allow for the inspections.

When it comes to monitoring, the old adage "work smarter, not harder" should be remembered.

Customer Surveys. Customer surveys are excellent tools to gain feedback related to how the contractor is providing the service to be delivered. Surveys are a sampling technique used for collecting data that can be used to grade performance standards.

Third-Party Monitoring. On very large-scale service contracts, it may be in the best interest of the government to turn monitoring activities over to a third-party contract expert. For example, an industrial hygiene firm may be hired to monitor the performance of an asbestos removal contractor.

Each of these major methods of monitoring has varying manpower and associated cost requirements. For example, monitoring using the 100% inspection method requires more monitoring time and greater attendant costs than random sampling. Third-party certification, on the other hand, involves the least amount of staff monitoring time and only marginal attendant costs. When it comes to monitoring, the old adage "work smarter, not harder" should be remembered. At the beginning of this chapter, the comment was made that principal/agent theory points out that governments have no economic incentive to monitor their contractors. When manpower and cost-intensive monitoring approaches are used, the probability increases that governments will not follow through on their monitoring responsibilities. Careful consideration should be focused on how each task specification or objective statement, and its related performance measure/performance requirement and performance standard/AQL, will be monitored. In the ongoing case example of elevator maintenance and repair services, the government demonstrates a preference for periodic inspection, which is a mid-range monitoring approach in terms of manpower requirements and attendant costs. Figure 36 is a case example from DeKalb County Georgia on using third-party certification for monitoring/quality assurance.

> As part of a plan to upgrade correctional health services at its county jail, DeKalb County, Georgia, decided to contract for services. The county chose to use a performance-based contracting approach. The contract contained a large number of design specifications dealing with such input and process issues as: staffing levels, staff qualifications, hours of operations, etc. However, rather than attempting to develop output, quality, and outcome performance standards for such a highly technical service as correctional health services, DeKalb County chose, instead, to include just one *quality/outcome* performance standard. Under the terms of the contract, the contractor has 18 months from the effective date of the contract to seek and secure accreditation from the National Commission on Correctional Health Care.

Figure 36. *Using Third-Party Certification for Monitoring/Quality Assurance.*

Source: Adapted from Martin (2002b) and DeKalb County Georgia (2000). *Request for proposals (RFP) no. 01-01 to provide inmate health care at the DeKalb County Jail.* Decatur, GA: DeKalb County; and Martin, L. L. (2002). *Making performance-based contracting perform: What the federal government can learn from state and local governments.* Arlington, VA: The IBM Center for the Business of Government.

Contract Types

There are many types of contracts based on the method used for pricing a service. The most common are the firm fixed price, fixed price with escalator (sometimes termed firm fixed price with economic price adjustment), fixed price with incentive, fixed price combined, cost plus fixed fee, percentage of revenue, and time and material contracts. The types are not mutually exclusive. Aspects of each may be incorporated into a hybrid type, when appropriate. The following are descriptions of the various contract types given by FAR (Federal Acquisition Circular [FAC] 90-32, Subpart 16).

> **Firm-fixed-price contract.** A firm-fixed-price contract provides for a price that is not subject to any adjustment on the basis of the contractor's cost experience in performing the contract. This contract type places maximum risk and full responsibility for all costs, and resulting profit or loss, upon the contractor. This provides maximum incentive for the contractor to control costs and perform effectively and imposes a minimum administration burden upon the contracting parties. (FAR 16.20)
>
> A firm-fixed-price contract is suitable for acquiring commercial items or for acquiring other supplies or services on the basis of reasonably definite functional or detailed specifications when the contracting officer can establish fair and reasonable prices at the outset, such as:
>
> a. There is adequate price competition;

    b. There are reasonable price comparisons with prior purchases of the same or similar supplies or services made on a competitive basis or supported by valid cost or pricing data;
    c. There is available cost or pricing information which permits realistic estimates of the probable costs of performance; or
    d. Performance uncertainties can be identified and reasonable estimates of their cost impacts can be made, and the contractor is willing to accept a firm-fixed-price representing assumption of the risks involved.

Fixed-price contracts with economic price adjustment. A fixed-price contract with economic price adjustment provides for upward and downward revision of the stated contract prices upon the occurrence of specified contingencies. Economic price adjustments are of three general types:
    a. *Adjustments based on established prices.* These price adjustments are based on increases or decreases from an agreed-upon level in published or otherwise established prices for specific items or the contract end items.
    b. *Adjustments based on actual costs of labor or material.* These price adjustments are based on increases or decreases in specified costs of labor or material that the contractor actually experiences during contract performance.
    c. *Adjustments based on cost indexes of labor or material.* These price adjustments are based on increases or decreases in labor or material cost standards or indexes that are specifically identified in the contract. (FAR 16.03.1)

  A fixed-price contract with economic price adjustment may be used when (i) there is serious doubt concerning the stability of market or labor conditions that will exist during an extended period of contract performance, and (ii) contingencies that would otherwise be included in the contract price can be identified and covered separately in the contract. Price adjustments based on established prices should be limited to contingencies beyond the contractor's control.

Fixed-price incentives contracts. A fixed-price incentive contract is a fixed-price contract that provides for adjusting profit and establishing the final contract price by a formula based on the relationship of final negotiated total cost to total target cost (FAR 16.204).

Fixed-price contracts with prospective price redetermination. A fixed-price contract with prospective price re-determination provides for (a) firm-fixed-price for an initial period of contract deliveries or performance and (b) prospective re-determination, at a stated time or times during performance, of the price for subsequent periods of performance. (FAR 16.205)

Cost-sharing contracts. A cost-sharing contract is a cost-reimbursement contract in which the contractor receives no fee and is reimbursed only for an agreed-upon portion of its allowable costs. A cost-sharing contract may be used if the contractor agrees to absorb a portion of the costs, in the expectation of substantial compensating benefits. (FAR 16.303)

Cost-plus-incentive-fee contracts. A cost-plus-incentive-fee contract is a cost-reimbursement contract that provides for an initially negotiated fee to be adjusted later by a formula based on the relationship of total allowable costs to total target costs.

Cost-plus-award-fee contract. A cost-plus-award-fee contract is a cost-reimbursement contract that provides for a fee consisting of (a) a base amount (which may be zero) fixed at inception of the contract and (b) an award amount, based upon a judgmental evaluation by the government, sufficient to provide motivation for excellence in contract performance. (FAR 16.305)

Cost-plus-fixed-fee contracts. A cost-plus-fixed-fee contract is a cost-reimbursement contract that provides for payment to the contractor of a negotiated fee that is fixed at the inception of the contract. The fixed fee does not vary with actual cost, but may be adjusted as a result of changes in the work to be performed under the contract. This contract type permits contracting for efforts that might otherwise present too great a risk to contractors, but it provides the contractor only a minimum incentive to control costs. (FAR 16.306)

Fixed-price incentive contracts. A fixed-price incentive contract is a fixed-price contract that provides for adjusting profit and establishing the final contract price by application of a formula based on the relationship of total final negotiated cost to total target cost. The final price is subject to a price ceiling, negotiated at the outset. A fixed-price incentive contract is appropriate when:

1) a firm-fixed-price contract is not suitable;
2) the nature of the supplies or services being acquired and other circumstances of the acquisition are such that the contractor's assumption of a degree of cost responsibility will provide a positive profit incentive for effective cost control and performance; and
3) if the contract also includes incentives on technical performance and/or delivery, and the performance requirements provide a reasonable opportunity for the incentives to have a meaningful impact on the contractor's management of the work. (FAR 16.403)

Requirements contracts. A requirements contract provides for fulfillment of all actual purchase requirements for supplies or services during a specified contract period, with deliveries or performance to be scheduled by placing orders with the contractor.

1) For the information of offerors and contractors, the contracting officer shall state a realistic estimated total quantity in the solicitation and resulting contract. This estimate is not a representation to an offeror or contractor that the estimated quantity will be required or ordered, or the conditions affecting requirements will be stable or normal. The contracting officer may obtain the estimate from records of previous requirements and consumption, or by other means, and should base the estimate on the most current information available.
2) The contract shall state, if feasible, the maximum limit of the contractor's obligation to deliver and the government's obligation to order. The contract may also specify maximum or minimum quantities that the government may

order under each individual order and the maximum that it may order during a specified period of time.

A requirements contract may be appropriate for acquiring any supplies or services when the government anticipates recurring requirements but cannot predetermine the precise quantities of supplies or services that designated government activities will need during a definite period. (FAR 16.503)

Indefinite-quantity contracts. An indefinite-quantity contract provides for an unspecified quantity, within stated limits, of supplies or services to be furnished during a fixed period, with deliveries or performance to be scheduled by placing orders with the contractor.

1) The contract shall require the government to order, and the contractor to furnish, any additional quantities, not to exceed a stated maximum. The contracting officer may obtain the basis for the maximum from records of previous requirements and consumption, or by other means, but the maximum quantity should be realistic and based on the most current information available.
2) To ensure that the contract is binding, the minimum quantity must be more than a nominal quantity, but it should not exceed the amount that the government is fairly certain to order.
3) The contract may also specify maximum or minimum quantities that the government may order under each task or delivery order and the maximum that it may order during a specific period of time. (FAR 16.504)

Time-and-materials contracts. A time-and-materials contract provides for acquiring supplies or services on the basis of (1) direct labor hours at specified fixed hourly rates that include wages, overhead, general and administrative expenses, and profit and (2) materials at cost, including, if appropriate, material handling costs as part of the material costs.

A time-and-materials contract may be used only when it is not possible at the time of contract award to estimate accurately the extent or duration of the work or anticipate costs with any reasonable degree of confidence.

(1) *Government surveillance*. A time-and-materials contract provides no positive profit incentive to the contractor for cost control or labor efficiency. Therefore, appropriate government surveillance of contractor performance is required to give reasonable assurance that efficient methods and effective cost controls are being used.

(2) *Material handling costs*. When included as part of material costs, material handling costs shall include only costs clearly excluded from the labor-hour rate. Material handling costs may include all appropriate indirect costs allocated to direct materials.

Labor-hour contracts. A labor-hour contract is a variation of the time-and-materials contract, differing only in that the contractor does not supply materials.

The preferred contract types for use in performance-based contracting are: (a) cost reimbursement contracts with incentives/penalties; (b) fixed-price contracts with incentives and penalties, and (c) fixed-fee or unit-cost contracts with incentives and penalties. The U.S. Federal Government prefers the use of fixed-price contracts with incentives and penalties. Figure 37 lists the common types of contracts.

Firm Fixed Price:	Contracts usually for one year or less and contracts not affected by market fluctuations.
Fixed Price with Escalator:	Primary multi-year contracts with pricing factors subject to market fluctuation.
Fixed Price with Incentive:	Single or multi-year contracts in which savings could result through increased productivity or cost reduction without affecting the quality of the service. Both the contractor and the local government can benefit from savings effected by the contractor.
Cost Plus Fixed Fee:	Single or multi-year contracts primarily in the fields of architecture, engineering, and other professional and consulting services.
Time and Materials:	Contracts for trades services and other areas in which the time of completion cannot be determined or the agreed-to price is based on hourly rates and material provided.
Percentage of Revenue:	Contracts in which the local government receives a portion of the revenue generated by the contract; examples are contracts for concessions and for adult education.

Figure 37. *Common Types of Contracts.*

Source: Adapted from Harney, D. (1992). *Service contracting: A local government guide* (p. 36). Washington, DC: International City/County Management Association.

Other Approaches to Performance-Based Contracting

There are other approaches to performance-based contracting in addition to the general approach to performance-based statements of work outlined above. Three other frequently used approaches include: (a) milestone contracting, (b) revenue enhancement and share-in-savings contracting, and (c) award fee contracting.

Milestone Contracting

Milestone contracting can be compared to project management for performance-based contracting. Any non-recurring public sector service that has a start date, an end date, and major tasks or milestones to be accomplished along the way can be conceptualized as a project and contracted using the milestone approach. Non-recurring public sector services that lend themselves to milestone contracting include management studies, financial and performance audits, and program evaluations. An example of a milestone approach to management consulting services is illustrated in Figure 38. In this simplified example, the government wants the management study to be completed within six months. The milestone performance-based contract has been constructed to motivate the contractor to complete the work within six months, or sooner, if possible.

Milestone	Due Date	% of Fee
1. Contract Award	January 1	
2. Submission and Approval of Management Study Plan	On or Beofre February 1	10%
3. Submission and Acceptance of 3 Month Progress Report (Output/Quality)	On or Before April 1	10%
4. Submission and Acceptance of Draft Final Report (Output/Quality)	On or Before June 1	10%
5. Submission of Final Report (Outcome/Quality)	On or Before July 1	30%
	After July1 Before July 15	20%
	After July 15	10%
6. Acceptance of Final Report (Outcome/Quality)	August 1	50%

Figure 38. *Milestone Performance-Based Contracting for Management Consulting Services.*

This example demonstrates several points: (a) the contract is a project because it has a start date, an end date, and major milestones; (b) the contract is performance-based because it ties compensation to output, quality, and outcome performance; and (c) the contract has both incentives and penalties. If the contractor completes the management study and submits an acceptable draft of the final report after July 1, but before July 15, it will earn 100% of its fee. If the contractor completes the management study and submits an acceptable draft final report early (on or before July 1), it will earn 110% of its fee. If the contractor completes the management study and submits an acceptable draft final report after July 15, it will earn 90% of its fee. Milestone contracting is essentially a fixed-price contract with progress payments and, in this respect, can be compared to contracting for construction.

Government human service agencies have been experimenting with a derivation of milestone contracting for recurring services by treating individual clients as projects. Figure 39 illustrates a milestone performance-based contracting approach used by the Oklahoma Department of Rehabilitative Services (Oklahoma DRS). Each person serviced is treated as an individual project with a definable start point (determination of need), end point (case closure), and major milestones along the way (e.g., job placement). A fixed-fee per person is established in the contract and the contractor earns a portion of that fee every time a person achieves one of the milestones. In this example, 55% of the contractor's fee is directly tied to output, quality, and outcome performance.

Milestone	Type of Milestone	% of Fee
1. Determination of Need	Process	10
2. Vocational Preparation	Process	10
3. Job Placement	Output	10
4. Job Training	Process	10
5. Job Retention	Process	15
6. Job Stabilization	Quality/Outcome	20
7. Case Closed	Outcome	25

Figure 39. *Oklahoma Department of Rehabilitation Services Milestone Performance-Based Contracting.*

Source: Adapted from Frumkin, P. (2001). *Managing for outcomes: Milestone contracting in Oklahoma* (p. 12). Arlington, VA: The IBM Center for the Business of Government; Oklahoma Department of Rehabilitation Services (Oklahoma DRS). (n.d.). *Milestone payment system* (pp. 1-2). Oklahoma City: Department of Rehabilitation Services.

An evaluation of 13 performance-based contracts awarded by the Oklahoma DRS between fiscal years 1992 and 1997 found that case closures increased 100% and contractor costs decreased 35% (Oklahoma DRS, n.d.). This approach is essentially a fixed-fee contract with progress payments.

Revenue Enhancement and Share-in-Savings Contracting

Revenue enhancement and share-in-savings is another approach to performance-based contracting. In revenue enhancement and share-in-savings arrangements, a proportion of a contractor's compensation is dependent upon their performance in either increasing revenues or decreasing costs—the desired outcome of the contract. In keeping with the basic orientation of performance-based contracting, payment mechanisms usually take the form of cost reimbursement with incentives or fixed price with incentives or fixed fee or unit cost with incentives, although other types of financial arrangements are possible. The most common uses of revenue/cost-savings-sharing performance-based contracts include:

- Recovery auditing (revenue enhancement);
- Building energy savings (share-in-savings);
- Innovations in leasing and the utilization of public buildings and properties (revenue enhancements and share-in-savings); and
- Management improvements (share-in-savings) (Beaulieu, 2000).

Figure 40 illustrates how a performance-based contract for share-in-savings can be structured. The case example involves the Metropolitan Government of Nashville/Davidson County Tennessee (Metro) and its performance-based contract for change management services. As an added touch, Metro included a "partnering" component that allowed government employees to share in any cost savings resulting from the implementation of the contractor's recommendations.

> The Metropolitan Government of Nashville/Davidson County Tennessee (Metro) entered into a share-in-savings performance-based contract for change management services to improve the operating efficiency of its Metro Water Services (MWS). Metro wanted to insure to the extent possible that the consultant's recommendations would be implemented by MWS staff, thereby increasing the probability that the recommendations would result in actual cost savings.
>
> Metro's performance-based contract requires the contractor to reduce the MWS's operating and maintenance budget from a base of $74 million in fiscal year 1999 to a level of $64 million in fiscal year 2002 and a level of $60 million in fiscal year 2003. As an incentive, 10% of the contractor's monthly compensation is to be held in escrow by Metro until MWS's budget is reduced to the $60 million level. As an incentive to both the contractor and the MWS staff, the contract also provides that:
> - For the first $4 million in additional savings (when the MWS's budget is between $60 and $64 million per year), the contractor and the MWS staff are to receive 15% of the annual cost savings.
> - For savings in excess of the $4 million (when the MWS's budget is less than $60 million per year), the contractor and the MWS staff are to receive 20% of the annual cost savings.
>
> According to the partnering provision of the contract, any share-in-savings is to be divided among the contractor, the MWS, and employees of MWS as follows: 15% to the contractor, 15% to MWS employees on payroll at the time the partnering provision becomes activated, and 70% to be carried over and available for use by MWS.

Figure 40. *Performance-Based Contracting for Change Management Services with Share-in-Savings and Partnering.*

Award Fee Contracting

Award fee contracting is a form of performance-based contracting used by the U.S. Federal Government when it is either not possible or extremely difficult to develop objective performance measures/performance requirements. In such situations, a contractor may earn an "award fee." The amount of the award fee as well as the performance conditions under which it can be earned are determined solely by the government. Under U.S. Federal Government procurement regulations, neither the amount of the award fee criteria nor the decision to award or not award the fee is subject to the disputes clause.

Performance-Based Contracting and Auditing Considerations

In performance-based contracting, the issue of data integrity is particularly important. When contractor compensation, either partially or in total, is tied to performance, the performance itself becomes subject to audit. If the performance data cannot be documented, verified and replicated, audit exceptions and questioned costs may arise. One solution is to include contract language that denies payments to contractors in situations where performance data is incomplete, inaccurate, or not verifiable.

Pinellas County Florida confronted the issue of data integrity problems when deciding to use performance-based contracting for ambulance services. Pinellas County included strong contract language that dealt with this potential problem (see Figure 41).

> When Pinellas County Florida decided to use performance-based contracting for ambulance services, one of the many issues it had to confront was data integrity (a *quality* performance standard). Third-party payers (e.g., insurance companies, managed health care programs, Medicare, Medicaid, and others) generally will not pay for services rendered unless complete and accurate data are provided documenting the need for the service, the type of service provided, and the name and relevant personal information of the person receiving the service. In order to insure that it would be able to properly invoice third-party payers, Pinellas County built stringent penalty language into its ambulance services contract. Pinellas County: "shall automatically deduct from the Additional Service Amount equal to the Wholesale Rate for one transport for every Patient served by Contractor for whom all the information required to be supplied by Contractor (i.e., dispatch record, Billable Run Report, and any required forms) is incomplete, illegible, inaccurate, altered, or lacking evidence of medical necessity, where such medical necessity exists, as to result in (Pinellas County's) [parenthesis added] claim for payment being denied by responsible payors, or to otherwise prevent (Pinellas County) [parenthesis added] from effectively utilizing its data processing, billing and collection procedures.

Figure 41. *Dealing with the Problem of Data Integrity in Performance-Based Contracting through Contractual Language.*

Source: Martin, L. L. (2002). *Making performance-based contracting perform: What the federal government can learn from state and local governments.* Arlington, VA: The IBM Center for the Business of Government; and Pinellas County, Florida. (1999). *Ambulance service agreement* (p. 58). Largo, FL: Pinellas County.

References

Arizona Department of Economic Security (Arizona DES). (2003). *Arizona dictionary and taxonomy of human services.* Retrieved December 10, 2003, from http://www.de.state.az.us/taxonomy.

Beaulieu, M. (2000). *Share in savings: Summary of interviews and comparison to federal agencies' missions.* Washington, DC: The Council for Excellence in Government.

Federal Acquisition Institute. (1979). *Principles of government contract law.* Washington, DC: Federal Acquisition Institute.

Governmental Accounting Standards Board (GASB). (1994). *Concepts statement no. 2 of the Governmental Accounting Standards Board on concepts related to service efforts and accomplishments reporting.* Norwalk, CT: GASB.

Gordon, S. (2001). *Performance-based contracting.* IQ Report. Washington, DC: International City/County Management Association.

Martin, L. L. (1999). Performance contracting: Extending performance measurement to another level. *The Public Administration Times, 22*(2), 1 and 8.

Martin, L. L. (2002). *Making performance-based contracting perform: What the federal government can learn from state and local governments.* Arlington, VA: The IBM Center for the Business of Government. Retrieved March 10, 2003, from htttp://www.businessofgovernment.org.

Martin, L. L., & Kettner, P. (1996). *Measuring the Performance of Human Service Programs.* Thousands Oaks, CA: Sage Publications.

Melkers, J., & Willoughby, K. (1998). The state of the states: Performance budgeting requirements in 47 out of 50. *Public Administration Review, 58*(1), 66-73.

National Association of State Procurement Officials (NASPO). (1997). *State and local government purchasing: Principles and practices.* Lexington, KY: NASPO.

National Institute of Governmental Purchasing, Inc. (NIGP). (2002). *Dictionary of purchasing terms* (5th ed.). Herndon, VA: NIGP.

Oklahoma Department of Rehabilitation Services (Oklahoma DRS). (n.d.). *Milestone payment system.* Oklahoma City: Department of Rehabilitation Services. Retrieved August 23, 2001, from http://www.onenet.net/~home/milestone.

Organisation for Economic Co-operation and Development (OECD). (1999). *Performance contracting lessons from performance contracting case studies: A framework for public sector performance contracting.* Paris: OECD.

Rogin, R. (n.d.). *Performance-based service contracting.* Washington, DC: U.S. Department of the Treasury. Retrieved February 1, 2002, from http://www.ustreas.gov/procurement/training.

Thoma, T. (2001). *Developing model performance contracts.* Presentation at the conference on "Performance-Based Contracting in the Public Sector." Ottawa, Canada, September 5 and 6.

U.S. Department of Defense. (2000). *Guidebook for performance-based services acquisition (PBSA) in the Department of Defense.* Washington, DC: U.S. Department of Defense.

U.S. General Accounting Office (GAO). (2001). Current condition of federal contracting. PowerPoint presentation to members of the Commercial Activities Panel. Retrieved December 10, 2003, from http://www.goa.gov/a76panel/powerpoint/ctcondition.

U.S. General Accounting Office (GAO). (2002). *Contract management: Guidance needed for using performance-based service contracting.* Washington, DC: GAO.

U.S. Office of Federal Procurement Policy (OFPP). (1997). Memorandum for agency senior procurement executives, the deputy under secretary of defense (acquisition reform) performance-based service contracting (PBSC) points of contact, subject: PBSC checklist. Washington, DC: OFPP.

U.S. Office of Federal Procurement Policy (OFPP). (1998a). *A guide to best practices for performance-based service contracting.* Washington, DC: OFPP. Retrieved December 10, 2003, from http://www.arnet.gov/Library/OFPP/Best-Practices/pbsc/library2.html.

U.S. Office of Federal Procurement Policy (OFPP). (1998b). *A report on the performance-based service contracting pilot project.* Washington, DC: OFPP. Retrieved December 10, 2003, from http://www.arnet.gov/Library/OFPP/PolicyDocs/pbscpilpro.html.

Wimmer, S. (2003). Contracting for performance: No more "acquisition think." *Government Procurement, 11*(5), 14-17.

Chapter 6

Proposal Evaluation and Contract Award

The process of contracting for services is similar to the contracting process used for supplies and equipment but with certain distinctions. One distinction: the evaluation process for Request for Proposal (RFP) is much more onerous. It has been previously stated that there are major differences between the RFP process and the Invitation for Bids (IFB) process. These differences are reflected throughout the contracting process. Cost factors are far more insignificant in the RFP process, while the timeline for awarding a service contract is much longer, depending on the complexity of the service. It is not unusual to re-offer a service contract several times in order to satisfy all of the constituents. The contract itself can take on various iterations, and it is important to work closely with the legal counsel of the government. The American Bar Association (ABA) recognizes the uniqueness of service contracts and has developed recommended clauses that should be inserted in all contracts for service. Performance contracts are much more demanding in terms of outcome quantification, and this has presented procurement officials with a different set of contractual issues, such as the inclusion of incentives and penalties. The contract phase must be approached very carefully because of its legal ramifications.

The Evolving Service Contracting Process

The process of receiving, evaluating, and awarding bids/tenders or proposals varies, depending on the jurisdiction. The process regarding bid openings is clear-cut and has been in place for many years. Service contracting—the process of soliciting and receiving proposals, and the subsequent award of a contract based on proposals received—is evolving.

A bid/tender opening is normally open to the general public, unless specifically prohibited by statute, ordinance, regulation, or policy. It is extremely rare for bids not to be made available to the general public; but, in the procurement of services, the actual opening of the proposals might be deferred in special circumstances. When this occurs, the methodology for proposal delivery and opening must be clearly stated in the solicitation.

Sound public procurement policy requires that, however well defined the process may be, safeguards must be in place to assure fairness and credibility. The procurement manager will be wise to address the following points in the solicitation document:

- Set a date and time for receiving offers. Indicate that late submissions will not be accepted and that they will be returned unopened.
- A debriefing will be conducted following a decision to award. Consideration should be given for a time that unsuccessful offerors might inspect the responses received from other offerors. Proprietary information and trade secrets will not be available for this inspection.
- Pricing is irrevocable for a given period of time following the opening of offers and may be extended by mutual agreement.
- There will be no questions taken from those in attendance at the opening. Questions or inquires regarding the opened offers will *not* be entertained during the evaluation process, with the exception of discussions as specified in the solicitation document.

Evaluation and Award

The evaluation of a bid/tender or offer is a critical element in the contracting for service process, and the role of the procurement office must be clearly defined (National Institute of Governmental Purchasing, Inc. [NIGP], 2001, p. 99). The procurement office may be solely responsible for evaluating offers or may coordinate with others, such as the evaluation committee or the project manager. If an end-user agency attempts to preclude procurement from the evaluation process, the procurement manager should request the involvement of senior management to discourage such a practice.

The evaluation process is dependent on the method of solicitation utilized, i.e., competitive negotiation, multi-step bidding, or competitive sealed proposals. With each method, the degree that price is a factor will vary, depending on the weight assigned to the evaluation criteria.

The evaluation must be based on the criteria developed by the Statement of Work (SOW) team and as stated in the solicitation's SOW. Evaluation criteria may be based on any or all of the following:

- Understanding and responsiveness to the solicitation;
- Appropriateness of methodology;

- Adequacy of the work plan;
- Focus on result;
- Capability and capacity (personnel, equipment, and materials);
- Adherence to time schedule;
- Management plan;
- Qualifications;
- Reputation and references;
- Price/cost of services provided;
- Quality of required submissions (resumes and past projects); and
- Disclosure of independence and relationships.

Usually, the procurement office will do an initial review of responses in order to identify those responses that are clearly unacceptable. Acceptable proposals must meet the minimum requirements of the solicitation and must not have any deficiencies. Acceptable proposals may have weaknesses; but, generally, weaknesses will not render a proposal unacceptable.

Unacceptable proposals are those that fail to meet all of the requirements of the solicitation because at least one serious deficiency exists in the response. Deficiencies do not render a proposal non-responsive; however, a deficiency can eliminate a proposal from consideration. A letter is usually sent to the offeror whose proposal has been eliminated from consideration.

Sound public procurement policy requires...fairness and credibility.

Best-Value Evaluation Process

Best value is the process used in competitive procurement to select the most advantageous offer through evaluation and comparison of factors in addition to cost or price. Best-value evaluation follows these guiding principles:

- Use best value when it is essential to evaluate and compare factors, in addition to cost, in order to identify and select the most advantageous offer.
- Always include cost or price as an evaluation factor.
- Include the offeror's relevant past performance as an evaluation factor, unless it would clearly serve no useful purpose.
- Structure evaluation criteria and the relative order of importance to clearly reflect the jurisdiction's need and to facilitate preparation of proposals that best satisfy that need.
- Limit evaluation criteria to those areas that will reveal substantive differences or risk levels among competing offers.
- Clearly state the basis on which the jurisdiction will make the best value decision in the solicitation.

- Request only the necessary information to evaluate proposals against the evaluation criteria.
- Ensure consistency among the objectives of the solicitation, the contracting strategy, the plan for selecting a method of solicitation, the solicitation contents, and the evaluation method and selection of an offeror.

Evaluation Committee

Many services are evaluated and awarded solely by the procurement staff without the need to convene an evaluation committee or panel. The following list will help to determine if an evaluation committee is needed:

- The size, scope, and complexity of the service;
- The type of procurement method utilized;
- The jurisdiction's procurement law, ordinance, and regulations;
- The judgment of the chief procurement officer; and
- The selection plan decided upon and stated in the IFB/ITT/RFP.

The evaluation committee will evaluate, score the responses, select a finalist and, if required by statute, ordinance, or regulation, make a recommendation for award. Members of the evaluation committee may include:

- Procurement staff (solicitation's procurement manager);
- Department or agency representative;
- Contract manager (project manager);
- Professional staff (engineering, medical, accounting, etc.);
- Representative from finance, budget, etc.; and
- Legal counsel (as advisory only).

The committee also may include other voting or non-voting members, such as consultants, citizens, legislators, or members of advisory committees (Harney, 1992, p. 100). The foundation of the committee is the chief procurement officer for the jurisdiction and the technical expert for the end-user agency. While the procurement staff actively participates in the evaluation process and may or may not have voting status, the head of the end-user agency is ultimately responsible for the final source selection.

The evaluation committee should include members of all functional areas in the jurisdiction in order to utilize the best talent available. In addition to being technically qualified, members should be unbiased, impartial, and free from any personal or business relationships with offerors that are submitting proposals. Ethics laws in some jurisdictions may detail criteria to be followed by public employees and private citizens who may serve on an evaluation committee.

Thought and consideration should be given when naming individuals to an evaluation committee. The committee needs to function efficiently, effectively, and in a timely manner. Members need to be motivated and posses excellent interpersonal and analytical skills.

The overall responsibility of the evaluation committee is to provide justifiable and defensible recommendation for award, based upon the evaluation criteria stated in the solicitation. Figure 42 provides a sample guideline for the evaluation committee members and, if required, could be presented at an orientation or training session prior to commencing with the process of evaluation.

Introduction
The Invitation for Bids/Invitation to Tender/Request for Proposal includes language concerning the evaluation process. The evaluation committee has been charged with the responsibility of determining which responses should be classified as *reasonably susceptible for award* and will recommend, from the highest rated responses, which will best serve the interests of the jurisdiction.

Mission
The primary mission of an evaluation committee includes:
  a) Review of all responses received to the solicitation, using the solicitation and the evaluation criteria as benchmarks;
  b) Individually rate each response;
  c) Meet in executive session to evaluate, discuss, and determine final ratings;
  d) Keep accurate records of all meetings, conferences, oral presentations, evaluations, and decisions (a recording secretary must be made a part of the committee);
  e) Issue a final report and recommendation to the chief procurement official.

If further clarification is needed, the following may be implemented by the procurement office for the evaluation of responses:
  a) Under the direction of the procurement office, informal contact may be made with offerors whose responses are not adequate for the purpose of clarification;
  b) For the purpose of discussion, give all offerors an equal opportunity to make a presentation and supplement an offer under the direction of the procurement office, if necessary.

Responsibilities
The responsibilities of the evaluation committee include:
  a) Familiarization with:
     1) The Evaluation Form;
     2) Scope of Work; and
     3) Technical Criteria.
  b) Review of each Technical Response:
     1) Independently;
     2) Thoroughly;
     3) Objectively; and
     4) Prior to committee meeting.
  c) Completion of an Evaluation Form for each Offeror:
     1) Independently;
     2) Thoroughly, with comments to justify scorings;
     3) Score independently; DO NOT compare individual response scores;
     4) Factors not specified in the solicitation document cannot be considered;
     5) Be consistent in ranking methodology of all responses; and
     6) Personal biases cannot be a factor in scoring, i.e., first-time offeror with no previous history with the jurisdiction, previous issues with a particular offeror, etc.

> *(Figure 42, continues)*
>
> **General Hints for Review of a Response**
>
> a) Allow sufficient time to read carefully all of the information received in the responses.
>
> b) Do not read technical information when tired or distracted.
>
> c) Do not read too many technical responses in a short period of time. The last one read might not receive the attention required.
>
> d) Use a pencil to complete the Evaluation Form. All preliminary evaluations are subject to change based on information exchanged at the evaluation committee meeting.
>
> **Committee Membership**
>
> For the majority of solicitations, committee membership should consist of a minimum of three and a maximum of seven members, depending on the complexity and Statement of Work requirements. Leadership, attendance, and good record keeping are vital to the success of the committee.
>
> **Confidentiality**
>
> Confidentiality and security of all responses received is an absolute requirement of all committee members. All contacts with offerors are to be made by the procurement office. Any compromise in the confidentiality or security of any response could result in the cancellation of the solicitation.
>
> **Procurement Office's Role**
>
> The procurement manager or designee should attend, at a minimum, the first and last committee meeting. At the initial meeting, this individual should review the procurement process to date, the evaluation criteria, and seek to identify and correct any misunderstandings and misconceptions of any committee member.
>
> **Final Ranking**
>
> Based on the evaluation of the Technical and Financial sections of the responses, the Evaluation committee will select, from among the highest scored responses, responses that will best serve the interest of the jurisdiction. The committee will make recommendations to the chief procurement official for the award to the response that receives the highest overall score. Technical merit may be given a greater value than price.

Figure 42. *Evaluation Committee Orientation Format.*

An orientation session also could include:

- Introduction of members and definition of roles;
- Selection of committee chairperson (preferably to be the procurement manager);
- Selection of a person to record all proceedings, not necessarily required to be a voting member of the evaluation committee;
- A summary of the solicitation;
- A review of the rules governing the evaluation process;
- Explanation of evaluation scoring procedures; and
- Instructions regarding the completion of the evaluation forms.

Mission of the Evaluation Committee

The mission of the evaluation committee has been described as follows (Short, 1990, p. 31):

- Review all proposals received in response to the RFP, using the RFP and the evaluation criteria as benchmarks.

- Conduct all formal conferences that are scheduled with proposers for the purpose of discussion.
- Give all proposers an equal opportunity to make a presentation supplementing a proposal (if presentations are permitted by the RFP).
- During competitive negotiation, give those proposers who are susceptible to possible award an opportunity to present a Best and Final Offer (BAFO).
- Meet in executive session to evaluate, discuss, and reach consensus.
- Keep an accurate record of all meetings, conferences, oral presentations, evaluations, and decisions.
- Issue a final report and recommendation.

A final report and recommendation is usually addressed to the head of the end-user agency with a copy to the chief procurement official.

The award is usually based on the evaluation committee's recommendation unless, after review by the procurement office or upon protest of a proposer, the recommendation is reconsidered because:

- Mathematical errors were committed in scoring the proposals.
- The recommended proposer should have been disqualified as not responsive to all the mandatory requirements of the solicitation.
- There was evidence of collusion or fraud involving either the proposer or a member of the evaluation committee.
- The evaluation committee failed to follow the evaluation criteria set forth in the solicitation.
- Violations of statutes, ordinances, regulations, or policies have occurred.

An example of a violation would be the disclosure of information contained in another proposal by a member of the evaluation committee to a proposer.

Administrative/Procedural Duties

Besides making a recommendation of award, the evaluation committee also has administrative and procedural duties, including:

- To keep a record of minutes of all committee deliberations;
- To keep a record of all correspondence files;
- To keep a record of all completed forms;
- To keep a record of all handwritten notes taken by all members throughout the process;
- To keep a record of all supplemental information provided by the finalists; and
- To organize all member scoring forms and justifications for final ranking. (NIGP, 2001, p. 103)

Attendance

It is extremely important that all voting members attend all scheduled meetings and oral presentations by the finalists. The absence of a voting member may render the final scoring void and establish grounds for a protest. This concern may be eliminated if each voting member designates an alternate who may substitute in the voting member's absence. If alternates are used, they also must attend all committee meetings (NIGP, 2001, p. 104).

Special Responsibilities of the Evaluation Committee

A fair and equal distribution of assignments within the evaluation committee is necessary if the committee is to function effectively. Special responsibilities may be assigned to the procurement manager and the project manager during the evaluation process. One of these managers may be required to:

- Contact all the references listed in the response to determine if the respondent successfully delivered similar services to other comparable jurisdictions.
- Make an assessment regarding the respondent's capability to accomplish the service delivery as outlined in the SOW. Can the respondent responsibly perform all of the service requirements, if awarded the contract?
- Determine if the references have experienced issues, poor performance, or were involved in any disputes or claims with the respondent.

The jurisdiction's financial staff may be called upon to calculate the total cost of the service delivery based on the cost and price information provided by the respondent. Finance and budget staff also may be required to evaluate other financial information, such as interest rates, the time value of money, energy savings, and special financing.

Evaluation Process for a Competitive Negotiation

Generally, the evaluation process for competitive negotiation consists of the following:

- Full evaluation committee plus alternates attend an orientation session, select a chairperson and recording secretary, receive scoring forms, and review scoring methodology.
- Committee determines acceptable and unacceptable proposals.
- Unacceptable proposals with a letter of explanation are returned in a timely manner.
- Committee members independently review and score acceptable proposals.
- Full committee meeting is convened to review the scores assigned by each committee member during the independent review.

- Adjustment of scores is made based on committee discussion.
- Respondents are ranked by total scores.
- Committee selects top-ranked finalists (usually no more than three) for further evaluation.
- Remaining respondents are eliminated, although proposals are retained.
- Finalists are invited to an interview that may be combined with an oral presentation.
- Committee members scoring the interview and oral presentations. Following the interview/oral presentation, the committee may require additional information or supplemental submission to be forwarded in writing to the committee chairperson. A date and time for submission should be given (normally 10 business days).
- Supplemental information is evaluated by the committee and may be scored.
- Oral presentations/interviews and supplemental information are ranked by score.
- Approval from the appropriate jurisdiction official to begin negotiations with the respondent receiving the highest score.
- Negotiation on those areas listed in the RFP as negotiable. The full committee may not participate in the final negotiations. Typically, no more than two or three members of the evaluation committee participate.
- All negotiated areas are agreed to, and a contract award is recommended.

Note: Price may be discussed at the interview/oral presentations and a non-binding estimate of cost may be asked for in the SOW or as supplemental information (NIGP, 2001, p. 105).

Evaluation Process for Multi-Step Offers

Multi-step offers involve a two-step process. The first step requires the submission of unpriced technical proposals. After the evaluations, the technical proposals are ranked by score, and the top two or three finalists are selected.

In the second step, the selected finalists are asked to submit price proposals. The sealed price proposals may be submitted with the technical proposals or when finalists have been selected. If either of these methods is used, discussion of price is *not* permitted during the technical phase. The award is then made to the lowest priced offeror whose technical proposal received the highest ranking (NIGP, 2001, p. 105).

After the evaluations, the technical proposals are ranked by score...

Evaluation Process for Competitive Sealed Bids

Competitive sealed bidding requires that the award is made to the lowest *responsive* and *responsible* bidder based solely on the response to the criteria in the IFB and does *not* include discussions or negotiations with the bidders (NIGP, 2001, p. 105).

Evaluation Process—Decision Rule for Competitive Sealed Proposals

Once the evaluation committee has selected the criteria to be used to evaluate the proposals, measures of their relative importance must be determined. This can be accomplished by stating the importance of the various criteria in the solicitation document or by establishing a mathematical system. These rules may encompass any one or combination of the following evaluation methods: (a) fixed weight, (b) variable weight, (c) trade-off analysis, or (d) go/no-go.

The evaluation committee may weigh the criteria by priority or trade-off statements, judgmental decision rules, or a combination of these elements. Weighing involves assigning a point value to each criterion according to its relative importance. Typically, a value of 100 to 1,000 points is used for distribution over the evaluation criteria.

Not all source selection officials like using specific numerical relationships. Some prefer using priority statements. For example, in a priority statement, cost may be said to be slightly more important than management, but slightly less that operational suitability. Examples of decision rules include:

> If management is rated anything less than satisfactory, the entire proposal is unacceptable, or If the proposal price is 30 percent higher than the agency estimate, it will be judged as being potentially unrealistic, the cost score will be penalized, and the technical proposal will be reevaluated to see if there is some misunderstanding of the requirements. (Cibinic & Nash, 1986, p. 548)

The evaluation committee can use any of the decisional processes in order to make a sound selection. In cases where a fixed relationship between evaluation criteria cannot be established in advance, the evaluation committee may use priority statements. In some cases, they may use variable relationships between criteria.

Columbia County, Georgia, has an excellent guide for the evaluation of proposals, which is included in their *Procurement Procedure Manual* (2004). The following is an excerpt from this manual:

Form for Evaluation of Responses

A. General

The evaluation criteria in the sample form are general in nature and not intended to apply to all projects. The Committee shall revise the form (with the assistance of the Procurement Manager) to match each solicitation being evaluated by adding or deleting criteria as appropriate. The form must be approved by the Procurement Manager prior to release of the responses from the Procurement Office. The inclusion of criteria not described or referenced in the original solicitation is prohibited.

B. Assigning Points

Points are assigned according to the degree of responsiveness of the information presented in the responses. The points indicate the *quality* of the response. Very low scores represent an unacceptable or poor response; low to middle scores represent satisfactory or average; middle and above scores represent a good or very good response. Excellent responses often are given all the points assigned for that category. The Committee can assign other numerical values to the range of points allowed for grading the quality of the response. It is important to note that the summation of the maximum points for all categories should total 100.

Only the best proposal for each category shall receive the maximum possible points for that category. The remaining responses receive fewer points for that category. Although the scoring of points is a matter of subjectivity, the Committee member's judgment must be based on the information presented in the offeror's proposal.

An offeror shall not be penalized due to lack of experience with the County or given a point advantage because of previous contract relationships with the County. The relevancy of such experience in terms of the RFP's scope of work may be judged as with any other reference of the offeror. When the County is used in this manner as a "reference," a reference check form must be completed and made part of the record. Point scores always shall be assigned in an impartial and objective manner.

C. Weighing Scores

Some criteria in the evaluation form are given more importance (weight) than others by assigning a higher maximum score to that criterion. Weights indicate the *relative importance* of the responses, not their quality. Criterion that have maximum scores 5, 10, or 15 points higher than other criterion rank either "moderately important," "important," or "very important" as compared to other criterion. In general, once a score value has been assigned to an evaluation criterion, it cannot be interpolated or otherwise changed by the Committee members.

D. Scoring Columns

During independent review (before the meeting of the full Committee), each Committee member reads the offeror's response and inserts a point score for each criterion. The best response for each criterion listed receives the highest point value for that criterion. The responses for that criterion from the remaining offerors receive fewer points according to their relationship to the "best" response.

Negative or "0" point values can be assigned to evaluation criteria by the Committee member. When an offeror states that a given critical requirement will not be provided, a negative score (-) can be assigned to that criterion that is equal to the highest point value allowed for that item. If an offeror did not address an RFP requirement, a point value of "0" is entered in the form. Negative scores are assigned only when the offeror takes exception to a required item or clearly states that the requirement is not part of its offer.

Insert brief comments under each criterion, explaining the reason for any unusually low or high scores. These notes may be needed for reference during the full Committee discussions if the points assigned are questioned by another Committee member, or to justify the Committee member's score in the event of a protest by an unsuccessful offeror. When finished with the independent review, total the scores for each offeror.

The most commonly used scoring system is fixed weights.

When the full Committee meets to review the responses, new information received by a Committee member from the discussions of the full Committee may result in the Committee member deciding that a score requires changing. It is not unusual to have a Committee member's original score changed because of new information discovered at the full Committee meeting. For example, one member could have "discovered" information that other members thought was apparently missing from a response because the offeror put the information in an attachment instead of in the main section of the proposal. The Committee member then enters the revised score on the final form. If there are no changes to the independent review, the same point value is transferred to the final form. After Committee discussions are complete, the scores are totaled. (last updated on 11/02/04)

A template that can be used as a guideline for scoring of oral and written presentations is included as Appendix I. This particular form, also taken from Columbia County Georgia's *Procurement Procedure Manual* (Columbia County, Georgia, 2004), was created for the scoring of oral presentations but could be adapted for use in the scoring of written proposals.

FIXED WEIGHTS

The most commonly used scoring system is fixed weights. This is a mathematical weighing system allowing the evaluation committee to assign weight to each designated criteria by a percentage distribution. Within each criterion, a 100% distribution may be used again to fix the relative importance of each criterion.

Since public procurement at the state and political subdivision is price driven, it is best to reserve a specific amount of points for price/cost. The use of the RFP method indicates that price is not the primary consideration for selection of an offeror. However, because price and cost must be considered, points must be allocated. For example, if the committee establishes a total of 1,000 evaluation points, between 250 and 400 of those 1,000 points must be reserved for pricing. The remaining points are allocated in descending order of importance for the remaining evaluation criteria. The price is not normally given to the evaluation committee until the technical portion of the response is evaluated and scored, thus reducing the possibility of influencing technical scores.

After all technical scores have been submitted, the highest scoring technical proposal receives the maximum amount of points allocated for price. By using a simple algebraic equation, a lesser amount of points are assigned to the remaining technically scored proposals.

For example, the evaluation committee assigns 1,000 total evaluation points and, of those, 250 points are for price. The highest scored technical proposal would receive 750 points (NIGP, 2001, p. 107). Table 10 is an illustration of how weights can be distributed.

TABLE 10

Evaluation Criteria

Area of Evaluation	Points	Total
I. Adequacy of Technical Proposal		400
a. Literature search and investigation methodology	150	
b. Proposed sources of information	100	
c. Plan for assessing the value of each publication	75	
d. Correlation of literature to economics aspects	50	
e. Presentation of findings	25	
II. Project Management		200
a. Previous experience with similar objects	90	
b. Company resources available to the project manager	60	
c. Proposed subcontracting effort	30	
d. Project management organization	20	
III. Personnel Qualifications		150
a. Technical experience of principal	100	
b. Education qualifications	30	
c. Consultant qualifications	20	
IV. Price/Cost		250

Source: Cibinic, J., & Nash, R. (1986). *Administration of government contracts*. Cambridge, MA: NIT Center for Advanced Engineering Study.

VARIABLE WEIGHTS

The evaluation committee may determine that fixed weights should not control the method of scoring in all situations. Often, the jurisdiction determines that cost or price should become as important if technical proposals are of relatively equal merit. For instance, the RFP may state that the degree of importance of cost as a factor could increase, depending upon the equality of the proposals for other criteria evaluated (NIGP, 2001, p. 108).

TRADE-OFF ANALYSIS

Trade-off analysis is a method that requires the evaluation committee to analyze the value of technical differences between proposals in order to determine if these differences justify the cost or price differential. Technical criteria are point scored, and the differences between the trade-offs are determined. In this case, the technical criteria are of more relative importance than price.

The evaluation committee has a great deal of discretion when using trade-off analysis. In competitive negotiation, procurement regulations do not require that awards be made on the basis of lowest cost. If a solicitation does not mention the relative importance of cost, then cost and technical considerations are given equal merit. The evaluation committee has broad discretion in determining the manner and the extent to which it will utilize technical and cost evaluation results. A procurement office may award an offeror that has earned higher technical scores and higher costs if the result is consistent with the evaluation criteria and if it is determined that the technical difference outweighs the cost difference (NIGP, 2001, p. 108).

When trade-off analysis is used, the RFP must inform offerors that the procurement office will determine the weight to be accorded cost criteria after determining the relative merits of the technical proposals. Cost factors are not scored. The weight to be accorded them can be given only after the relative merits of the proposals have been determined from a technical standpoint.

Go/No-Go

Another method of evaluating proposals is known as go/no-go. It can be applied to major areas and elements of management, operational suitability, and other criteria when identified for evaluation. This method is frequently used in situations where the product is subject to testing. This plan must adequately meet the requirements of the management section of evaluation. During evaluation, the management plan proposed by the offeror is either "go" (adequate) or "no-go" (inadequate). If it were inadequate, the evaluation committee would solicit a revised proposal from the offeror designed to make management adequate. In a "go" situation, the element will not be further scored or summarized.

If an element is scored adequate, it is no longer relevant in the evaluation process, and an award is made on the basis of other criteria. An adequate score in an area is a minimum requirement for selection. The RFP may provide for award to the offeror with the lowest overall price among those offers found acceptable in the technical and management areas. Technical and management criteria are scored on a "go/no-go" basis (NIGP, 2001, pp. 108-109).

Lowest Priced Acceptable Proposal

The lowest priced, acceptable proposal is an alternative method that entails awarding to the lowest priced proposal among all proposals found acceptable in both technical and management areas. All evaluation criteria, except price, are scored on a go/no-go basis. Technically unacceptable proposals still may be included in the competitive range if it is possible that they may become acceptable. For instance, an award on a fixed-price solicitation can be made to the lowest priced offeror meeting the RFP technical specifications (NIGP, 2001, p. 109).

Drafting the Contract

Once the successful offeror has been identified and all negotiations are completed, the formal contract should be created with the help of the jurisdiction's legal counsel. The formal contract document will incorporate all plans and specifications that formed the basis of the offer, including the RFP or IFB /Invitation to Tender (ITT) document, the offer or proposal, all terms, conditions, and pricing that was negotiated, and any other contractual requirements.

> NIGP's *Dictionary of Purchasing Terms* defines contract as:
>
> 1: A legally binding promise enforceable by law; 2: an agreement between parties, with binding legal and moral force, usually exchanging goods or services for money or other consideration; 3: all types of agreements regardless of what they may be called, for the procurement or disposal of supplies, service, or construction; 4: (CN) an agreement between a contracting authority and a person or business unit to provide a good, perform a service, construct a work, or lease real property for appropriate consideration.

In order to be legally enforceable, all contracts must have the following essential elements:

- Offer and acceptance (mutual assent);
- Definiteness;
- Legal consideration;
- Mutuality of obligation;
- Capacity of the parties; and
- Legality of purpose.

Two of these elements, legal consideration and mutuality of obligation, are related. Because of the formal nature of the public contracting process, there is seldom a dispute about whether the government and its vendor have complied with some of these elements (Thai, 2004, p. 79).

> A contract for services should:
> - Protect the interest of the jurisdiction;
> - Identify the responsibilities of the parties to the contract;
> - Define what is to be delivered;
> - Document the mutual agreement, substance, and parameters of what was agreed upon; and
> - Identify the audit trail.

No oral or written communication between the successful offeror and the jurisdiction can be considered, including any and all negotiated areas, unless it is incorporated in written form into the final contract document. The offeror to whom the contract is awarded is only obligated to perform those duties set forth in the contract document.

Contract Format

Protests, disputes, and other situations may impede the contract award process. Following the resolution of such issues and other necessary approvals of boards, commissions or other higher authority, the procurement officer will prepare a contract document for execution. The procurement officer may decide the form of contract document or may defer this decision to legal authority. The entire effort of the service contracting process culminates with the execution of the contract. The preparation of the contract document leaves no room for error. The contract will dictate performance, price and all agreements, as well as understandings and expectations, which are to be clearly stated in precise and explicit language. The government generates the contract document. It should never be forwarded to the prospective contractor until it has been reviewed for completeness by the contract administration team and the legal department as to form and legal sufficiency. If an error occurs, but is not discovered until after all parties have executed it, it may be impossible to rectify the error without great difficulty and added expense. The SOW is the heart of the contract along with the cost or price proposals. All other documents (bonds, insurance certificates, boilerplate, addendum, etc.) must also be incorporated into the final contract document.

There are multiple options relative to contract form that may include: (a) purchase-order contract, (b) short-form contract, (c) standard-form contract for contractors, or (d) formal contract.

Purchase-Order Contract

The purchase-order contract is the simplest contract format and may be used for services that are simple, uncomplicated, and have been procured using a competitive sealed bidding, negotiation, or small value RFP. In some cases, the purchase order itself becomes a cover sheet that references other attachments. When it is necessary to encumber funds, the purchase order contract may be the preferred document (Harney, 1992, p. 124). The purchase-order contract should, at a minimum, include the following information:

- Contract term,
- Unit price or pricing/cost schedule,
- Designation of government contract monitor or manager, and
- Scope of Work.
- Contract price,
- Insurance requirements,

Short-Form Contract

Generally, a short-form contract document is used for contracting for services made under the RFP or IFB process. It may be a brief one-page contract in a template format on a resident database that can be easily edited (Harney, 1992, p. 125).

The short-form contract language is generally pre-approved by the legal staff and is more detailed than the purchase-order contract. It also requires written execution by both parties. The short-form contract will include, by reference, other contract documents. Figure 43 depicts a short-form contract template.

City of America, USA Contract

THIS AGREEMENT, made this the ____ day of ____, 2002, by and between the City of America, hereinafter called "Owner," and the ABC Company, a corporation in the City of America, and State of _____, hereinafter called "Contractor."

WITNESSED: That the Contractor and the City, in consideration of the mutual covenants, promises, and agreements contained herein, agree as follows:

Scope of Work: (*summarize the scope of work*)

Contract Documents: The contract documents consist of this signed contract, any and all amendments, exhibits, and other supporting documentation contained in Bid or Request for Proposal submitted by the Contractor, all of which are incorporated herein by reference.

Compensation and Method of Payment: (list the prices submitted in the bid or proposal/cost schedule, or refer to appropriate submission pages)

IN WITNESS WHEREOF, the parties to these agreements have executed this Contract in three (3) counterparts, each of which shall be deemed an original, in the year and day first above mentioned.

Attest: (Seal)   Contractor:
_____   By: _____

Attest: (Seal)   City of America
_____

                                            By: _____

Figure 43. *Sample of Short-Form Contract.*

Source: Adapted from Harney, D. (1992). Service contracting: A local government guide (p. 126). Washington, DC: International City/County Management Association.

Standard-Form Contract for Contractors

Certain corporations, engineers, architects and other professional groups may insist that the government execute a standard contract form developed by their professional association or a corporate contract form prepared by their legal office. Quite often, these contracts will favor the contractor to the detriment of the government. If all other contract form options have been exhausted and the government decides to execute the contractor's contract, it should be reviewed in great detail by the government's legal office. Harney's (1992) text details the provisions to watch for in a contract document prepared by a contractor (see Figure 44).

Proposed Contractors' Standard Contract Provisions

Applicable law. Enforcement and interpretation are to be according to the laws and the courts of another state.

Limitation of Liability. The contractor's liability for damages is lower than required by the local government. Some provisions may prohibit consequential damages of any kind, however caused; others may limit the contractor's liability to an amount equivalent to the value of the contract.

Termination. Renewal or termination clauses may conflict with the bid document. Clauses allowing the contractor to terminate at its convenience on short (thirty- or forty-five-day) notice are not uncommon.

Arbitration. An arbitration clause may require contract disputes to be submitted for resolution by a professional arbitrator, a procedure that could deny the governing body its right to settle contract disputes without the intervention of a third party.

Indemnification. The local government may be required to indemnify the contractor for acts or omissions of the local government, pay attorney's fees or costs of collection, reimburse expenses for termination of the contract by the local government, even if termination was the result of an action of the contractor.

Unusual Rights of the Contractor. The contract may permit the contractor unusual discretion in making unilateral changes to the work, rather than making recommendations for decision by the local government contract manager.

Limiting Services. The contract may limit contract services to a level below that agreed to during negotiations.

Nonsubstitution. A nonappropriation clause may contain a nonsubstitution requirement that prohibits the local government from obtaining an equivalent or better product or service for several years after cancellation by the local government for nonappropriation. The local government should not agree to more than a six-month nonsubstitution clause, if any.

Insurance. The contract may require the local government to purchase builder's risk or contractor's liability coverage or other insurance at its own expense, instead of having the contractor provide it, and may limit the contractor's liability for damage directly caused by the contractor.

Payments. The contract may require advance or down payments. Public funds should not be used to pay for a service that has not yet been received.

Figure 44. *Provisions to Watch for in Standard Contracts Provided by Contractors.*

Source: Adapted from Harney, D. (1992). *Service contracting: A local government guide* (p. 127). Washington, DC: International City/County Management Association.

Formal Contract

Procurement officials have a close working relationship with the government's legal staff. Often, an attorney representing the government has served on the SOW team and is familiar with the service to be contracted. Frequently, a contract form is included in the RFP document, and the contractor is advised that if they are awarded the service contract, this will be the legal document that they will be expected to execute.

In the formal contract document, all terms, conditions, amendments, addenda, exhibits, appendices, the RFP, and all other pertinent information are incorporated into the contract document. The formal contract document will contain information specific to the service. Extraneous material, not directly related to contract performance, will not become a part of the contract document. This may include promotional marketing information, resumes, instructions to the offerors, minutes of meetings, etc. The formal contract document is generally not executed until the contractor has submitted all necessary and required documents, such as bonds, insurance certificates, licenses, etc. The contract start date and its completion date should be clearly stated as well as the total contract cost. Upon its execution by all parties, it is the responsibility of the purchasing official to assure that copies of the contract document are distributed internally to all necessary staff. Original copies should be retained by the agency for whom the service was contracted, the law office, and the purchasing office. Many jurisdictions are now scanning contract documents into a shared database for easy access and retrieval.

Exhibits

There are various exhibits that may be included with the contract form. Three exhibits in particular are critical components to the final contract document: (a) Statement of Work exhibit, (b) Unit Price exhibit, and (c) Insurance exhibit.

Statement of Work Exhibit. This exhibit details the final outcome of negotiations between the contractor and the contracting agency. The final SOW reflects how the service will be performed, the duties and responsibilities of the contractor, and often differs from the initial SOW found in the RFP. During discussions between the successful contractor and the jurisdiction, the original SOW and the terms and conditions of the solicitation are refined and expanded. The result of the discussions exists primarily in the form of written reports or memoranda and addenda to the RFP issued during the solicitation process. Following award of a contract, the SOW is the only codified document that describes the requirements the contractor is legally bound to follow.

There are two options for deciding who should prepare the Statement of Work Exhibit. The jurisdiction, preferably the procurement office, should be responsible for preparing the contract, including exhibits and attachments. This task often proves to be time-consuming, as the document may need to be created from scratch. However, the use of standardized contract formats often facilitates the process by establishing the contractual boilerplate or outline of the legal requirements of the agency. Should the successful contractor present the contract documents to the agency, it is imperative that the purchasing department ensure that the final Statement of Work Exhibit reflects verbatim the agreed-upon changes to the technical requirements, price changes, delivery requirements, and standards of measuring performance effectiveness and achievement both during the contract performance as well as upon contract completion. Further, the final Statement of Work Exhibit must establish a base line from which any contractual changes are determined.

> *The final SOW reflects how the service will be performed, [and] the duties and responsibilities of the contractor...*

Unit Price Exhibit. The contract amount should be identified in the main section of the contract under the heading Contract Amount. In addition to the contract amount, a Unit Price Exhibit may be included when the contractor uses many individual prices and invoices for supplies or services. Unit prices, for example, may include hourly labor rates for various classes of workers, equipment rental charges, and percentage discounts that apply to materials used.

Insurance Exhibit. An important detail of the competitive negotiating process is to make sure the risk to the jurisdiction is minimized in the procurement. There should be careful review and approval of insurance certificates provided by the contractor. The following clauses must be a part of any insurance certificate provided to the jurisdiction:

- *Identification of Contract.* The contract number and title must appear on the insurance certificate. The jurisdiction should not allow the contractor's insurance agent to issue a certificate without knowing the risks of the contract.

- *Name of Insured.* The name of the contractor should be on the insurance certificate. If the contractor is a subsidiary, do not accept just the name of the parent organization on the certificate. Make sure the name of the subsidiary is also on the certificate.

- *Certificate Holder.* The complete legal name of the jurisdiction and the name and address of the individual or office responsible for approval of the contractor's coverage must be included on the certificate of insurance. Cancellation notices are sent to the person or office reflected on the certificate.

- *Insurance Company Rating.* All insurance carriers providing coverage for the contract should have a minimum "Best's" rating. A. M. Best is a publisher of guides that rate the financial and management strengths of insurance carriers. The jurisdiction's risk manager or legal counsel should determine if the rating furnished on the certificate meets the required minimum.

- *Liability Limits.* The insurance coverage must meet or exceed the contract requirements. Since insurance is a cost factor in the IFB/ITT/RFP, the coverage and cost should be determined during discussions and before the best and final offer.

- *General Liability Endorsement.* The certificate must include all endorsements or special provisions that expand or modify the coverage or specific types of liability required. The insurance certificate should also identify the endorsement and each type of liability coverage required as part of the comprehensive general liability insurance. For example, independent contractors, products, completed operations, and personal injuries are types of liability coverage. If there are doubts about the coverage being provided, request a copy of the affected policy to determine if there are any exclusions that could affect the coverage provided by the certificate.

- *Effective Dates.* All certificates must show the expiration date of each policy carried by the contractor. If any of the policies are going to expire during the contract term, contact the contractor at least 30 days before the expiration date and obtain a current certificate that reflects that coverage is extended to at least the end of the contract term; or require that the effective dates of the initial certificate cover the full term of the contract.

- *Cancellation Notice.* Most insurance agents issue a standard insurance certificate form titled ACORD (Association for Cooperative Operations Research and Development). This preprinted form contains a clause that releases the insurance agent from the responsibility of notifying the certificate holder of a cancellation of listed policies, even though insurance carriers always notify the insured party (the contractor) and the contractor's insurance agent of cancellations. The jurisdiction can request and receive a modification to the clause that requires the insurance agent to notify the jurisdiction at least 30 calendar days before a cancellation.

- *Bid, Performance, and Payment Bonds.* Like insurance certificates, bonds must be reviewed carefully to ensure they are executed properly, are in the required form with an attached power of attorney, and that the bonding company is authorized to conduct business in the state where the work is performed. (Harney, 1992, pp. 135-136)

Bid, Performance, and Payment bonds may be signed by a local representative of the bonding company, by insurance brokers, or by agents who have been given this authority through a Power of Attorney. A copy of the Power of Attorney for the person signing the bond must accompany each bond submitted to the jurisdiction.

Some contractors submit a combination Performance and Payment Bond that may have abbreviated language and limited information about the procedures to follow in the event of default and the extent of the bonding company's liability. It is recommended that separate Performance and Payment bonds are provided and that the jurisdiction's legal counsel review and approve the language in each. Some jurisdictions create their own bond forms that are included as exhibits in the original solicitation.

American Bar Association Clauses

The ABA's *2000 Model Procurement Code for State and Local Governments* provides recommended contract clauses that should be inserted in all contracts for services.

- A clause giving the jurisdiction the unilateral right to order, in writing (i) changes in the work within the scope of the contract; and (ii) temporary stopping of work or delaying performance.
- The unilateral right to adjust or vary between estimated units of service and actual quantities.
- A clause addressing price adjustments. The trigger mechanism and method of computation will depend on the type of contract.
- Liquidated damages as appropriate.
- Specific excuses for delay or nonperformance.
- Procedure for termination of the contract by default.
- Procedure for termination of the contract, in whole or in part, for the convenience of the jurisdiction. (Section 6.101)

Other common contractual clauses include: (a) time and location; (b) identification of personnel; (c) objectives to be accomplished; (d) Scope of Work; (e) deliverables; and (f) funding responsibilities/limitations.

Contract Incentives and Penalties

Many governments, especially those that have embraced performance-based contracting, are including incentives and penalty provisions as part of the RFP. Many fixed price, performance-based contracts are designed to reward the contractor if performance, savings, or other deliverables exceed the agreed-upon thresholds. In the more traditional cost type contract, the contractor has no risk and, hence, no incentive to improve performance. The cost-type contract reflects the "you call and we haul" mentality. We tell the contractor what to do and they do it. The contractor bears no risk. Under a fixed price incentive contract, the risk is shifted to the contractor. If performance outcomes are exceeded, an agreed-upon incentive award is given. If the contractor fails to meet the performance outcomes, the contractor is penalized. Such penalty provisions should not be confused with liquidated damages provisions. Liquidated damages are not penalties. They are used in an entirely different context and apply to default and contract breaches. Under the design-based RFP, there are no incentives for the contractor to reduce costs or other administrative and operational expenses.

Incentive contracts can bring the added benefit of increased competition and be creatively designed with contractor input. Frequently, during the RFP phase, contractors are asked to describe where incentives can be included in the contract. Contractors are willing to point out areas within the SOW that, if implemented, will result in cost savings through reorganization and streamlining work processes. The potential for future improvement on the part of the contractor should not be restricted but tied to predefined goals. Some service contracts are works in progress. Everything cannot be identified prior to award so the wise contracting officer will creatively identify certain areas within the scope of work that can result in future cost reductions, which then result in financial incentive to the contractor. As incentives are identified, the contract can be amended accordingly.

Negative incentives or performance penalties also can be used to improve contractor performance and behavior. For example, the SOW may indicate that a deduction (penalty) will be applied to the monthly billing if certain performance requirements are not met.

- If the contractor fails to satisfy certain quality requirements of the deliverables, the government will deduct 10% of the amount billed.
- Customer complaints in excess of an agreed-upon number may result in a 5% penalty applied to the monthly charges.

The penalty amounts are arbitrary and should not be excessive. Excessive penalty provisions will repress competition, so a delicate balance should be maintained between incentives and penalties. Needless to say, contractors are concerned about penalties and the fact that each minor glitch could result in another deduction. On the other hand, the government wants protection from service or performance problems. Hayes (1994) identified several approaches that attempt to mitigate the penalty concern issue.

> *Earn Back*—giving the contractor the opportunity to "earn back" previously assessed penalties by exceeding performance standards in a future time period.
>
> *Positive Performance Credit*—allow the contractor to exceed performance during a specified period thus allowing them to offset previously assessed penalties.
>
> *Dual-Set Weighting Factors*—individual performance standards should be weighted according to importance. If weights are not assigned, the contractor could conceivably take advantage of the "earn back" and "positive performance" provisions by performing poorly in important areas and exceeding performance standards in less important areas.

References

Cibinic, J., & Nash, R. (1986). *Administration of government contracts*. Cambridge, MA: NIT Center for Advanced Engineering Study.

Columbia County, Georgia. (2004). Evaluation guidelines for requests for proposals. In *Columbia County, Georgia's procurement procedure manual (Appendix A)*. Columbia, GA: Columbia County.

Harney, D. (1992). *Service contracting: A local government guide.* Washington, DC: International City/County Management Association.

Hayes, D. (1994). *Advanced issues related to outsourcing agreements.* San Francisco: Fenwick & West LLP.

National Institute of Governmental Purchasing, Inc. (NIGP) (2001). *Contracting for services.* Herndon, VA: NIGP.

National Institute of Governmental Purchasing, Inc. (NIGP) (2002). *Dictionary of purchasing terms* (5th ed.). Herndon, VA: NIGP.

Short, J. (1990). The contract cookbook for purchase of services (2nd ed.). Lexington, KY: Council of State Governments.

Thai, K. V. (2004). *Introduction to public procurement.* Herndon, VA: National Institute of Governmental Purchasing, Inc. (NIGP).

Chapter 7

Protests and Disputes

Various types of protests and disputes can arise at some point during the award of hundreds of contracts for service amounting to millions of dollars. The procurement process is, by its very nature, subject to litigious challenges. The procurement officer will always be on the front lines of contractor protests. Because the Request for Proposal (RFP) process is more subjective than the Invitation for Bids (IFB) process, protests may occur more frequently. Governments must have clearly articulated protest procedures in place. The protest procedure should be spelled out in the boilerplate language of the RFP document.

The integrity of the contracting process requires that the resolution of protests and responses to protests be fair, objective, and timely. The courtroom has been the final resting place for many unresolved protests. The procurement officer must make every attempt to resolve a protest or potential protest at the lowest possible administrative level. Frequently, a well-reasoned response to a contractor's letter of concern would quickly resolve the issue and avoid a possible protest threat.

The introduction of alternative dispute resolution (ADR) is now being used more frequently to resolve contractor dispute issues and has eliminated many expensive court proceedings. A wise procurement official, when faced with a potential or real protest, should immediately seek the advice of the government's legal council.

Protests

Aside from the legal nature of a contract, contracts are about relationships and partnerships. The dynamics of human nature will dictate that any contractual relationship may involve disagreements. In the area of service contracts, these disagreements can be informal or formal. Informal disagreements may be easily and quickly resolved. Formal disagreements will manifest themselves as protests. Contractors familiar with public procurement know that some form of protest process is available to them. Most protests are resolved administratively, but there is always the possibility that a protest will be advanced through a judicial process. Contractors may challenge the procurement at any stage prior to the award of a contract. Addressing protests varies greatly, and an agreement on terms and definitions assists in understanding the general nature of protests.

> **Protest:** a written objection by an interested party to the solicitation or to a proposed award of a contract, with the intention of receiving a remedial result.
>
> **Dispute:** a disagreement between parties to a contract over performance or other contract terms requiring administrative action to resolve.
>
> **Arbitration:** a process by which a dispute between two contending parties is presented to one or more disinterested parties (arbitrators) for a decision. It is also the resolution of a disagreement by such a process.
>
> **Alternative Dispute Resolution (ADR):** any procedure used voluntarily to resolve issues in controversy without the need to resort to litigation. These procedures include, but are not limited to mediation, fact-finding, and arbitration.
>
> **Claim:** a written assertion or demand by one of the parties to a contract which seeks, as a contractual right, payment of money, adjustment of contract terms or other relief for injury or loss damage arising under or relating to a contract.
>
> **Change Order:** a written alteration to a contract or purchase order, signed by the procurement authority, in accordance with the terms of the contract, unilaterally directing the contractor to make changes. (The National Institute of Governmental Purchasing, Inc. [NIGP], 2002)
>
> **Appeal:** the re-submission of a protest, contract dispute, or claim to a higher authority, with the intent to overturn a decision of a lower authority (Harney, 1992, p. 140).

Bidders and offerors will normally file a protest if they feel that a wrong decision has been made regarding a recommendation to award a contract. Protests are usually filed prior to contract award. The jurisdiction's administrative procedures should clearly state the steps an alleged aggrieved contractor must take when filing a protest. Many jurisdictions will include protest procedures in the solicitation document. At a minimum, protest procedures should have:

- A notification to all bidders of the intent of the jurisdiction to award the contract, which should contain the date and the time that the award will be made;
- A timetable indicating the deadline for protest filing, because timeliness is critical in any protest action;

- To whom the aggrieved bidder must submit the protest and in what form; and
- A statement regarding the appeal process and how appeals are made.

In many jurisdictions, legal counsel addresses all protests, claims, and disputes due to the fact that there may be potential litigation. In some jurisdictions, the protest may be as simple as sending a letter to the chief procurement officer. The procurement officer conducts an informal meeting and renders an opinion. If the bidder is not satisfied with the opinion, the only recourse is the judicial system. In other jurisdictions, an elaborate protest procedure may include a formal hearing by elected officials, an arbitration process, or perhaps ADR. Most parties would prefer to avoid litigation and amicably resolve the protest. For a more comprehensive study of ADR, refer to Alternative Dispute Resolution (Martin & Miller, 2005), which serves as an implementation guide to negotiation, mediation, arbitration and mini-trial for Public Contracting Professionals.

A major decision that procurement officials must make, based on legal counsel opinion, is whether the award should be delayed pending the resolution of the protest. When determining whether the protest should impact the award of the contract, administrative procedures usually make provisions so that if the protest is received before contract performance begins and delay would not have an adverse effect on government operations, the award process will be stopped and the start of work delayed until the protest is resolved (Harney, 1992, p. 141).

> *A major decision... is whether the award should be delayed pending the resolution of the protest.*

Claims and contract disputes occur after the award of the contract. Frequently, a claim or contract dispute may result in the issuing of a change order to the master contract. Claims and contract disputes, if not quickly resolved to the satisfaction of both parties, may result in payment delays and possibly penalty charges or liquidated damages. Local and state laws frequently stipulate the procedures for resolving contract disputes involving monetary claims against the government and may require a hearing with a governmental body before the contractor can apply to the courts for relief (Harney, 1992, p. 142).

Figure 45 is an example of protest language used in an RFP issued by the State of Alaska.

> **3.12 Aggrieved Respondents**
>
> 3.12.1 Protests
>
> An interested party may protest the award of a contract, the proposed award of a contract, or a solicitation for professional services by an agency. The protest shall be filed in writing with the Project Procurement Officer, within ten (10) days after a Notice of Intent to Award the contract is issued and include the following information:
>
> 1. The name, address, and telephone number of the protestor;
> 2. The signature of the protestor or the protester's representative;
> 3. Identification of the contracting agency and the solicitation or contract at issue;
> 4. A detailed statement of the legal and factual ground of the protest, including copies of relevant documents; and
> 5. The form of relief requested.
>
> The project procurement officer shall issue a written decision containing the basis of the decision within the statutory time limit. A copy of the decision shall be furnished to the protester by certified mail or another method that provides evidence of receipt.

Figure 45. *Protest Language Example—State of Alaska.*

Sources of Protests

There are countless reasons as to why a protest may occur, the most common of which include:

Restrictive Specifications. Competition is the hallmark of public procurement. When specifications are written in such a way as to preclude certain service providers, the public interest is not being served. Requirements must be clear and reasonable. Restrictive specifications must be qualified. Pre-solicitation conferences are always a good forum for hearing the concerns of competing offerors, and their input will provide the procurement officials the opportunity to reconsider those areas of the specifications or areas within the Statement of Work that have been designated as being too restrictive. If the Statement of Work team feels strongly that certain language labeled as *restrictive* must remain, a justification should be prepared in order to defend the team's position. Arbitrary language should be avoided and reasonableness should prevail.

Non-Conforming Response. Substantive exceptions to the terms and conditions of the solicitation that cannot be accepted without affecting the price or quality of the services delivered may cause the offer to be non-conforming. The *NIGP's Dictionary of Purchasing Terms* (5th Edition) defines non-conformance as: the failure of material or service to meet specified requirements for any characteristics or quality. To minimize the risk of receiving protests involving non-conforming responses, procurement regulations should specify clearly the rules for rejection and incorporate those rules in the solicitation document.

Submission of Deficient Surety. A bond is a form of financial protection against damages and a surety is legally liable for the debt, default, or failure of the principal to satisfy the obligations of the contract. Surety bond amounts are specified in the solicitation document. Many times, the offeror will submit a surety bond less than what was specified. This is a reason to declare the response deficient and unacceptable. A response should not be accepted from an offeror who submits a deficient surety.

Failure to Provide Required Information. A response that does not include certain required information may be accepted if the missing information does not affect price, quality, or the delivery schedule for the service. Certain categories of requested material, such as critical work references, are closely related to the evaluation of the quality of the offeror's service, and failure to submit such documentation may mandate rejection. The solicitation document should clearly identify what information must be submitted by the offeror and what the penalty is for failure to do so.

Late Responses. Jurisdictional administrative policy varies concerning the acceptance of a late bid or offer. The majority opinion is that a late bid or offer will not be accepted under any circumstances. There are jurisdictions that will accept a late bid or offer depending on a variety of circumstances. Accepting a late bid or offer will usually generate a protest. A jurisdiction should have a procedure in place that details the conditions under which a late bid or offer can be accepted. (Harney, 1992, pp. 142-143)

In addition to the aforementioned causes of protest, the following may also generate a protest:

- Failure to comply with Minority and Women's Business Enterprises (MWBE) requirements;
- Clerical mistakes;
- Failure to sign the solicitation document;
- Unbalanced pricing;
- A substantial deficiency; or
- Arbitrary evaluation criteria.

Debriefing

Many jurisdictions will debrief unsuccessful offerors before the final award of the contract. When the successful offeror has been selected and a recommendation for award has been made, the unsuccessful offerors are notified and, at their request, may be debriefed as to the basis of the selection process. A procurement official usually conducts the debriefing. The official then explains the results of the jurisdiction's evaluation of the proposal to the unsuccessful offeror. This is done without making any point-by-point comparison with other proposals. The debriefing may help avoid or minimize future protest action because it provides the rationale as to why the response was deemed unacceptable for award. The debriefing also enables contractors to improve their future competitive position. They can gain a better understanding of why certain areas of their proposal were deemed deficient.

Responding to Protests

It is essential that the full nature and extent of the protest be known before a jurisdiction can respond to a protest. An effective protest procedure should state that all protests be in writing and submitted within the required time frames. It is essential that the procedures clearly articulate a timeline for filing the protest. The procedures should indicate that the written protest should be sent to the chief procurement official for the jurisdiction. This first step in the process could eventually lead to litigation. Frequently, the protest is mailed to the governor, county executive, president of the university, comptroller, etc. When this occurs, it may take weeks before the chief procurement official receives the protest. When the protest is received, it should be reviewed promptly with the jurisdiction's legal counsel.

Many jurisdictions include a section in the solicitation document detailing the steps to be taken when filing a protest. The following points could be useful in establishing a well-defined procedure for filing a protest:

- Require that all protests be in writing.
- Specifically state to whom (name, title, address) the protest should be directed.
- Establish a definition for timely submission of a protest and the specific time after which a protest will not be accepted.
- Review the protest with the appropriate legal counsel.
- Draft a protest response letter and circulate it to appropriate internal staff (i.e., legal, SOW team, end-user agency) for their approval; and
- Mail the protest decision response by Registered Mail, return receipt requested.

If the protestor is not satisfied with the decision, they may opt to pursue litigation through the appropriate judicial process. If this occurs and if the courts hear the protester, an injunction may be filed that stops the contracting process. The jurisdiction might be prohibited from awarding the contract until the process is completed. Many jurisdictions have established a hearing process that must be followed prior to appealing to the courts. Following the written response to the protest, the contractor may be required to have a hearing with the chief procurement official or another jurisdiction official. This administrative hearing between the jurisdiction and the protesting contractor (offeror) may also be referred to as the ADR. The purpose of ADR, or other forms of administrative hearings, is to resolve controversial issues relative to the contracting process so that litigation can be avoided.

Whatever the process, the jurisdiction will be in a position to defend, explain, and justify all of the many decisions manifested in the solicitation. As a protest escalates from protest, to response, to hearing, to possible litigation, the burden of proof is on the jurisdiction's procurement and contracting officials. They must demonstrate, without a doubt, that the entire process was not arbitrary, capricious, or done in bad faith and that the processors did not show favoritism while they worked with the best interests of the jurisdiction in mind. This reinforces the need to document every step of the contracting process and to retain the documentation in the contract file for the period of time recommended on the record retention schedule.

Alternative Dispute Resolution

Many jurisdictions have established a hearing process that must be followed prior to appealing to the courts. Quite often, this process is detailed in the boilerplate or reflected in the contract document. All protests should be in writing. Following the contractor's written response to the protest, the protestor may be called upon to attend a hearing with the chief procurement officer or another jurisdiction official. A good rule of thumb to remember: negotiate before you litigate.

Procurement agencies are adopting administrative procedures to deal with protests and disputes. ADR is being embraced as a wise alternative to litigation. NIGP offers a course that addresses this topic in its entirety. ADR is defined as, "any procedure that is used to resolve issues in controversy including, but not limited to, conciliation, facilitation, mediation, fact-finding, mini-trials, arbitration and use of ombudsmen, or any combination thereof" (*Administrative Dispute Resolution Act* [Pub. L. No. 101-552], 104, Stat. 2736). In some cases, litigation is important and should be pursued. Litigation will: (a) interpret the law; (b) establish precedent; and (c) deter future wrongdoing. Compared to litigation, ADR has its own advantages, which include: (a) cost effective (litigation is expensive); (b) quick resolution of disputes; and (c) generally less adversarial.

A good rule of thumb to remember: negotiate before you litigate.

Protest Avoidance Strategies

There is no way to design a protest avoidance strategy that will guarantee a protest-free process. There are strategies that can be utilized to minimize the possibility of protests. The following could be helpful in mitigating contractor protest during the service contracting process:

- Issue a Request for Information (RFI) prior to the issuance of an RFP. The RFI solicits contractor input and ideas early. The RFI indicates to the marketplace that the government is open to suggestions and removes the appearance of an arbitrary or proprietary process.

- Post the RFP on the Internet. This lets the world know that the government is serious about competition and again brings "openness" to the contracting process.
- After completion of the evaluation process the contract negotiations and at least 10 days prior to the formal award, issue a "Notice of Intent to Award" to all respondents.
- Debrief successful offerors before the final award of the contract.
- Keep the communication lines open with all finalists, especially those that are providing best and final offers. If contractors feel that they have been "shut out" of the process, they will be more inclined to protest.
- Always respond to a protest in the most diplomatic manner. Harsh or negative responses may push the protestor in the direction of the courtroom.
- Agree with the protestor whenever possible, but always return to the principal points of your justification for non-award.
- Assure that the relationship does not turn adversarial. The true purchasing professional will maintain a sense of calm and composure throughout the pre-award discussions.

Disputes

Disputes generally result from various interpretations of the contract language. Interpretation cannot be arbitrary or without thoughtful deliberation. Quite often, the legal experts are consulted, and it is not unusual for the legal staff to be present when the disputes are being discussed with the contractor. All contracts should contain a disputes clause that provides a foundation for the resolution of disputes that may arise from unsettled claims. This clause should contain applicable procedural language in addition to the rights and responsibilities of both parties.

The Disputes Clause

The disputes clause should provide a mechanism for appeal of the contracting officer's decision to a higher authority in accordance with established governmental procedures. The government disputes clause normally encompasses disputes arising "under the contract" and those "relating to the contract." The effect of the latter component expands the scope of the dispute process to any claims for which no specific remedy is provided under a contract clause. As a result, the volume of litigation is potentially reduced. Other key provisions you should consider for inclusion in a disputes clause include:

- A requirement that contractor claims must be submitted in writing to the contracting officer;
- A time limit for issuance of a decision by the contracting officer;
- The stipulation that decisions rendered by the contracting officer are final unless an appeal or suit is filed;
- A time limit for filing an appeal; and
- A requirement that the contractor continue to perform pending final resolution of any relief, claim, appeal, or action arising under the contract.

Assertion of Claims

The disputes process is set in motion by the submission of a claim that triggers the contracting officer's obligation to render a timely decision. Routine requests by the contractor for equitable adjustments, progress payments, etc., are not claims unless and until it has been established that the government disputes the contractor's right to recovery or the amount of recovery. For a dispute to exist, there must be some evidence of a disagreement or controversy between parties.

The mere occurrence of a dispute or controversy is not enough to establish the existence of a claim. The contractor must submit a written demand to the contracting officer for relief as a matter of right. A contractor's claim must be sufficiently detailed to enable the contracting officer to give reasonable consideration to the merits of the claim.

The disputes clause included in contracts should establish the conditions with which a contractor's claim must comply. It also establishes certification requirements tied to the dollar value of the claim.

The Role of the Contracting Officer

Disputes between the parties to a contract are frequently unavoidable. When they do occur, the contracting officer is responsible for facilitating a resolution. The first priority of the contracting officer should be to reach a settlement through negotiation.

In dealing with disputes, the contracting officer acts in a dual capacity. First, as an advocate of the government, the contracting officer represents the government's position with respect to the dispute. When a settlement cannot be reached, the contracting officer acts in a quasi judicial capacity in rendering a final decision. This final decision represents the government's settlement offer and serves as a prerequisite to access by the contractor to the appeals process.

The contracting officer should make every effort to obviate litigation by negotiating a settlement. Settlement can occur at many stages of the administrative process. Routine requests can be settled before they become claims. Actual claims can be settled before or after issuance of a final decision, or during subsequent stages of the litigation process. The contracting officer, like most purchasing officials, has reasonably broad authority (within the limits of their delegation) to settle a claim up to the point where litigation has commenced in a court.

Appeals

All government organizations must have an appeals process through which unresolved claims are settled by negotiation, arbitration, or adjudication. Inability to settle an appeal may prompt the contractor to seek relief in the state or federal courts. Harney (1992) defines an appeal as the resubmission of a protest, contract dispute, or claim to a higher authority, with the intent to overturn a decision made by a lower authority.

Administrative procedures for handling protests, contract disputes, claims, and appeals should be a part of every government's contracting program, and formal procedures are necessary to supplement purchasing statues or regulations. Without formal procedures, the simplest protest, dispute, or claim could escalate until it requires resolution by the governing body or the courts.

References

Harney, D. (1992). *Service contracting: A local government guide*. Washington, DC: International City/County Management Association.

Martin, L. L., & Miller, J. R. (2005). *Alternative dispute resolution*. Herndon, VA: National Institute of Governmental Purchasing, Inc. (NIGP).

National Institute of Governmental Purchasing, Inc. (NIGP) (2002). *Dictionary of purchasing terms* (5th ed.). Herndon, VA: NIGP.

Chapter 8

Contract Administration and Monitoring

Tom Olsen, Director of Enterprise Development for the City of Indianapolis, makes an important observation about monitoring and evaluating contractor performance:

> For politicians and the media, the exciting part of privatization projects is doing the new deals. Managing and monitoring the contract relationships is a lot more pedestrian and a lot less sexy. But make no mistake about it, it is every bit as important.

Much time and effort is devoted to the Request for Proposal (RFP) process and contract award. The award of a service and the execution of the contract is just the start of a long-term relationship. It is a prologue to what may possibly become years of service delivery. Contract monitoring is the primary means of safeguarding against contractor performance problems. How the contractor is to deliver the service, be it design-based or performance-based, has been articulated in the SOW/RFP. It is now incumbent upon the government to have the required surveillance and quality assurance in place that ensures that the contractor is conforming to the contract requirements. Dr. Jonas Prager of New York University states, "Efficient monitoring, though costly, pays for itself by preventing overcharges and poor quality performance in the first place, by recouping appropriate outlays and by disallowing payment for inadequate performance" (Eggers, 1997, p. 21).

Contract Administration

Contract Administration can be defined as the management of all actions taken after the award of a contract to ensure compliance with the contract, e.g., timely delivery, acceptance, payment, and contract closing. The broad objectives of the contract administration function include:

- *Satisfying the Requirement*: assuring that the government agency receives the services and the outcomes specified in the contract;

- *Ensuring On-Time Delivery*: assuring that the government agency acquires the services and outcomes contracted for within the timeframe specified in the contract; and

- *Protecting Financial Interests*: payments must be reviewed, approved and monitored in order to ensure that payment conforms to the payment methods specified in the contract. In certain contracts, it means reviewing the charges submitted by a contractor to make certain that they are allowable.

Achieving these objectives requires significant diligence on the part of the contract monitoring team, but the potential cost of inadequate administration demands such diligence.

Figure 46 illustrates best practices that may be utilized to monitor service contracts.

In conjunction with Andersen Consulting, the New York-based Outsourcing Institute has identified seven common elements of well-managed outsourcing relationships. These are:
- Objective performance criteria that are negotiated, measured, and reviewed
- Formal reporting structure
- Performance-based pricing
- Internal training and communications on the company's business goals and on how to manage the relationship
- Vendor training on a customer's business environment and goals
- Cultural normalization (the provider must understand that every organization has its own culture)
- Ongoing exchange of knowledge and expertise.

Figure 46. *Best Practices for Monitoring and Managing Outsourcing Contracts.*

Source: The Outsourcing Institute, New York, NY, 1-800-421-6767.

The Nature and Purpose of Contract Administration

Contract administration revolves around the management of the various relationships resulting from the contractor's performance of the contract. Contract administration begins when the contract is awarded and ends when all of the work is delivered, completed, and accepted.

Establishing a cooperative and effective working relationship with the contractor is the key to good contract administration. It needs to be balanced with strong ethical considerations. A relationship that is too close may breed ethical dilemmas; therefore, the contract administrator must establish an arm's-length relationship. "Good faith" is used to describe a contractual relationship. Failure of the contractor to cooperate, performance failures, and abuse of power are all examples of "bad faith" on the part of the contractor.

Timely resolution of contract problems is also a major goal of effective contract administration. *Federal Acquisition Regulation* (FAR) Subpart 42.5 speaks to issues that can help in the avoidance of contractual problems:

> (a) A post-award orientation aids both the government and the contractor personnel to (1) achieve a clear and mutual understanding of all contract requirements, and (2) identify and resolve potential problems. However, it is not a substitute for the contractor's full understanding of the work requirements at the time offers are submitted, nor is it to be used to alter the final agreement arrived at in any negotiations leading to award.

It is important to note that generally, the rules of contract administration are derived from policies, procedures, statutes, and regulations as well as from federal, state and local court decisions. While the genesis of good contract administration may be legalistic, most of the operational actions are in the form of problem resolution.

"Good faith" is used to describe a contractual relationship.

Monitoring

The SOW team must consider contract monitoring and how it will be effectively implemented during the early planning stages of the SOW/RFP. Monitoring and quality assurance cannot be an afterthought. The monitoring plan, sometimes referred to as the Quality Assurance Plan (QAP), defines precisely what a government must do to guarantee that the contractor's performance is in accordance with contract performance standards (Eggers, 1997, p. 21).

> The following is illustrative of a federal government approach to quality assurance.
>
> **Quality Assurance.** Agencies shall, to the maximum extent practicable, assign contractors full responsibility for quality performance. Agencies shall develop formal, measurable (i.e., in terms of quality, timeliness, quantity, etc.) performance standards and surveillance plans to facilitate the assessment of contractor performance and the use of performance incentives and deduction schedules. Agencies shall, to the maximum extent practicable, avoid relying on cumbersome and intrusive process-oriented inspection and oversight programs to assess contractor performance (Cullen & Broadbent, 1998).

FAR is very precise in terms of the government's quality assurance plan (46.401). The monitoring plan (quality assurance plan) should be quantifiable, specific and include requirements such as: (a) contractor reports, (b) inspections, and (c) citizen complaints and surveys.

Contractor Reports. Contractor reports are contractor-generated statements of progress. The report details the work completed to date and compares work with the contract requirements and previous periods. The report lists expenditures to date and forecasts work for the entire contract period. In addition, the report should give a narrative account of problems encountered during performance and should mention any contract adjustments believed necessary. When verified by the government monitor, this report becomes the formal statement of contract compliance. Verification is more than a cursory review of the data and normally requires independent inspections and confirmation of accuracy.

Inspections. Inspections and observations vary greatly and depend on a number of considerations, such as the function contracted, the interest of the unit in serious monitoring, and the type of monitoring conducted. Some functions, such as solid waste collection, may require little monitoring because poor performance will trigger citizen complaints. However, even with this service, most agencies should check performance through some formal measures such as spot-checking the number of disposal bins unemptied. Other services such as nursing home care may require surprise inspections; while still others, fleet maintenance, for example, may require periodic or individual inspection. In any case, monitoring must be flexible. For example, a swimming pool inspection should not inconvenience users on hot summer weekends (Rehfuss, 1993, p. 10).

Many inspections use a rating or scorecard system that indicates the number of waste disposal spills or the cleanliness of streets (by a visual rating scorecard). Rating scores and other formal evidence of contractor performance reduce the possibility of arbitrary inspector action.

Citizen Complaints and Surveys. A third major type of monitoring activity is conducted through citizen complaints and surveys. Complaints should be formally documented and can be taken either by the contractor and forwarded to the agency or taken by the agency and forwarded to the contractor. In the former case, the contractor has a chance to handle the matter first, although the monitor should be alerted that a complaint has been registered. Complaints can be supplemented by citizen surveys. Surveys are useful because they also measure citizen satisfaction with the service, while complaints measure only *dissatisfaction* (Rehfuss, 1990, p. 10).

Some government units rely almost entirely on complaints for contract monitoring. This is done for a variety of reasons including: (a) the unit does not know how or does not want to monitor; (b) the unit does not believe monitoring is important; or (c) the unit feels that complaints alone provide enough control (as in waste disposal and other high-visibility functions, where it is assumed that if citizens do not complain, things are going well). While complaints and surveys are useful, they should not, in most cases, entirely take the place of actual inspections and contractor reports. Figure 47 lists several elements of a monitoring program.

Contractor Relations
- Initial meeting with contractor after bid award
- Continuous monitor-contractor interaction
- Formal and informal contractor feedback from monitor

The Contract
- Specific performance standards
- Penalties for nonperformance spelled out

The Contract Manager
- Comprehensive list of duties
- Training programs for contract managers

Citizen Relations
- Formal complaint system
- Citizen surveys

Figure 47. *Elements of a Complete Monitoring Program.*

Source: Rehfuss, J. (1989). *Contracting out in government* (p. 100). San Francisco: Jossey-Bass.

Performance Standards

The best way to monitor programs is to set reasonable but explicit performance standards in the contract and inspect closely enough to ensure that the contractor meets these standards. Performance standards are specific indicators of the level of contractor performance. Without careful attention to standards, it is impossible to determine if the contractor's performance meets the contract specifications. Standards also help contractors by protecting them from arbitrary monitoring.

Output measures can be used to gauge whether performance standards are being met. The number of street miles cleaned or solid waste collected and calculated in tons are examples of output measures. Standards also can rely on more complex metrics such as patient satisfaction levels of nursing care.

Another option is to use input measures such as the number of registered nurses per shift at a nursing home. However, the problem with relying primarily on input standards is that they fail to measure the actual performance of the contractor. Having five registered nurses on a shift may meet state standards and the agency contract, but it does not prove the level of care the patients are receiving. Therefore, performance measures, based solely on input standards, should be avoided whenever possible.

Performance also can be measured by using efficiency or effectiveness measures. Efficiency measures demonstrate how inputs relate to outputs. One could measure the hours expended mowing lawns versus the actual acres mowed. Effectiveness measures, on the other hand, assess the impact of the service on customers. Efficiency and effectiveness measures are usually better criteria than output or input measures for judging contractor performance. They also are more inherently complex, making them more difficult and time-consuming to calculate.

Monitoring Strategies

There is no limit to the amount of time, energy, and resources that a government could expend on contract quality assurance. Priorities need to be decided for the degree of monitoring applied to particular types of service contracts. How much monitoring and at what level are usually dependent upon the size and complexity of the contract. Monitoring strategies that would be very effective for street resurfacing may be inappropriate for a complex technology contract (Eggers, 1997, p. 24).

Some services require less overt monitoring than others. For highly visible service contracts that have a direct impact on the public, such as snow removal and garbage pickup, poor service will usually be exposed through citizen complaints. For large technical service contracts, it might make sense to hire a third party to monitor the contract. Determining the appropriate technique for monitoring and to what extent it should be done depends on several factors, including the level of acceptable risk for nonperformance. Where there exists a high level of risk for even minor problems, e.g., aircraft maintenance, high-cost and high-control preventive monitoring techniques are necessary (Eggers, 1997, p. 24).

Creating Trust

Monitoring should not be viewed in an adversarial fashion. The contractor should be considered a strategic partner and given incentives to innovate, improve, and deliver better customer service (Eggers, 1997, p. 24). Establishing a trust relationship requires structuring the right risks, rewards, benefits, and opportunities in the early stages of the contract negotiation phase.

Outsourcing requires managing the relationships and the cornerstone of any successful relationship is effective communication. If communication opportunities are created, the need for direct monitoring will be reduced.

- *Schedule regular contract status meetings.* Depending on the size and scope of the contract, schedule meetings once or twice a month to review the status of the outsourcing relationships.

- *Invite prospective contractors to explain how to assess their performance.* Though public officials are ultimately responsible for determining what outcomes and outputs they want achieved, contractors can provide helpful advice in developing the performance indicators that tie a vendor's performance to these objectives.

An informal survey of contractors can assist public officials in figuring out which performance indicators are important for a particular service. In many cases, the individual drawing up the RFP or contract may be unfamiliar with the intricacies of the service and, thus, unaware of the full range of possible performance indicators.

An advantage to this type of approach is that it reduces the likelihood of serious misunderstandings arising over the nature of the performance standards during the course of the contract. Furthermore, it should result in a more precise SOW that, in turn, should increase competition because all contractors will be submitting proposals based on mutually developed performance indicators rather than on differing interpretations.

- *Create a management information system to evaluate contractor performance.* The best performance indicators in the world are useless unless they are accompanied by a system to track whether the standards are being met. Monitoring technology must be in place to track and record performance. With the data in place, contract managers can better measure performance and determine areas where improvement may be needed. Meetings can be scheduled with the contractor to review data and discuss areas of concern.

Outsourcing Manager

As governments continue to move in the direction of outsourcing and contracting for various services, management should consider creating a position in which an individual would be solely responsible for managing the outsourcing functions. Some governments have decided to create a position for a high-level executive who would manage outsourcing relationships. This individual would have experience in, or need to be trained in:

- Identification of privatization opportunities and potential contractors;
- Oversight of the RFP process;
- Evaluation of vendor proposals;
- Management of outsourcing relationships; and
- Monitoring of contractor performance.

Most government organizations have individuals in their purchasing departments with some or all of these skills. However, as privatization becomes an increasingly important component of a government's mission, more senior and politically connected individuals will be needed to standardize the process, develop performance standards that adhere to the administration's mission, and drive the privatization process through the bureaucracy. These new government executives will have to handle a variety of complex issues and relationships, such as employee transitions; asset transfers; developing outcomes, performance goals, and penalties; termination; dispute resolution; and risk management (Eggers, 1997, p. 31).

Outcome Monitoring

Outcome monitoring is the analysis of results based on user-provided data on the service quality. In the instance of a street-sweeping contract, the number of miles swept becomes the measure of output. The outcome analysis would focus on citizen feedback rating regarding the cleanliness of the streets. The SOW should include monitoring procedures (Harney, 1992, p. 160).

Outcome measures should assess some aspect of the effect, result or quality, such as:

- Number/percentage of clients who were helped to a significant extent, according to creditable, objective evidence;
- Number/percentage of clients who reported satisfaction or dissatisfaction with the service received; and
- Response time or length of wait for the service.

The ultimate goal of contracting for any service is to satisfy a public need. Outcome monitoring is an analysis process that will assist public managers in determining how well the intended service delivery has been accomplished. It is a quality control technique that will improve service delivery to the citizen. Some service contracts do not directly impact the public. A management study contract should be subject to the same outcome study as a citizen service contract (National Institute of Governmental Purchasing, Inc. [NIGP], 2001, p. 144).

Poor Performance

Most contracts for service will experience some type of performance issue. The procurement office must be immediately involved in any situation regarding poor or inadequate performance. Policies and procedures should be in place that address how the jurisdiction will respond to the contractor's failure to adequately perform. Most contractors will perform effectively, but unforeseen events can occur that will impact performance. The contract administration team will be challenged to deal with the day-to-day operational issues of contract performance.

Contract Interruptions. Contract interruptions will occur; and, when they do, the contractor cannot continue to provide the service. Bankruptcy and strikes are just two examples of the types of interruptions. Performance bonds or interruption insurance may protect the jurisdiction financially but may not assist in creating a back-up service provider to ensure continued service performance.

Liquidated Damages. Liquidated damages are an option when performance falls below an acceptable level. Whenever this action is considered, the legal counsel for the jurisdiction should be consulted. Legal counsel will review precedence-setting court opinions that could apply. In most cases, the contractor must be allowed a period of time to cure any deficiency before liquidated damages can be assessed. Liquidated damages cannot be applied as a penalty, and the jurisdiction must be able to prove the amount of monetary damages. While liquidated damages afford some financial protection, they may not help in the performance interruption.

Action Plan for Addressing Poor Performance

A five–step action plan is recommended to address poor contractor performance.

Step 1. The project manager attempts to resolve the issue by working directly with the contractor's on-site supervisor. The project manager should notify the procurement manager of the nature of the issue and what action has been taken to date.

Step 2. If the project manager cannot resolve the performance issue, the project manager calls the contractor, explains the issue, and asks the contractor to resolve the issue within a specified time period (i.e., five days, two weeks, etc.). A letter or a fax is also sent to confirm the conversation that restates the nature of the issue and the time period allowed for correction.

Step 3. If the issue persists, a formal meeting is held with the contractor and the contract administration team. The contractor's on-site supervisor should also be in attendance. Minutes of the meeting are taken. The contractor should be reminded of the possible course of action authorized by the contract if corrective action is delayed any further, including enforcement of the liquidated damages provisions.

Step 4. At this step, the procurement manager should render an enforcement decision. Enforcement requires the procurement manager to issue a letter, often referred to as a Nature of Default letter, which is sent to the contractor with a copy furnished to the bonding company. Before issuing the Nature of Default letter, the procurement manager should consult with the jurisdiction's legal counsel. The Nature of Default letter must contain sufficient information for the contractor to cure the issue. Specific dates and a description of any liquidated damages that the jurisdiction intends to assess if the contractor fails to cure must be stipulated. The letter should also advise the contractor that failure to cure the issue within the specified period of time would be cause to cancel the contract.

Step 5. If all attempts to resolve the issue have failed, the procurement manager will need to cancel the contract. Simultaneously, action must be taken by legal counsel to attempt to collect a settlement from the contractor's bonding company. Never assume that the bonding company will agree with the jurisdiction's legal counsel. It is not unusual for a bonding company to defend the actions of the contractor and refuse to satisfy a jurisdiction's claim of contractor default. (NIGP, 2001, p. 145)

Suspension and Debarment

If a contractor defaults on a contract, procurement officials normally will enact suspension or debarment proceedings against the defaulting contractor. The American Bar Association's (ABA) *2000 Model Procurement Code for State and Local Governments* (S-9-102) lists the reasons for suspension and debarment. A definition of each is included in NIGP's (2002) *Dictionary of Purchasing Terms*.

Suspension: the temporary exclusion of a person or company from participating in a procurement activity because of previous illegal or irresponsible action.

Debarment: the temporary exclusion of a person or company from participating in a procurement activity for an extended period of time, as specified by law, because of previous illegal or irresponsible action.

There are two types of debarment.

- *Without Prejudice*. The debarred person or company is kept from submitting responses to solicitations for a period of time not to exceed 24 months.

- *With Prejudice*. The debarred person or company is permanently kept from submitting responses to solicitations.

Termination

Termination clauses cover either termination for default or termination at the convenience of the government. Decisions regarding termination should be made after thoughtful consideration of the consequences and with input from a variety of sources, such as law and the impacted governmental agencies.

Termination for Default

When you exercise the right to terminate a contract for default, you effectively inform the contractor that its performance failure has caused the government to terminate the agreement as set forth in the contract. There are several issues to contemplate when considering this option.

- For the contractor, the consequences of a default termination can be very serious; so do not take the decision lightly.
- Termination for default may not be in the government's best interest, there are alternatives.
- Termination for default cannot happen arbitrarily, such a decision must be preceded by certain conditions and procedures.
- Intervening factors can render a default termination inappropriate or unenforceable.

Consequences of a Default Termination

The impact of a default termination will vary, depending on a number of considerations. The most important of these is the type of contract. The potential consequences for a contractor of a default termination under a fixed-price contract are far more serious than those experienced under a cost-reimbursement contract.

Any default termination threatens the contractor's opportunity for future business; but, under cost-reimbursement contracts, the contractor can be assured of payment for all allowable costs, regardless of whether or not any portion of the work is accepted. However, under a fixed contract, a contractor faces the following consequences:

- The contractor is entitled to compensation only for work that you accept.
- The government can demand return of progress or partial payments already given to the contractor.
- The government has the right, but not the duty, to appropriate the contractor's material, inventory, and construction plant and equipment at the site, subject to a negotiated compensation.
- The contractor is liable for excess costs of re-procurement or completion.
- The contractor may be liable for actual or liquidated damages.

Alternatives to a Default Termination

It does not follow that you should necessarily terminate just because you have the right to do so. Termination for default is rarely a satisfactory solution to unacceptable performance.

Actually, it should be a decision of last resort. Terminating for default will not solve the critical needs. However, in certain instances, alternatives are available.

Considerable time and effort may be expended while defending a default termination. These costs may not be recoverable; and, as a result, termination is not always cost effective. Finally, terminating for default will do nothing to promote timely delivery of a requirement. Therefore, before taking this action, consider the following grounds:

- Whether it would be effective to withhold payment until satisfactory performance is demonstrated;
- Whether, if termination action is taken, there is an alternative source of supply;
- Whether the contractor's financial condition precludes recovery for the excess cost of re-procurement;
- Whether continued performance under a revised delivery schedule would serve the government's interest; or
- Whether, where the requirement for the supplies or services no longer exists and the contractor is not liable for damages, a no-cost termination agreement should be executed.

The Right to Terminate for Default

The right to terminate is dependent upon two prerequisites. First, reasonable grounds for termination must exist. One cannot issue a default termination arbitrarily. Second, there are certain procedural requirements with which the government must comply. The most fundamental condition warranting a default termination is the failure to perform or deliver within a prescribed time period.

There are additional performance breaches that generally serve as reasonable grounds for termination. One should exercise discretion in defaulting a contractor. Be sure that default is the best course of action, no excusable condition exists, and rights have not been waived to default through some unintentional action. The additional grounds of default are: (a) failure to make progress; (b) noncompliance with other contracted provisions; and (c) failure to proceed, e.g., noncompliance with a duly authorized change order.

Cure Notice

In a case of the contractor failing to perform some provisions other than those dealing with the timely delivery or failing to make progress as to endanger performance altogether, the procurement officer must give the contractor notice of the failure and allow at least 10 days for cure (remedy) of the failure before issuing a termination notice. The government should reserve the right, unilaterally, to extend the time for cure if it is in the best interest of the government, without waiving the right to default. This "10-day cure notice" should:

- State that a termination for default may arise unless the failure to perform or make adequate progress is cured within 10 days;
- Call the contractor's attention to its contractual liabilities in the event of default;
- Request an explanation of the failure to perform;
- State that failure to present an explanation may be taken as an admission that there is no valid explanation;
- Where appropriate, invite the contractor to discuss the matter at a conference; and
- Require the contractor to immediately inform you of how it intends to cure the deficiency.

References

American Bar Association (2000). *The 2000 model procurement code for state and local governments.* Chicago: American Bar Association.

Cullen, J., & Broadbent, M. (1998). *Managing financial resources* (3rd ed.). London: McGraw-Hill.

Eggers, W. (1997). *Performance-based contracting.* Los Angeles: The Reason Public Policy Institute.

Harney, D. (1992). *Service contracting: A local government guide.* Washington, DC: International City/County Management Association.

National Institute of Governmental Purchasing, Inc. (NIGP). (2001). *Contracting for services.* Herndon, VA: NIGP.

National Institute of Governmental Purchasing, Inc. (NIGP). (2002). *Dictionary of purchasing terms* (5th ed.). Herndon, VA: NIGP.

Rehfuss, J. (1990, Winter). Contracting out and accountability in state and local government: The importance of contract monitoring. *State & Local Government Review, 22,* 44-48.

Chapter 9

Extensions, Renewals, and Transitional Contract Issues

Effective contract administration and monitoring are important components in the contractual relationship. How a contractor performs according to the contract terms will help determine if the contract will be renewed. Fortunately, there are more successful contracts and contractors than unsuccessful ones. Relationship management defines contract administration. It is unequivocally a people business. Service contracts are people contracts. The management function consists of getting work accomplished through people, and the same principle applies to managing the service contracts. If we fail to manage people, we fail to manage the contract. The principles of partnering, for example, are based on the Golden Rule, "Treat others as you would like to be treated yourself." When there is a contract failure, government officials must examine their various options: Do we re-offer the contract? Do we litigate? Do we enact liquidated damages? Do we award to the next lowest offeror? How do we successfully transition from an outsourced contract back to providing the services with government workers? If procurement professionals are well schooled in the myriad intricacies of service contracting, successes will outnumber failures.

Contract Renewal Terms

Until recently, most public purchasers have issued service contracts with relatively short terms and limited renewal options. A one-year term with two one-year renewal options was standard. Many service contracts require the dismantling of jurisdictional, in-house services and dictate that term contracts of 5 to 10 years are needed. This is evident in service contracts where rapid contractor turnover can have an adverse effect on clients. Longer-term contracts are also necessary in service contracts that require large capital investments.

Longer-term contracts will usually produce benefits of economies of scale and greater savings over the life of the contract. When contracts are for services with limited competition, a longer-term contract may be advantageous to the jurisdiction. Longer-term contracts are recommended when:

- There is a large capital investment;
- It is difficult to return to in-house service delivery;
- There is limited competition; and
- Program needs call for a longer term (i.e., a human services contract covering transportation of senior patients).

Service contracts should never be automatically renewed. Procurement must recognize that renewal is a joint decision made by the end-user agency and the procurement office. A unilateral decision to renew should never be made by procurement or by the end-user agency. Issues that will impact the decision to renew include: (a) economic, budgeting, and fiscal factors; (b) program changes or a restructuring of the service delivery; and (c) unsatisfactory contractor performance.

Renewal and Extension Issues

Generally, a contract for service will be either a one-time service commitment or an ongoing service. The Statement of Work (SOW) will address the length of the service as well as contemplate issues such as renewal or extension. The delivery of professional services may be both one-time and ongoing. For example, a management study may be a one-time service contract, while an auditing service may be ongoing. Client services, however, may be either one-time or ongoing.

Ongoing service contracts should contain a renewal clause. Typical contract language would state, "This is a two-year contract with a one-year renewal option. The contract may be renewed upon the mutual agreement of both parties." Contract renewal requires that the original contract contain a renewal clause. If the original contract does not contain a renewal clause, the contract may not be renewed. Without an escalator clause or a defined methodology that will be used to calculate price escalation, the contract must be renewed under the same price, terms, and conditions as the original. To renegotiate any part of the contract is to essentially enter into a new contract. A contract that is renewed is the same contract that was originally entered into. If the contract did not contain an escalator clause or specific language as to how the renewal pricing was to be agreed to, the price under the original contract must remain firm.

When a published escalator clause is used to determine successive years' pricing in a multi-year contract or in one with an option to renew, the contract document must include three key dates:

- *Escalator Date*: date used to calculate the price for the subsequent year's contract;
- *Anniversary Date*: date on which the contract expires, unless the government has taken action to renew;
- *Decision Date*: date by which the contractor must decide whether to accept a renewal offer.

The contract must include enough time between the decision date and the anniversary date to allow the government to re-bid the contract if it chooses not to renew or if the contractor declines the renewal offer (Harney, 1992, p. 184).

A contract extension is not the same as a contract renewal. A contract extension changes and extends the contract termination date. Upon mutual agreement of both parties, contracts may be extended to some future date. Contracts may be extended in time due to excusable delays. The contractor must clearly demonstrate that the event caused delay to the overall completion of the contract. For example, rain, snow, or other inclement weather may be cause for an excusable delay resulting in a contract extension.

The extension of a contract will always raise legal issues, so it is important to contact your attorney in order to be sure that extensions are based on sound legal advice. Unsuccessful bidders are sometimes poor losers; and, if they are made aware of a contract extension, they may challenge it, protesting that the extension is a change in the scope of work and should be disallowed.

Strategies to Consider

Procurement professionals might be challenged by every service delivery request. Facts, figures, and technical details will be required from the end-user agency that is requesting the service. In addition to qualitative and quantitative information, the procurement professional must also rely on experience and judgment as the solicitation process proceeds. The following points might be of assistance in making sound decisions:

- Promote an understanding of procurement;
- Executive approval;
- Quick study;
- The customer lives with the contract;
- Ethics;
- Options; and
- Newspaper test.

Understand Procurement. To elected and senior management leadership of a jurisdiction, the application of the terms *purchasing* and *procurement* are sometimes used interchangeably. Purchasing is only a part of the function of procurement. These two terms are not interchangeable, and the professional procurement official should attempt to convey the actual meaning of purchasing and procurement to senior management and, if asked, to elected officials.

To assist the professional procurement official, the jurisdiction should have ordinances and possibly state laws that clearly identify the procurement responsibilities and duties of the procurement office. These ordinances and state laws should also reflect the ramifications of procurement delegation external to the procurement office. An absence of ordinance and state law that would clearly establish procurement authority and responsibility will seriously affect the procurement office's ability to function properly.

Executive Approval. Decisions to outsource or privatize a service must be made at the jurisdiction's highest level. If lower-level managers become involved in a procurement of services that has not been approved by senior jurisdiction officials, wasted effort and lost productivity will result.

Decisions regarding the outsourcing process should be made openly and honestly. Misinformation can create unnecessary stress within the jurisdiction, especially when organized labor is involved. Multitudes of stakeholders are involved in the decision to contract out, and credibility among all parties is essential. Senior management and elected officials must be kept fully informed.

Public trust...

is critical to the

integrity of the

entire contracting

process.

Quick Study. The procurement professional that becomes involved in a major service contract must quickly understand all of the processes. Procurement should take the lead and control the process. Social and economic considerations may be of primary importance along with issues of cost benefit. Hidden agendas should be uncovered and quickly dismissed, as they will undermine the process.

The Customer. Procurement provides the service for the end-user agency. When issues go wrong, the end-user agency bears most of the pressure and discomfort of complaints about the service or criticism of the contractor (Rehfuss, 1989, p. 220). When the garbage is not collected, the unhappy taxpayer will call the sanitation department, not the procurement office. An arbitrary procurement decision, while technically correct, may create havoc between the contractor and the end-user agency.

Ethics. Public trust in the procurement process is critical to the integrity of the entire contracting process. Even the perception of wrongdoing will damage well-intended efforts.

Options. A "what if" analysis of all the major issues should be conducted. What if citizen complaints reach an unacceptable level? What if the contractor files for bankruptcy, has a major strike, or walks off the job? Back-up options are critical to the jurisdiction's ability to provide service in the wake of a major issue.

Newspaper Test. Government will always be under public scrutiny. Improprieties, especially in government contracting, make great newspaper stories. The following items are watched closely by newspapers and may raise questions in the public's eye:

- Sole-source contracts;
- Secret meetings with contractors;
- Incomplete public information about a contract;
- Favoritism to a particular contractor;
- Failure to disclose a jurisdictional official's ties to contractors;
- Who may bid, tender, or offer;
- Contracts awarded to family members of procurement and/or elected officials;
- Change orders for work already completed or for work that may not have been done; and
- Contracts that were awarded under delegated authority but fail to comply with the procurement ordinances, rules, regulations, or law.

Unsolicited Proposals

Procurement officials should be prepared to receive an unsolicited proposal. A private contractor sends a proposal to elected officials and states that contracting for a particular service will result in enormous savings to the jurisdiction. Often, these unsolicited proposals are dismissed and may be of no consequence. On occasion, the unsolicited proposal may have merit and generate attention. Procurement may be asked to participate in a review of such a proposal in order to determine if the alleged savings are factual.

Some jurisdictions seek outsourcing, while others have it thrust upon them (Gardner, 1997). San Bernardino, California, received an unsolicited proposal from a private company that proposed to assume complete responsibility for the operation and management of the county's waste system. Extensive cost analysis determined that the proposal could generate savings to the county, and competitive negotiations were held. The contract brings approximately $1 million a year into the general fund, and the contractor receives an 11.5% profit on what the county defines as allowable costs, such as permits. The outsourcing of the waste system to a private company resulted in the layoff of 119 county employees, the elimination of a county department, and the sale of equipment.

Unsolicited proposals need to be thoroughly analyzed both in terms of what is said in the proposal and what is left unsaid. The procurement office must ascertain if the unsolicited proposal constitutes a valid sole source or merely suggests a new approach to a service that will lead to competitive solicitation.

Publicization

Publicization is the opposite of privatization. Publicization moves the service into the public sector and out of the private sector. In the San Bernardino example, publicization would require the county to rehire the 119 employees, repurchase equipment, and recreate the department. If the contractor fails, files for bankruptcy, or defaults, the process would have to move quickly in order to maintain the necessary sanitation services for the public. Privatization efforts sometime fail, and the jurisdiction must accept the fact that it is not always in the jurisdiction's best interest to continue with the private contractor.

If time permits, a good first step towards publicization is to name a task force responsible for planning, organizing, and managing the process of returning the service in-house (Harney, 1992, p. 195). The task force may consist of:

- A management level staff person (project manager) from the department that normally provided the service;
- The members of the contract administration team that are overseeing the contract;
- Representatives of other departments that may be affected by the return of the service in-house;
- Representatives from legal, finance, and auditing;
- Employees and labor representatives; and
- When needed, cost management or industry consultants.

The procurement office is also represented on the task force; because, in most cases, a contract is in place that will be terminated. A primary reason to return the service in-house is due to unsatisfactory contractor performance. It is important to document all contract performance issues. A contractor may not willingly walk away from a lucrative public contract. If the situation turns adversarial, the contractor may sue for breach of contract.

When the decision has been made to return a service in-house, cost factors must be taken into consideration in order to support the decision. The argument for privatization is savings and productivity. The reasons for returning a service to the jurisdiction may not be based on savings or productivity. The jurisdiction knows what costs it has been incurring with the private contractor and must determine, for budgetary purposes, what the ongoing costs will be to the jurisdiction.

Partnering for Successful Service Contracting

Partnering is a concept that jurisdictions are embracing in order to take contractual relationships beyond the formal offer and acceptance of most traditional contracts. Partnering is a concept that requires the contractor to actually become an extension of the jurisdiction. Partnering can be defined as a contractual relationship that seeks to provide shared benefits to the mutual satisfaction of both parties in terms of creating value, continuous improvement, issue resolutions, and information access. Procurement officials have always been concerned about close relationships with contractors and have attempted to maintain a distant association. The new paradigm of privatization has caused procurement professionals to reassess partnering and how it can best be structured.

Longer contract terms and the recent change in Internal Revenue Service guidelines extending the length of time allowed for private providers to operate, maintain, and manage contracts has been a contributing factor to the ongoing dialogue. Under the new IRS guidelines, jurisdictions can extend contract terms for up to 20 years. A partnering agreement can be incorporated into the final contract and should be addressed in the SOW. A partnering agreement will generally include:

- A clause stating the process that will be used to prevent disputes;
- A statement regarding litigation avoidance (conflicts will be resolved outside the courtroom);
- An emphasis on effective and frequent communication and adherence to meeting schedules;
- A strategic alliance that will result in building interdependence rather than independence;
- A relationship based on total quality and continuous improvement;
- A free exchange of cost and budget information;
- A reward for labor-saving ideas that increase productivity;
- A commitment to teamwork;
- Monitoring that is based on the *Trust but Validate* premise;
- Dedication to the principle of "optimize, not compromise"; and
- A shared savings incentive clause for both the contractor and the jurisdiction to benefit from cost-conscious decisions.

Partnering may create issues for the jurisdiction. There has been litigation on the status of *permatemp* employees in both the private and public sectors. Permatemp is a combination of the words *permanent* and *temporary*. It is a modern employment situation in which an employee does long-term, on-site work for a company but receives all pay and benefits from a third-party staffing firm. Employees hired as contractors rather than employees, whose service is protracted, have sued to be allowed to participate in benefits extended to full-time employees. When the jurisdiction's employee benefits exceed those of the partnering contractor, it might generate similar action.

Principles of Partnering

The foundation of any successful partnering relationship is the code of conduct required for good teamwork. Such partnerships must reflect the Golden Rule: "Treat others as you would like to be treated yourself"; but, unfortunately, this adage has been transformed by a litigious society into "Those who have the gold, rule." When owners and contractors behave ethically and morally, neither have a need to go to court.

Ethical and moral behavior can be easily compromised during tough times when contractors are going broke and owners are struggling to do more with less. Such situations require that a "code of conduct" be included as part of the partnering agreement.

According to *Partnering: A Concept for Success*, published by the Associated General Contractors of America, there are seven key elements involved in partnering, the first three of which are character traits, or principles. The first three elements are: (a) commitment, (b) equity, and (c) trust. If one can establish these, the next four fall into place: (d) development of mutual goals and objectives, (e) implementation, (f) continuous evaluation, and (g) timely responsiveness (Harisenrider, 1994).

Commitment is critical to the success of any relationship, both inside and outside of the workplace. In order to decide if a partnering relationship can be achieved, one has to determine if there exists the willingness and ability to make and keep promises to one another. The project team must have the support from upper management in order to be able to make and keep promises. In a heavily controlled bureaucratic environment, this first principle could easily become an immovable barrier. Many contracting firms tout partnering in their marketing departments but practice profit maximization in their financial departments. After all, isn't it the objective of any corporation to maximize ownership wealth? When this edict is passed along to the field managers, they are hard pressed to be in a position to make the type of commitments required in a team-minded partnering agreement. The fact is that team-minded commitments are not possible when all the owner and contractor have known for years is that 99 cents is less than a dollar.

Equity and trust are the next two principles that are mentioned. They go hand in hand because money is involved. Both the owner and contractor's representatives are expected to make the best possible use of money (Harisenrider, 1994, pp. 82-83).

Contract Interruptions

No matter how qualified contractors may be, they are subject to events that might not be under their direct control. Bankruptcies, strikes, and delivery failures on the part of their suppliers are all reasons for contract interruption. These possibilities should be anticipated when the decision to contract is being considered. When the contract is awarded and the government employees are no longer in place, the concern about continuity of service delivery in the event of interruption becomes problematic.

Certain safeguards can be included in the contract provisions that will mitigate these concerns. Inclusion of a performance bond in the contract and purchasing interruption insurance can minimize financial risks. Agencies should consider three alternatives to complete dependence on the contractor:

- Use of contingency contracts with other providers;
- Partial contracting (dividing the contract among competing contractors); and
- Competing themselves with the contractor (dividing the contract between the contractor and the agency itself).

Contingency contracts bind a secondary contractor to provide services in the event that the primary contractor cannot or does not perform (Rehfuss, 1989, p. 108). Partial contracting is another technique. Under partial contracting, the service may be divided geographically among multiple contractors. This also may include dividing work into functions or type of work. For example, a painting contract may be structured so that part of the work, i.e., interior painting, is done by the government's painters; and all outside painting is done by the contractor. The final way of avoiding dependence on contractors is to have city workers share the contract with private contractors (p. 109). Refuse collection and janitorial contracts are examples of contract sharing.

...government officials are tasked with the responsibility of minimizing the risk of contract interruption.

Whatever the strategy chosen, government officials are tasked with the responsibility of minimizing the risk of contract interruption. This is especially critical in areas that directly impact public safety, such as juvenile detention centers, police fleet maintenance, and medical services. There will also be risks associated with outsourcing services, but creative risk avoidance strategies will help establish a certain comfort level.

Final Report

At some point, all contracts terminate. Many will have happy endings, and a few will leave a trail of destruction. It is recommended that upon termination of major service contracts, a final report should be generated. The final report is an account of activities to upper management that retrospectively reviews the efficiency of the contractor's performance and the success or shortcomings of the contracting effort.

The report should summarize the work performed and describe any problems encountered and how they were resolved. The report should not recite the technical specification but should describe the accomplishments and the successful outcomes. It should include a section addressing "lessons learned." It can articulate things and events that were done right as well as what was done wrong. Successes should be replicated, and failures should be a learning experience not to be repeated.

The final report should have multiple authors. The SOW team could collaboratively write it, with the procurement officer or contract administrator generating the first draft. The report is a learning tool that can assist in the development of future contract efforts. It should be a "snapshot" of the entire contracting effort, and a copy should reside in the official contract file. The contractor also should receive a copy.

Transition Issues

Service contracts will go through various transitional phases. Contracts may be renewed, extended, or offered again. Upon expiration of one contract, a new contract will be awarded. In some cases, the incumbent contractor will win the new contract; but, quite often, the contract will be awarded to a new contractor. This interim period between the exiting of the incumbent and the advent of the new contractor can create concern, anxiety, and problems if not carefully managed.

There always will be some resistance to change. Employees establish a comfort level with the contractor, and they would prefer that the relationship continue. In large multi-layered service contracts, the transition period may take months. It is important to closely monitor and manage the transition period. Contract transition should be managed around intended consequences (planned change) rather than unintended consequences (unplanned change). If there was an adversarial relationship with the incumbent, the transition to the new contractor will be much more difficult to manage. If a contract is terminated for cause or if a contractor defaults and the performance bond is enforced, the transitional issues become extremely complicated. It is rare that the incumbent will hand over the contract to the new contractor with well wishes and a pat on the back. There are some techniques that transition managers might consider that will make for an effective transition.

- At the time of re-bid or re-offer, meet with the contractor and the agency in order to review the possibility of contract transition.
- Develop and follow a detailed transition plan.
- Ensure that there is sufficient time allowed for the transition period.
- Determine any critical positions that may require special training.
- Inventory equipment and inspect public facilities that were used by the incumbent contractor.
- Ensure that the current contractor completes all assigned work without leaving a backlog of work or problems for the incoming contractor.

- Consider overlapping contracts in order to minimize transitional issues. (This approach may be problematic and might have limited application.)
- Develop a "customer first" attitude. The goal is to make sure that the transitions have no, or minimal, impact on service delivery to the customer.
- If necessary, require the incoming and outgoing contractors to meet and agree to a written *contract transition protocol.*

Large service contracts or construction-related contracts might require the incoming and outgoing contractors to agree to sign a Contract Transition Protocol agreement. This protocol agreement is a formalized approach that requires both the entering and exiting contractors to agree to certain provisions, which may include:

- *Noninterference.* Prior to the legal commencement date of the contract, the incoming contractor will not interfere with the performance of services by the outgoing contractor.

- *Non-solicitation.* The newly awarded contractor agrees not to solicit, meet with, or in any way interfere with the existing employer-employee relationship between the incumbent and its employees prior to the contract commencement date.

- *Cooperation for Continued Employment.* At the commencement of the contract but not before, a meeting of the incoming and outgoing contractors will be held to determine whether the incoming contractor may hire employees of the outgoing contractor. Agreement also should be reached to respect any confidentiality, nondisclosure, or non-competition agreements that may exist between the employee and the employer.

- *Mediation.* Should any disputes arise between the incoming contractor and the outgoing contractor, the parties agree to submit their dispute to a mutually agreed-upon mediator.

Contract transition can be a destabilizer if not managed properly. Purchasing officials may become heavily involved in transition issues and should be familiar with the various dynamics that will be in play during this critical time.

References

Associated General Contractors of America (AGC). (1992). *Partnering: A concept for success*. Washington, DC: AGC.

Gardner, B. (1997). Outsourcing waste facilities. *Governing Magazine*. Washington, DC: Congressional Quarterly, Inc.

Harisenrider, T. (1994). *Partnering—A concept for success*. Arlington, VA: Associated General Contractors of America.

Harney, D. (1992). *Service contracting: A local government guide*. Washington, DC: International City/County Management Association.

Rehfuss, J. (1989). *Contracting out in government*. San Francisco: Jossey-Bass.

Appendix A – Table 1

*Service Contracting By City and County Governments—1982-2003
(Public Works and Transportation)*

Service	1982 For Profit (%)	1982 Non-Profit (%)	1988 Private (%)	1992 For Profit (%)	1992 Non-Profit (%)	1997 For Profit (%)	1997 Non-Profit (%)	2003 For Profit (%)	2003 Non-Profit (%)
Residential Solid Waste Collection	35	0	36	37	1	49	0	39	1
Commercial Solid Waste Collection	44	0	38	54	1	60	0	43	0
Street Repair	23	0	36	29	1	34	0	35	0
Street/Parking Lot Cleaning	9	0	15	16	1	20	0	18	1
Traffic Sign Maintenance	26	2	27	24	1	24	0	27	0
Tree Trimming & Planting	31	1	36	31	2	36	2	38	3
Cemetery Administration	11	8	11	11	6	14	8	12	4
Inspection Code Enforcement	7	1	9	5	2	8	0	7	0
Bus System Operations	23	21	26	14	8	22	8	21	11
Para-Transit System Operations	22	20	30	19	15	22	16	19	16
Parking Lot/ Garage Operations	12	2	14	13	2	15	2	21	1
Airport Operations	24	4	30	16	3	19	1	21	0
Utility Meter Reading	10	1	7	18	2	17	1	12	1
Utility Billing	13	1	32	27	2	13	1	12	1
Hazardous Waste Disposal	*	*	44	35	3	37	2	38	4

*Data not available or question not asked

Sources: Adapted from Farr, C. (1989). *Service delivery in the 90s: Alternative approaches for local governments.* Washington, DC: International City/County Management Association; Martin, L. L. (1999a). *Contracting for service delivery: Local government choices.* Washington, DC: International City/County Management Association; and Moulder, E., Director of Survey Research and Information Management. (2003). *Contracting for service delivery: Local government choices,* Special Data Issue No. 4. Washington, DC: International City/County Management Association (ICMA).

Appendix A – Table 2

Service Contracting By City and County Governments—1982-2003
(Health and Human Services)

Service	1982 For Profit (%)	1982 Non-Profit (%)	1988 Private (%)	1992 For Profit (%)	1992 Non-Profit (%)	1997 For Profit (%)	1997 Non-Profit (%)	2003 For Profit (%)	2003 Non-Profit (%)
Sanitary Inspections	1	6	3	2	2	4	1	4	0
Insect & Rodent Control	14	5	15	14	1	20	2	16	0
Animal/Rabies Control	6	9	11	5	9	8	10	6	9
Animal Shelter Operations	13	18	17	11	23	11	23	6	22
Child Day Care Facility Operations	35	37	34	53	35	48	31	38	35
Child Welfare Programs	5	24	17	4	13	8	19	11	25
Programs for the Elderly	4	29	19	6	24	8	26	7	31
Public Housing	13	18	14	*	*	*	*	*	*
Hospital Operations	30	27	24	31	30	36	36	25	28
Public Health Programs	8	27	19	5	8	16	14	11	19
Drug & Alcohol Treatment	6	41	34	20	34	20	35	18	47
Operation of Homeless Shelters	*	*	43	5	54	5	61	5	62
Operation of Mental Health & Mental Retardation Programs & Facilities	7	40	35	15	29	17	28	19	36

*Data not available or question not asked

Sources: Adapted from Farr, C. (1989). *Service delivery in the 90s: Alternative approaches for local governments.* Washington, DC: International City/County Management Association; Martin, L. L. (1999a). *Contracting for service delivery: Local government choices.* Washington, DC: International City/County Management Association; and Moulder, E., Director of Survey Research and Information Management. (2003). *Contracting for service delivery: Local government choices*, Special Data Issue No. 4. Washington, DC: International City/County Management Association (ICMA).

Appendix A – Table 3

Service Contracting By City and County Governments—1982-2003 (Public Safety)

Service	1982 For Profit (%)	1982 Non-Profit (%)	1988 Private (%)	1992 For Profit (%)	1992 Non-Profit (%)	1997 For Profit (%)	1997 Non-Profit (%)	2003 For Profit (%)	2003 Non-Profit (%)
Crime Prevention & Patrol	3	2	4	1	1	0	0	0	0
Police & Fire Communications	1	3	1	1	1	1	1	0	1
Fire Prevention & Suppression	1	3	1	1	3	1	2	1	2
Emergency Medical Services	14	10	18	14	8	16	8	13	8
Ambulance Services	25	10	24	27	10	28	9	21	8
Traffic Control & Parking Enforcement	1	1	1	1	0	1	0	1	0
Vehicle Towing & Storage	80	0	80	83	3	79	4	80	2

Sources: Adapted from Farr, C. (1989). *Service delivery in the 90s: Alternative approaches for local governments.* Washington, DC: International City/County Management Association; Martin, L. L. (1999a). *Contracting for service delivery: Local government choices.* Washington, DC: International City/County Management Association; and Moulder, E., Director of Survey Research and Information Management. (2003). *Contracting for service delivery: Local government choices*, Special Data Issue No. 4. Washington, DC: International City/County Management Association (ICMA).

Appendix A – Table 4

Service Contracting By City and County Governments—1982-2003
(Parks, Recreation, Arts, and Cultural Services)

Service	1982 For Profit (%)	1982 Non-Profit (%)	1988 Private (%)	1992 For Profit (%)	1992 Non-Profit (%)	1997 For Profit (%)	1997 Non-Profit (%)	2003 For Profit (%)	2003 Non-Profit (%)
Recreation Services	4	13	8	5	3	10	5	9	7
Parks Landscaping & Maintenance	9	2	13	9	2	18	2	18	2
Operation of Convention Centers & Auditoriums	5	6	11	8	6	14	8	15	9
Operation of Cultural & Arts Programs	7	39	23	6	41	7	36	10	45
Operation of Libraries	1	10	1	1	4	1	5	0	7
Operation of Museums	4	32	8	2	37	5	39	5	35

Sources: Adapted from Farr, C. (1989). *Service delivery in the 90s: Alternative approaches for local governments.* Washington, DC: International City/County Management Association; Martin, L. L. (1999a). *Contracting for service delivery: Local government choices.* Washington, DC: International City/County Management Association; and Moulder, E., Director of Survey Research and Information Management. (2003). *Contracting for service delivery: Local government choices,* Special Data Issue No. 4. Washington, DC: International City/County Management Association (ICMA).

Appendix A – Table 5

Service Contracting By City and County Governments—1982-2003
(Support Services)

Service	1982 For Profit (%)	1982 Non-Profit (%)	1988 Private (%)	1992 For Profit (%)	1992 Non-Profit (%)	1997 For Profit (%)	1997 Non-Profit (%)	2003 For Profit (%)	2003 Non-Profit (%)
Building/ Grounds Maintenance	20	1	27	20	2	26	2	30	2
Building Security	8	1	13	12	1	19	1	19	1
Fleet Maintenance (Emergency Vehicles)	31	0	41	27	2	34	3	40	1
Fleet Maintenance (Heavy Equipment)	32	0	41	27	2	33	2	37	1
Fleet Maintenance (All Other Vehicles)	29	0	38	25	2	32	2	36	1
Data Processing	23	2	17	8	1	15	1	17	0
Legal Services	49	2	55	47	2	51	2	56	2
Tax Bill Processing	11	6	9	*	*	*	*	7	0
Tax Assessing	7	4	10	6	1	6	1	8	0
Delinquent Tax Collection	10	3	14	*	*	*	*	18	1
Secretarial Services	4	0	7	5	0	7	1	5	0
Labor Relations	23	1	33	*	*	*	*	*	*
Personnel Services	*	*	*	4	0	7	1	9	0
Public Relations & Information	7	2	10	6	1	9	2	12	1

*Data not available or question not asked

Sources: Adapted from Farr, C. (1989). *Service delivery in the 90s: Alternative approaches for local governments.* Washington, DC: International City/County Management Association; Martin, L. L. (1999a). *Contracting for service delivery: Local government choices.* Washington, DC: International City/County Management Association; and Moulder, F., Director of Survey Research and Information Management. (2003). *Contracting for service delivery: Local government choices,* Special Data Issue No. 4. Washington, DC: International City/County Management Association (ICMA).

Appendix B

Colorado State Auditor's Office Privatization Profile Summary Form (without weights)						
	Government Provision			Contract Provision		
Factor	Scoring					
Market Strength	-3	-2	-1	+1	+2	+3
Political Resistance	-3	-2	-1	+1	+2	+3
Service Quality	-3	-2	-1	+1	+2	+3
Impact on Employees	-3	-2	-1	+1	+2	+3
Legal Barriers	-3	-2	-1	+1	+2	+3
Risk	-3	-2	-1	+1	+2	+3
Resources	-3	-2	-1	+1	+2	+3
Control	-3	-2	-1	+1	+2	+3
Cost	-3	-2	-1	+1	+2	+3

Source: Adapted from Colorado State Auditor's Office. (1989, 1997). *Privatization assessment workbook*. Denver: Colorado State Auditor's Office.

Appendix C

| Colorado State Auditor's Office Privatization Profile Summary Form (with weights) ||||||||
| Factor | Government Provision ||| Contract Provision ||| Weight | Weighted Score |
	Scoring							
Market Strength	-3	-2	-1	+1	+2	+3		
Political Resistance	-3	-2	-1	+1	+2	+3		
Service Quality	-3	-2	-1	+1	+2	+3		
Impact on Employees	-3	-2	-1	+1	+2	+3		
Legal Barriers	-3	-2	-1	+1	+2	+3		
Risk	-3	-2	-1	+1	+2	+3		
Resources	-3	-2	-1	+1	+2	+3		
Control	-3	-2	-1	+1	+2	+3		
Cost	-3	-2	-1	+1	+2	+3		

Source: Adapted from Colorado State Auditor's Office. (1989, 1997). *Privatization assessment workbook.* Denver: Colorado State Auditor's Office; and Martin, L. L. (1993). *Evaluating contracting out.* Washington, DC: International City/County Management Association.

Appendix D

Public-Private Competition Checklist

Service Considerations	Favors Public-Private Competition
1. Service is ancillary	X
2. Service is hard	X
3. Service is stand-alone	X
4. Service precedent exists	X
5. Multi-year contract can be awarded	X
External Market Considerations	
6. High private sector interest	X
7. High private sector competitiveness	X
Internal Market Considerations	
8. High in-house and public employee interest	X
9. High in-house and public employee competitiveness	X
Other Considerations	
10. Low political opposition	X

Source: Adapted from Martin, L. L. (1996). *Selecting services for public-private competition.* Washington, DC: International City/County Management Association.

Appendix E

Level Playing Field Checklist

Process Issues	Tends to Favor the Public Sector	Competitively Neutral	Tends to Favor the Private Sector
1. Type of Competition - Sequential Process - Parallel Process			
2. Public Sector Access to Outside Consultants - YES/NO			
3. Independent Review of Public Benchmarks, Bids, and Proposals - YES/NO			
4. Separation of Purchaser and Provider Functions - YES/NO			
Costing Issues			
5. Mandated Private Sector Wage Scales - YES/NO			
6. Mandated Private Sector Employee Benefits - YES/NO			
7. Minimum Cost Savings Threshold - YES/NO			
8. Cost Comparison Approach - Fully Allocated Costs Approach - Avoidable Cost Approach - State of Texas Approach			
9. Transition Costs - Private Sector Only - Public and Private Sectors - Excluded			
10. Contract Administration and Monitoring Costs - Included for Private Sector Only - Included for Both - Excluded			
Contract Administraion Issues			
11. Public Sector Memorandum of Understanding - YES/NO			
12. Penalties for Public Sector Failure to Perform - YES/NO			
13. Provisions for Monitoring - Private Sector Only - Private Sector and Public Sector			

Source: Martin, L. L. (1999). *Developing a level playing field for public-private competition.* Arlington, VA: The IBM Center for the Business of Government.

Appendix F

Examples of Alternative Surety

Cash Escrow Deposit

A Cash Escrow Deposit requires the service provider to place cash, equal to the contract amount, in an escrow deposit. Normally, it requires the signature of the jurisdiction's chief financial official and the service provider to release funds from a Cash Escrow Deposit. The advantage to this type of bond is that funds are available if the service provider defaults. The service provider normally is allowed periodical interest accrual on the deposit until the contract is completed.

Certified or Cashier's Checks

The offeror purchases a certified or cashier's check from a bank or a savings and loan institution, which is usually provided in lieu of a Bid Bond. The check is written in the name of the jurisdiction, and the offeror cannot stop payment. However, the financial institution that issued the check can stop payment under special circumstances. Most progressive jurisdictions deposit the check immediately into a special fund and then reimburse the offeror with a jurisdiction check. This type of alternative instrument is rarely used for a high-value service delivery solicitation.

Irrevocable Letter of Credit

An irrevocable Letter of Credit, issued by a bank or savings and loan institution, can be used to guarantee performance or payment. The face amount of the Letter of Credit, usually equal to the contract amount, is released to the jurisdiction by the financial institution upon receipt of a written claim that the service provider has defaulted. Payment by the financial institution to the jurisdiction is immediate. If the instrument provided by the service provider does not have the term irrevocable, the service provider can cancel it at any time. Caution should be exercised when considering an Irrevocable Letter of Credit. In the event of a bankruptcy or takeover by the Federal Deposit Insurance Corporation, letters of credit can be among the first monetary instruments to be voided. Before accepting a Letter of Credit, the jurisdiction's finance office should review the financial statement or credit rating of the issuing institution.

The Letter of Credit, like the Cash Escrow Deposit, is an infrequently used performance guarantee because the service provider might have to deposit cash, savings bonds, or real estate with the issuing financial institution as collateral.

Payments as a Guarantee

A consideration for unacceptable service is to withhold a certain amount from monthly payments that the service provider has earned. This provides the jurisdiction considerable financial leverage against a service provider who is performing at unsatisfactory service delivery levels. Interruption of a service provider's cash flow is often more effective than a declaration of default and attempting to enforce the Performance Bond. The criteria for applying this method of deduction must be in the Special Conditions of the solicitation.

Personal Bond
A Personal Bond is a guarantee that the personal assets of the service provider are pledged and will be used to pay any claims for failure to enter into the contract, to perform the contract, or to pay debts incurred in the performance of the contract. A Personal Bond must be certified by the jurisdiction's financial office and then supported by an agreement approved by the jurisdiction's legal counsel. Collection against a Personal Bond may be time-consuming and legally complex, depending on the conditions of the approved agreement and the time required to convert pledged assets to cash. Litigation may be required to collect this type of bond.

Property Bond
The Property Bond is similar to a Personal Bond with the exception that the assets pledged by the service provider consist of real property. The same limitations and issues apply to a Property Bond as to the Personal Bond.

Appendix G

Standard Clauses Included in the RFP Boilerplate

Instructions to Bidders/Proposers
The instructions to bidders/proposers section of the boilerplate explain how to submit a response to a solicitation and list the conditions that must be met in order to submit a bid or proposal.

Statutes, ordinances, regulations, policy, or procurement procedures may require special clauses. If these clauses apply to actions that are required to qualify as a bidder/proposer or that otherwise take place before the award of a contract–for example, attending a mandatory pre-bid/proposal conference, making a presentation to an evaluation committee–they would be included in the instructions to bidders/proposers section of the solicitation document.

Acknowledgement of Amendments
The Acknowledgment of Amendments clause requires that bidders/proposers acknowledge any amendments, either by written acknowledgment on the bid/proposal form or by returning the amendment with the form.

Alternative Bids
The Alternative Bids clause states that bidders offering service delivery methods other than those permitted in the Statement of Work in response to a competitive sealed bid may submit an envelope clearly marked alternative bid. However, if the jurisdiction believes that a service delivery method offered in an alternative bid is valid, this clause permits the jurisdiction to cancel the solicitations and re-bid with a revised Statement of Work that includes the alternative method. Although the jurisdiction is not required to award any contract and can cancel a solicitation at any time before award, an explanation is expected by those who submitted bids. This clause provides an explanation when an alternative bid identifies an exceptional idea or service delivery method.

This clause is discussed at the pre-bid conference and encourages bidders to advise the jurisdiction of alternative service delivery methods well before the date set for receipt of bids. Advance notice permits the jurisdiction to amend the Statement of Work before bid opening. Each bidder then has the opportunity to submit a response on the basis of the same specifications, as required under competitive sealed bidding procedures, including acceptable alternatives offered by other bidders, thus avoiding the inconvenience and expense of canceling and re-bidding a solicitation.

Bid/Proposal Acceptance Period
The bid/proposal acceptance period is the length of time (usually in calendar days) that the response is binding on the bidder/offeror. This clause advises the bidder that the response

cannot be withdrawn before the specified time has elapsed, which is normally 45-60 days after bid opening.

Bid/Proposal Form Submission

Submission instructions tell the bidder/proposer when and where to submit the solicitation response, how to submit it, and how many copies to submit with the original. (The number of copies is usually equal to the number of members on the evaluation committee.) Also included in the bid/proposal submission instructions are procedures for the disposition of late responses, how to mark the response envelope, the rules regarding a bidder's/proposer's change to his or her response, and the rules governing withdrawals before and after bid/proposal opening.

Bid Withdrawal

A bidder is permitted to withdraw or amend a solicitation response before the date and time set for receipt of a response upon written request to the jurisdiction, and no reason is required. A bid cannot be amended after bid opening unless the amendment does not affect the price, quality, quantity, or delivery of the service. Bidders occasionally request an opportunity to withdraw a bid after bid opening because of a clerical error. The withdrawal of a bid after bid opening is irreversible. Bidders who bid the project too low and want to be released from their bid may also use the claim of a "clerical error." Unless a bidder can prove beyond a reasonable doubt that there was a clerical error, not an error in judgment, the bid response cannot be withdrawn; this sometimes forces a bidder who does not want an award to accept it. This rule follows the basic premise of public procurement; once a bid is opened, it cannot be withdrawn without a valid reason.

Bidder Certification

This clause states that the bidder/proposer agrees to accept the award and enter into a contract if the award is offered.

Bidder Investigation

Bidders may claim that they discovered a fact or condition only after the time set for receipt of bid responses or after being awarded the contract. They usually request additional payments to offset the added cost created by the fact or condition. The Bidder Investigations clause makes the bidder responsible for conducting all investigations a reasonable firm would conduct before making a business decision. Of course, the Statement of Work team must include in the Statement of Work any information that could affect the cost of the service. Failure to disclose known conditions can jeopardize the jurisdiction's defense against a claim that the information withheld damaged a bidder in some way.

Certification of Independent Price Determination

This clause protects the jurisdiction against collusion. Each bidder/proposer is required to certify that the response was prepared independently and that the price submitted will not be disclosed to any other person.

Collusion among Bidders/Offerors
This clause, derived from the Sherman Antitrust Act, describes prohibitions against collusion and the submission of more than one response from each bidder. This does not apply to the Alternative Bids clause.

Debarment
By requiring bidders/proposers to certify that they are not currently debarred from submitting bids/proposals, the Debarment Status Clause helps reduce the possibility of receiving a response from a bidder/proposer whose past performance led to debarment by another public jurisdiction.

Economic Price Adjustment
This clause explains how the jurisdiction evaluates an economic price adjustment formula submitted by the bidder/proposer when the solicitation document does not include a provision for that adjustment. It also explains how the jurisdiction evaluates a bidder/proposer exception to an economic price adjustment formula when a formula is included in the solicitation document.

* * * * * * * * *

The language and intent of the following clauses must be adjusted and approved by the jurisdiction's legal counsel to comply with state statute/ordinance/regulation or policy.

Expenses Incurred in Bid/Proposal Preparation
This clause states that the bidder/proposer is responsible for all costs associated with submitting the solicitation response.

Informalities and Irregularities
Most solicitation documents include a statement that the jurisdiction has the right to waive *informalities* and *irregularities* as minor defects in a bid response or variations from the exact requirements of the solicitation, provided that the defects or variations do not affect the price, quality, quantity, or delivery of the service. This clause can help prevent an otherwise excellent bid response from being rejected because of a minor defect. As in every decision to accept or reject a non-conforming bid response, consult with legal counsel.

Late Submissions
Some jurisdictions accept late bids/proposals under certain conditions. This clause describes the most common conditions considered in acceptance of a late bid. The most common conditions are when the delay is caused by the handling of the mail and the late bid is the only one received.

Non-conforming Terms and Conditions
Bidders sometimes submit responses that include corporate forms, brochures, or sample contract forms, any of which may contain terms and conditions that do not conform to the solicitation document. Examples include a provision that the contract is to be adjudicated

under the laws of another state or under corporate requirement for arbitration of contracts, both of which may not be allowed under statute, ordinance, regulation, or policy. Bidders may be unaware that their boilerplate violates the terms and conditions of the solicitation document, but some bidders may intend for their boilerplate conditions to supersede the terms and conditions of the solicitation document.

Some jurisdictions reject non-conforming bid responses as non-responsive. Others ignore non-conforming terms and conditions, consider the bid to be responsive, and proceed with the evaluation process. If the jurisdiction awards the contract to a bidder who has submitted non-conforming terms and conditions, the bidder may perform according to the non-conforming terms and conditions, not those of the jurisdiction. Moreover, the acceptance of a technically non-responsive bid gives other bidders grounds to protest the award. The Non-Conforming Terms and Conditions clause allows the jurisdiction to request the bidder to withdraw non-conforming terms and conditions that do not affect the price, quality, or delivery of the service. If price, quality, or delivery is affected, the principles of public procurement require that the bid be rejected as non-responsive.

Qualifications of Bidders/Proposers
This clause is used when the jurisdiction wants to obtain information from bidders/proposers through a Request for Information (RFI). The clause protects the jurisdiction from the claims of a bidder/proposer who interprets an RFI as a request for consulting services and bills the jurisdiction for services received.

Unnecessarily Elaborate Responses
Some bidders/proposers may submit a bound 100-page response with brochures, advertising releases, and technical manuals when a two- or three-page attachment is adequate. This clause advises bidders/proposers that elaborate responses are not required or advisable. It also helps to reduce the amount of material that the Procurement Evaluation team must read.

General Terms and Conditions
The general terms and conditions section of the boilerplate includes the terms and conditions that will be included in the final contract. In this section, the bidder/offeror is referred to as the contractor.

The language of the clauses in the general terms and conditions section must be approved by the jurisdiction's legal counsel and adjusted to comply with statute, ordinance, regulation, or policy. Like the instructions to bidders/proposers section, the general terms and conditions section of the solicitation document may include clauses that apply to almost every contract and some that are used only in specific instances.

Antitrust
The Antitrust clause permits a jurisdiction to benefit from an antitrust action if a resulting financial award affects a contractor or items or services provided by the contractor. If a paving supplier is convicted of an antitrust violation for price fixing, the paving contractor could receive treble damages for the material it procured from the supplier. If the jurisdiction had been paying

inflated prices to the paving contractor, the jurisdiction has standing in the settlement.

Applicable Law
Contractors based in another state usually want litigation to be brought in their home state. The Applicable Law clause specifically requires that litigation be brought in the state of the jurisdiction that issues the solicitation.

Assignment
The Assignment clause prohibits the contractor from transferring or assigning the contract to another party without written consent of the jurisdiction.

Certificates and Licenses
State statute and jurisdiction ordinance set out the requirements for certification, i.e., business licenses, occupational licenses, professional licenses, exterminating licenses, hazardous waste hauling and disposal licenses, and asbestos abatement licenses, to name a few. Do not assume that a contractor has the required certificates or licenses. When a professional license is required to perform the contract, the contractor should be required to submit a copy of the license with the solicitation document or prior to award.

Changes in the Statement of Work
The jurisdiction must plan for possible modifications to the contract after award is made and the contract is signed. The Changes in the Statement of Work clause sets forth the rules governing changes to the contract that the jurisdiction makes or requests. It also describes the resources available if the contractor and the jurisdiction disagree on changes that require additional compensation to the contractor.

Cost Reimbursement
The Cost Reimbursement clause prohibits a contractor from marking up the price of any material provided under a time and materials contract. The clause specifically prohibits the *use of cost plus a percentage of cost* pricing methods.

Employee Discrimination
An Employee Discrimination clause must be included in every public contract. If the contract is financed in part or in whole, federal requirements will apply. Most states and progressive jurisdictions have a statute or ordinance that addresses employee discrimination, and the statute or ordinance must be included in the solicitation document.

Ethics in Public Contracting
This clause is included to advise the contractor of statute, ordinance, or regulation requirements regarding gifts, inducement, or kickbacks to jurisdiction employees.

Failure to Enforce
It is common for a contract provision not to be enforced for a considerable length of time. This clause states that past failure to enforce a contract provision does not mean that the jurisdiction has waived its right to enforce that provision or any other provision.

Force Majeure
The Force Majeure clause excuses the contractor from performance due to conditions beyond the contractor's control. Use the clause carefully, making sure it applies to the solicitation's needs. For example, the clause should not be used, unless amended, when contracting for services to be provided during emergencies (natural disasters, hazardous materials use, riots, etc.). If a contract contains a standard Force Majeure clause, a contractor whose assistance is expected during an emergency can refuse to provide services. The specific events that can excuse a contractor from performing should be carefully defined for each contract.

Indemnification
The Indemnification clause is intended to help the jurisdiction in the event of negligent performance or non-performance by the contractor. It is best to have the jurisdiction's legal counsel provide the language for this clause.

Non-substitution
In competitive negotiation, some contractors may propose a non-substitution requirement. The intent of the contractor is that if the jurisdiction terminates the contract for non-appropriation of funds (see Chapter 4), it will not fund a project for that same or similar service in order to take advantage of a higher level of service or service technology. When negotiating, do not accept a non-substitution period of longer than six months; three months is preferable.

Oral Statement
This clause states that written modifications, issued from the procurement office, are the only acceptable method of modifying the contract and that the contract will not be affected by any oral statement made by any jurisdiction employee.

Patents, Copyrights, and Royalties
The contractor may use patented or copyrighted material or procedures in the performance of the work. A specially adapted hold-harmless clause written by the jurisdiction's legal counsel protects the jurisdiction from claims filed for patent or copyright infringement.

Procurement Regulations
To ensure that procedures for the resolution of contract disputes and other pertinent information are a part of the solicitation and contract documents, incorporate the jurisdiction's procurement regulations into the terms and conditions by reference.

Recovery of Money
The jurisdiction may have difficulty obtaining money due from a contractor. The Recovery of Money clause allows the jurisdiction to deduct money owed from payments due to the contractor.

Estimate of Requirements
Occasionally a jurisdiction can only estimate the amount of service it will require. Contracts for trade services involving electricians and plumbers or seasonal services such as snow removal are usually structured as Requirements contracts. The Estimate of Requirements

clause states that the jurisdiction offers no guarantee as to the extent of work during the contract term. The clause protects the jurisdiction if the estimate in the solicitation document is lower or higher than the amount of work actually performed.

Right to Audit
The right to audit the contractor's books is a standard clause of the contract. In practice, contractors are usually not audited unless there is evidence of fraud or dishonesty, the exposure to cash or securities, or the contract is based on a percentage of the contractor's revenue. Because contractors are aware that a jurisdiction seldom enforces a Right to Audit clause, they usually pay little attention to it, no matter how stringent the clause.

Termination
A Termination clause addresses termination for default or at the convenience of the jurisdiction. Termination for default allows the jurisdiction to terminate the contract when requirements in the contract are not met. Although termination at the convenience of the jurisdiction may generate opposition from contractors, some contracts should include this clause to protect the jurisdiction. Examples of such contracts are unknown duration, dependent on grants or other outside funding; enabling legislation; and requirements contracts.

Contracts with a Termination for Convenience clause will often cause a contractor to request the unilateral right to terminate. If this becomes an issue, the jurisdiction should forego the clause *Terminate for Convenience* rather than give a contractor the same right. To permit a contractor to unilaterally terminate a contract is, in effect, valid only for the period of notification of termination. Such contracts provide no incentive to improve unacceptable performance. Also, a threat to take action against the contractor or to assess penalties for poor performance could be answered with a contractor's notice of termination for convenience.

The only allowable termination initiated by a contractor should be on the anniversary date of a multi-year contract, and then only if the contractor gives reasonable notice of termination. Reasonable notice is considered 120 calendar days before the anniversary date. This allows the necessary time to re-solicit.

Traffic Control
If the contractor's operations affect the flow of vehicle or pedestrian traffic, this clause must be included with specific instructions for traffic management. Without this clause, the contractor who blocks a main street or sidewalk during rush hours and is directed by the jurisdiction to provide traffic management, could file a claim for lost time and added costs.

Vehicle and Equipment Buy-Back
The Vehicle and Equipment Buy-Back clause establishes a reserve position for the jurisdiction in the event the contractor defaults during the contract term. The clause allows the jurisdiction to retrieve vehicles or equipment that were specifically procured by the contractor for contract performance.

Source: Adapted from Harney, D. (1992). *Service contracting: A local government guide*. Washington, DC: International City/County Management Association.

Appendix H

Performance-Based Statement of Work Template

Service:

Service Definition:

Specifications of Tasks/ Statement of Objectives	Performance Measures/ Performance Requirements	Performance Standards/ Acceptable Quality Level	Incentives/ Penalties	Monitoring/ Quality Assurance Plan

Appendix I

Guideline Template for Scoring of Oral and Written Presentations

EVALUATION OF FINALIST'S ORAL/WRITTEN PRESENTATION

RFP# _____ TITLE: _____

FIRM NAME: _____

SUBJECTIVE SCORING

ENTRY SCORING METHOD

(C)	COMFORTABLE WITH OFFEROR –	INSERT A PLUS 1 (1)
(N)	NEUTRAL ABOUT OFFEROR –	INSERT A ZERO (0)
(U)	UNCOMFORTABLE WITH OFFEROR –	INSERT A MINUS 1 (-1)

Section Scores: Using The Assigned Points For Each Of The Four Sections, Insert Your Scores By Section.

ITEM DESCRIPTION — SUBJECTIVE SCORE SECTION (C) (N) (U) SCORES

I. PERSONNEL
1. Has key management been identified?
2. Have the key consultants and other team members been identified?
3. Has the presentation been clear as to the role and responsibilities of each of the above (1 & 2) will be?
4. Will the project manager and other presenter(s) be able to communicate with elected officials, staff, and the public?
5. Do you have confidence in the Project Manager?
6. Do you have confidence in the individual team members?
7. Do the individuals act as a team?
   TOTAL (SUBJECTIVE ENTRIES):
   SECTION SCORE (MAXIMUM ____ POINTS)

II. PAST WORK
1. What is your overall impression?
   TOTAL (SUBJECTIVE ENTRIES):
   SECTION SCORE (MAXIMUM ____ POINTS)

III. TEAM ISSUES
1. Has the firm assigned roles and responsibilities to specific individuals?   ___ ___ ___
2. Is the team leadership apparent?   ___ ___ ___
   TOTAL (SUBJECTIVE ENTRIES):   ___ ___ ___
   SECTION SCORE (MAXIMUM ___ POINTS)   _____

IV. APPROACH TO THE PROJECT
1. Does the team understand the unique qualities and nature of the project?   ___ ___ ___
2. Has the team been specific in identifying the issues to be dealt with in this project?   ___ ___ ___
   TOTAL (SUBJECTIVE ENTRIES):   ___ ___ ___
   SECTION SCORE (MAXIMUM ___ POINTS)   _____

V. REFERENCES AND ADDITIONAL TECHNICAL RESPONSES
1. Technical responsiveness at Committee meeting   ___ ___ ___
2. Results of reference checks   ___ ___ ___
   TOTAL (SUBJECTIVE ENTRIES):   ___ ___ ___
   SECTION SCORE (MAXIMUM ___ POINTS)   _____
   GRAND TOTAL (I - V):   _____

COMMITTEE MEMBER CERTIFICATION:

I certify that I have independently reviewed, evaluated and rated the firm identified on this form and that the point awards above reflect my best judgment of the merits of the offeror.

                               Signature: _____

                               Date: _____

Appendix I (Cont'd) on next page.

Appendix I (Cont'd)

Comments On The Form For Evaluation Of Oral/written Presentations

When the initial scoring of proposals is completed, all selected finalists are considered capable of performing the work. The purpose of the oral presentation is to obtain additional information about each finalist to enable Committee members to determine which of the selected finalists is (are) the best qualified.

The standard evaluation scoring form can be used in evaluating oral presentations. The Committee, together with the Procurement Manager, will make any adjustments to the form that may be necessary to make it conform to the specific RFP.

The scoring form is divided into four Sections: "Personnel" (the offeror's project team); "Past Work" (the offeror's experience with other clients); "Team Issues" (how the tasks will be managed by the team); and "Approach to the Project" (how well the team matches the project).

Maximum points allowed for each Section are determined by the Committee and the Procurement Manager and should be preprinted on the form for each Section in the space marked "SECTION SCORE (MAXIMUM ____ POINTS)." The maximum point values assigned may be weighted according to the importance of each Section. Section maximums could be 25, 50, 75, etc., as long as the total for all sections equals 100 points, depending on the importance of the Section.

When scoring, the three subjective entries—Comfortable (C or +1), Neutral (N or 0), and Uncomfortable (U or -1)—are entered for each evaluation criterion to help determine the final points awarded to each finalist.

The relative frequency of particular entries in a Section should impact on the final score assigned to that Section. For example, if a Section contained all Comfortable (C) values, the finalist should receive a high score for the Section; if all the entries were Uncomfortable (U), a much lower score may be appropriate; and, if half of the impressions were Comfortable (C) and half Uncomfortable (U) or all Neutral (N), a score in the middle range of the maximum score would be appropriate.

At the conclusion of each presentation, each Committee member shall assign points to Sections I through IV of the evaluation form and compute the grand total score for that finalist. The grand total scores for each finalist are used to rank the finalists. In general, if the evaluation is for a professional services firm, negotiations will start with the highest ranked finalist. If the evaluation is for services that are other than professional, negotiations start with the two highest ranked firms.

Source: Columbia County, Georgia. (2004). Evaluation guidelines for requests for proposals. In *Columbia County, Georgia's procurement procedure manual (Appendix A, revised 11-2-04)*. Columbia: Columbia County.

Index

- A -

ABA (American Bar Association), 135
ABA (American Bar Assoc.) Model Procurement Code, 77, 79, 157, 182
Acceptable Quality Level (AQL), 115-116, 118, 217
Acceptance document, 92
Accounting principles, generally accepted, 108
Accuracy Rates, 118
Acknowledgement of Amendments Clause, 210
ACORD (Association for Cooperative Operations Research & Development), 156
Activity-based costing, 40, 47
Actual cost, 37, 43, 90, 102, 125-126, 131
Ad hoc approach, 49, 51-52
Administration
  costs, 7, 36-37, 39, 41-45, 50, 56, 64, 68, 207
  function, 174
  staff, 37
  team, 80, 85, 151, 181, 192
Administrative
  Dispute Resolution Act, 167
  expenses, 127, 157
  functions, 81
  procedures, 162-163, 167, 170
  requirements, 90
ADR (Alternative Dispute Resolution), 161-163, 166-167
Advantages of Public-Private Competition, 52
AFSCME (American Federation of State, County and Municipal Employees), 4, 18
After-the-Fact Notification, 71-72
AGC (Associated General Contractors of America), 197
Agreed-to price, 128
Alabama, 8-9
Alaska, 63-64
Allocation methodology, 40
Alternative
  Bids clause, 210, 212
  Dispute Resolution (ADR), 24-25, 161-163, 167, 170
  guarantees, 100

service delivery, 2-3, 46, 51, 199-203, 210
Surety, 84, 100, 208
American Bar Association (ABA), 18-19, 77, 103, 135, 157, 182, 185
American Federation of State, County & Municipal Employees (AFSCME), 4, 19
Ammons, D. & Hill, D., 7, 19
Analysis process, 77, 180
Ancillary Services, 15, 26, 56
Andersen Consulting, 174
Anthony, R. & Young, D., 40, 44, 46
Antitrust clause, 212-213
Applicable Law clause, 214
AQLs (Acceptable Quality Levels), 118-119, 120, 122
Arbitration, 24, 153, 162-163, 167, 170, 213
Arizona, 3, 10, 26, 28, 36, 43, 51-52, 116-117
Arlington County, VA, 10, 57
Assertion of Claims, 169
Assignment clause, 214
Attendant costs, 37, 123-124
Audit Commission, 27, 46, 57
Auditing Considerations, 131
Australian, 10, 20, 62, 73
Award Fee Contracting, 128-129, 131
Award process, 77, 88, 135, 149, 151, 154, 163, 173

- B -

Back-up service provider, 181
Bad faith, 167, 175
BAFO (Best and Final Offer), 141
Bailor/Bailee insurance coverage, 99
Bank of Canada, 1, 19
Bankruptcy, 181, 190, 192, 194, 208
Beaulieu, M., 130, 132
Becker, F. & Mackelprang, D., 26-27, 46
Bell, A.K., 6, 21
Benchmarks, 50-52, 65-66, 68-69, 71, 122, 139 140
Best
  and Final Offer (BAFO), 140
  practices, 28, 35, 122, 133, 174

-Value Evaluation Process, 137
Bid
  Bond, 99-101, 208
  document, 153, 213
  /proposal, 36, 52, 58, 65-66, 68-69, 72, 78, 88,152, 210-212
  response, 210-212
  /tender, 77-78, 136, 191
Bidder Investigation, 211
Bidders, 17, 58, 65, 77, 88, 144, 162, 189, 210-213
Bidding, informal, 49, 52
Bids/Tenders, 50-52, 65, 75-76, 78-79, 88, 135-136, 139, 144, 161
BOB (Federal Bureau of the Budget), 3
Boilerplate, 76, 87-88, 161, 210, 213
Bond, 99-101, 156-157, 165, 195-196, 208-209
Bonding surety, 99-100
Boyne, G., 11, 19
Budget office, 3, 21, 35, 37, 47, 51, 74, 83
Budget policy, 25
Bundling, 57
Burt, D., 91, 103

- C -

Calendar of Events, 83, 88
California, 9, 43, 191
California Supreme Court, 17-19
CalTrans (California Department of Transportation), 17
Cancellation notices, 155-156
Capacity of the parties, 150
Capital equipment, 102
Cash Escrow Deposit, 100, 208
Cashier's Checks, 208
CCA (Corrections Corporation of America) vs. Malesko, 16
Certificate Holder, 155-156
Certificates, 88, 151, 154-156, 214
Certification requirements, 169, 214
Chairperson, committee, 79, 140, 142-143
Change Management Services, 130-131
Charlotte, NC, 19, 28, 43, 54

Chi, K. & Jasper, C., 1, 3-4, 7, 12, 19
Chief Procurement Officer, 138, 163, 167
Cibinic, J. & Nash, R., 144, 148, 158
CIPFA (Chartered Institute of Public Finance & Accountancy), 57, 73
Circuit-Riding Contract Manager, 81
Citizen complaints, 176, 178, 190
Citizen surveys, 176-177
Civic Federation, The, 4, 19, 53-55, 73
Clause, incentive, 193
Clauses, standard, 210, 215-216
CN (Canadian), 76, 150
Code of conduct, 194
Collaborative effort, 87, 93
Collusion, 88, 141, 211-212
Colorado approach, 28, 31-34
Colorado Commission on Privatization, 18-19
Columbia County, GA, 144, 146, 158, 220
Commencement of the contract, 196-197
Committee members, 80, 138-140, 142-143, 145, 211, 220
Commonwealth of Australia, 3, 7, 51, 53-55, 62
Competitive
  Negotiation, 16, 79, 136, 141-142, 149, 151, 191, 215
  neutrality, 54, 62, 73
  proposals, 76-78, 82, 136, 144
  Sealed Bids, 76, 78, 144
  Sealed Proposals, 76-78, 136, 144
  solicitation, 76, 78, 136, 191
Completion date, 154
Compulsory competition, 3, 51, 73
Compulsory competitive tendering, 3, 22, 74
Confidentiality, 29, 140, 197
Consultants, 50, 63, 65, 80, 82, 138, 192, 207, 218
Consulting services, 81, 103, 128-129, 213
Consumer price index, 7, 102
Contingency contracts, 195
Contract
  Administration And Monitoring, 36-39, 41, 50, 56, 64, 68, 82, 85, 173
  Administrator, 81-82, 95, 97, 196
  Award, 78-79, 126-127, 129, 135, 143, 151, 154, 162-164, 173, 210
  costs, 25, 28, 35-37, 39, 41-46, 56, 64, 68, 93
  Documents, 152, 154-155
  employees, 16, 96
  Extension, 83, 101, 110, 119-121, 188-189
  Format, 115, 151-152
  Incentives, 107, 119, 121, 125-126, 129, 135, 157-158
  informal, 139
  Interruptions, 181, 194
  management, 3, 25, 37, 81, 121, 130-131, 133, 153, 174, 180, 187
  Manager, 79-82, 138, 152-153, 177
  monitoring, 106-107, 115, 121-123, 173-176, 178
  price, 36, 38-39, 41-45, 102, 124-126, 143, 151, 155, 157, 188, 208
  Renewal, 83, 101-102, 110, 120, 153, 187-189
  Service Delivery, 7-8, 18, 23, 28, 39-41, 55, 66, 68, 73, 86, 90, 106, 173
  term, 40, 68, 97, 101, 120, 151, 156, 216
  transition, 50, 187, 196-197
  types, 76, 106, 124, 126, 157, 183
Contractor
  compensation, 110, 119-120, 130-131, 183, 214
  costs, 124, 130, 157, 183
  files, 190, 192
  protest, 161, 166-167
  Qualifications, 75, 83, 85, 87, 113
  Reports, 176
Contractor's
  experience, 75, 124
  financial condition, 184
  insurance, 155-156
  performance, 82, 120, 174-175, 177, 195
  right, 169, 216
Contractual
  boilerplate, 155
  clauses, common, 157
  requirements, 75, 150
  services, 73, 75
Copyright infringement, 215
Core services, 14-16, 23, 26-27, 29, 49, 56, 79
Corporate contract form, 153, 212
Corrections Corporation of America (CCA), 16
Cost
  approach, 31, 43-45, 50, 64, 67
  comparisons, 18, 34-36, 40, 46, 66
  overage, 36, 69
  -effective method, 98
  -plus-award-fee (CPAF)contract, 126
  -plus-fixed-fee (CPFF) contract, 124, 126
  -plus-incentive-fee (CPIF) contract, 126
  -reimbursement contract, 38, 111, 125-126, 127, 183
  -sharing contract, 125
  -type contract, 157
Costing terms, 39
Costs/Revenues, 36, 39, 41-43, 45, 130
Costs, unavoidable, 39-40, 44-45
Council of State Governments, 1, 12, 19, 159
Court decisions, 16-17, 175
CPPB (Certified Professional Public Buyer)
CPPO (Certified Public Purchasing Officer), i, iii, v
Creating Trust, 178
Criteria, technical, 139, 149
Critical service delivery, 58, 100
Crosby, P., 11, 19
Cullen, J. & Broadbent, M., 175, 185
Cultural normalization, 174
Cure Notice, 185
Customer
  complaints, 122, 158
  satisfaction, 111, 114, 122
  Surveys, 122-123
Cutler, T. & Waine, B., 54

- D -

Damages, 84, 94, 97-98, 153, 157, 163, 165, 181-184, 187, 213
Davis, H., 3, 7-10, 22, 36, 47, 51, 55, 59, 62, 74
Deadline, 99, 162
Debarment, 88, 182, 212
Debriefing, 136, 165-166, 168
Decatur, GA, 124
Decision
  Date, 189

of last resort, 184
unilateral, 188
Declaration of default, 209
Default Termination, 157, 182-185, 216
Defects, 122-123, 212
Deficient surety, 164-165
Definiteness, 150
DeHoog, R., 10, 19
DeKalb County, GA 124
Deliverables, 84, 94-95, 98, 157-158
Delivery
   failures, 194
   lapses, 97
   requirements, 23, 66, 94, 126, 155
   schedule, 94, 165, 184
Denver, CO, 32-34, 204-205
Department of Defense (DOD), 9, 46, 54, 109, 118-119, 122, 133
Design specifications, 57, 94, 110, 112-114, 117-118, 124
Design-based RFP, 157
Design-based SOW, 94
DFA (Department of Finance & Administration), 46, 58, 62, 73
Dilger, R., 7-8, 19
Direct costs, 7, 39-45, 94, 127
Direct government service delivery, 4, 7-8
Disallowing payment, 173
Discrimination, 88, 214
Disputes Clause, 131, 153, 168-169
Dobel, J., 4, 19
Dobler, D., 91, 103
Doctrine of substantial compliance, 118
DOD (Department of Defense), 109, 114, 117, 119, 122
Domberger, S & Hall, C., 51, 54, 73
Domberger, S. & Rimmer, S., 3, 7, 19
Donahue, J., 3, 19
Drucker, P., 2-3, 19

- E -

Economic price adjustment, 88, 124-125, 212
Effective cost controls, 127
Effective Dates of Insurance, 156
Elling, R., 26-27, 47
Emergency Assistance, 4, 97, 215

Employee benefits, 50, 64, 67, 193, 207
End-users, 29, 86, 88-89, 98
Equal opportunity, 65, 139, 141
Equipment Buy-Back clause, 216
Escalator clause, 188
Escalator Date, 189
Ethics, 18, 88, 138, 189-190, 214
Evaluation
   Committee, 138-143
   criterion, 145, 220
   form, 139-140, 145, 220
   guidelines, 158, 220
   methods, 89, 97, 102, 137, 144, 148
   of Performance, 25, 82, 84, 89, 97
   of proposals, 25, 144, 179
   Process/Methodologies, 83, 90, 136, 138, 140, 168, 179
   team, 32, 213
Ewoh, A., 3, 19
Ex ante (before the event), 105-107
Excessive penalty, 158
Exclusivity arrangements, 106, 121, 123
Excusable condition, 184
Excusable delays, 189
Execution of the contract, 151, 173
Executive approval, 189-190
Executive session, 139, 141
Expanded Systems Model, 108-110, 113-114, 117
Expiration date, 156
Explicit language, 151
Extended period, 125, 182
Extensions, 101, 106, 110, 119, 121, 123, 187-189

- F -

FAC (Federal Acquisition Circular), 124
Facilities management, 3, 40-43, 45
Fact-finding, 25, 162, 167
Failure of the contractor, 175, 185
Fantauzzo, S., 53, 73
FAR (Federal Acquisition Regulation), 109-110, 124-127, 135, 175, 183
Farr, C., 199-203
Favoritism, 55, 167, 191
Federal
   Acquisition Circular (FAC), 124
   Acquisition Institute (FAI), 118, 132

Acquisition Regulation (FAR), 109, 175
antitrust laws, 78
Bureau of Prisons, 17
Deposit Insurance Corporation (FDIC), 208
Fenwick, J., 70, 74, 159
Fidelity Bond, 100
Field Manager, 79-80, 82, 194
Final
   document, 83, 87, 151, 154
   negotiations, 143, 154
   offer, 16, 141, 156
   price, 125-126
   Report, 54, 129, 139, 141, 195-196
   score, 146, 220
Finance department, 40, 42, 46, 58, 73
Financial
   Interests, 174
   protection, 165, 181
   stability, 87, 100
Firm-fixed-price contract, 124, 126
First-line supervisors, 89
Fiscal Considerations—Non-Appropriations Clause, 101
Fiscal year, 1, 101, 105, 112, 131
Fixed
   Weights, 144, 146-148
   -fee contract, 16, 38, 130
   -price contract, 111, 125-127, 129, 183
   -price incentive contract, 125-126
   -price solicitation, 149
Flanagan, J., 54
Florida, 27, 76, 132
For-profit, 5, 13-15
Foreman, A., 70, 74
Formal
   amendment, 86
   Bidding, 49, 52, 76
   Contract, 52, 150-151, 154, 176-177
   solicitation, 75, 86
Fraud, 141, 216
Frumkin, P., 130
FTE (Full-Time Equivalent), 36
Fully Allocated Costs Approach, 41-42, 44, 64, 67, 207

- G -

Gabor, A., 11, 20
Gaebler, T., 3, 21

Gansler, J., 7, 20
GAO Commercial Activities Panel, 1, 21, 52, 54, 62, 73-74, 133
Gardner, B., 191, 197
Garrison, R., 44, 46
GASB (Governmental Accounting Standards Board) SEA (Service Efforts & Accomplishments) Reporting, 108-110
General Liability Endorsement, 156
General Terms and Conditions, 88, 213
Georgia, 124, 144, 146, 158, 220
GFOA (Government Finance Officers Association), 36
Go/No-Go, 144, 149
Good faith, 71, 175
Gordon, S., 105, 132
Gore, A., 3, 20
Government
  Finance Officers Association (GFOA), 36, 46-47
  Performance and Results Act (GPRA) of 1993, 107-110
Governmental Accounting Standards Board (GASB), 107-108, 132
GPRA (Government Performance and Results Act), 107-109

- H -

Hall, C., 20, 51, 54, 73
Hamilton, D., 17, 20
Hard services, 38, 49, 56-57
Harisenrider, T., 194, 197
Harney, D., 80, 84, 88, 103, 128, 138, 151-154, 156, 158, 163, 165, 170, 172, 180, 189, 192, 198, 216
Hartley, K., 57, 74
Hatry, H., 4, 20
Hayes, D., 158-159
Hazardous materials, 99, 215
Hearing process for protests, 166-167
Henry, N., 4, 20
Hill, D., 7, 19
Hinke, J., 7, 20
Hodge, G., 7-8, 20
Hold-back compensation, 120
Hold-harmless clause, 215
Hurdle Rates, 45-46
Hybrid type contract, 124

- I -

ICMA (International City/County Management Association), 1, 12-14, 28, 36, 55, 199-203
Identification of Contract, 38, 155
Identification of personnel, 84, 96, 157
IFB/ITT (Invitation for Bids/Invitation to Tender), 76-77, 87, 103, 138, 150, 156
IFB process, 135, 152, 161
Illinois, 8, 17
Illinois DCF (Department of Children and Families), 112
Illusory Competition, 6
Impartial treatment, 77
Imprecise statements of work, 109
Improprieties, 191
In-house employees, 2, 23, 49-55, 57-60, 67, 72, 81
Incentives/Penalties, 105-107, 115-116, 119-122, 127-129, 135, 157-158, 217
Incoming contractor, 196-197
Incumbent contractor, 196
Indemnification clause, 215
Indianapolis, IN, 3, 59, 62, 173
Indirect cost, 40
Industrial relations, 20-21, 73
Industry consultants, 192
Inferior performance, 107, 119
Information asymmetry, 105-106
Inherent competitive advantage, 62
Inherently Governmental Functions, 24-26, 29, 47
Inherently Governmental Services, 49, 56
Input measures, 177-178
Input standards, 177-178
Inputs, 107-110, 113-114, 117, 122, 178
Inspections, 25, 95, 122-123, 176, 200
Insurance
  brokers, 156
  carriers, 155-156
  certificates, 151, 154-156
  Company Rating, 155
  Exhibit, 154-155
  policy, 100
  requirements, 99, 152, 156
Integrity of the process, 82, 161, 190

Interdepartmental Committee Model, 70
Internal Revenue Service (IRS) guidelines, 193
Interruption insurance, 181, 195
Inventory equipment, 183, 196
Involuntary restrictions, 16
Irrevocable letter of credit, 100, 208
IRS Guidelines, 193
ISM (Institute for Supply Management), 89,93, 103
ITT (Invitation to Tender) (CN), 76-77, 87, 103, 138, 150, 156

- J -

Jasper, C., 1, 3-4, 7, 12, 19
Jeffries, M., 54
Jensen, R., 4, 7, 19-20, 51, 73
Johnson, R., 94
Johnson R. & Walzer, N., 8, 20
Joint Center for Political Studies, 9, 21
Judicial process, 162, 166
Judicial system, 163
Jurisdiction's procurement law, ordinance and regulations, 92, 138, 214
Jurisdictional Responsibilities, 84, 90-91
Justice Kennedy, 17

- K -

Kavanagh, I. & Parker D., 1, 20
Keene, W., 3, 20
Kelly, J., 36, 43, 46
Kessel, C., 121
Kettner, P. & Martin, L.L., 7-8, 20, 59, 73, 108, 132
Kickbacks, 6, 214
Kiesling, H., 4, 20

- L -

Labor costs, 99, 125
Labor-hour contract, 127
Lawther, W., 11, 20
Legal
  advice, 26, 161, 189
  and/or regulatory restrictions, 52
  authority, 151
  Barriers, 28, 30, 32-34, 204-205

document, 149, 153
staff, 152, 154, 166, 168
Legality of purpose, 150
Letter of Credit, 100, 208
Level Playing Field, 50, 62-63, 65-68, 71, 73
Level Playing Field Checklist, 63-64, 69, 207
Liability Limits, 156
Licenses, 214
Limited competition, 58, 188
Long-term, 19, 173, 193
Longer-term contracts, 187-188
Los Angeles County, CA, 9
Loss damage, 98, 162
Lowest priced offeror, 143, 150
Lowest priced proposal, 143, 149

- M -

Mackelprang, D., 26-27, 46
Make-or-buy decisions, 2-3, 24, 27, 33, 56
Management consulting services, 81, 103, 129
Management staff, 81, 192
Mandatory pre-bid/proposal conference, 210
Marginal performance, 97
Market Strength, 28, 32-34, 204-205
Market Testing, 71
Martin L.L. & Kettner, P., 7-8, 20, 59, 73, 108, 132
Martin L.L. & Miller, J.R., 163, 170
Material-related costs, 39
Materials management, 103, 137
MCD (Minimum Cost Differential), 46
McDavid, J., 6-7, 20
McGillicuddy, J., 28, 47
McNamee D. & Selim, G., 37, 47
McRobb, M., 11, 20
Measurable performance standards outputs, 109
Measure of output, 180
Mediation, 162-163, 167, 197
Melbourne, Australia 20, 51, 73
Melkers J. & Willoughby, K., 110, 133
Memorandum of Understanding (MOU), 50, 64, 68
Meta-analysis, 7-8
Method of Payment, 115, 152
Metro Water Services (MWS), 131
Michel, G., 34, 47

Michigan, 26, 27, 47
Milestone
   Contracting, 120, 128-130
   payment system, 130, 133
   performance-based contract, 129-130
Miller, J.R., 51, 163, 170
Miller, S., 74
Mini-trials, 163, 167
Minimum Cost Differentials (MCDs), 45-46
Minimum Cost Savings Threshold, 50, 64, 67, 207
Minnesota DHS (Department of Human Services), 111-112
Minority business enterprises, 100, 165
Minority public employees, 5, 9, 11, 30
Moffett, R., 7, 19
Monitoring
   and Managing Outsourcing Contracts, 174
   Costs, 36
   procedures, 69, 180
   /Quality Assurance Plan, 115-116, 122-124, 175-176, 217
   resources, 38
   responsibilities, 123
   risk factors, 38
   Strategies, 178
   techniques, 80, 178-179
MOU (Memorandum of Understanding), 50, 65, 68
Moulder, E., 13, 21, 199-203
Muller, T., 4, 20
Mullins D. & Zorn, K., 37, 47
Multi-Step Offers, 15, 79, 136, 143
Multi-year contracts, 57, 59, 128, 188, 216
Mutual agreement, 102, 136, 150, 188-189
Mutuality of obligation, 150
MWBE (Minority and Women's Business Enterprises), 165
MWS (Metro Water Services), 131

- N -

NAPM (National Association of Purchasing Management), 89, 103
National Commission for Employment Policy (NCEP), 9, 21, 124
National League of Cities (NLC), 21, 36

Nature of Default letter, 181-182
NCEP (National Commission for Employment Policy), 9, 21
Needs Statement, 91
Negotiation phase, 178
Negotiation process, 77, 79, 142
New Zealand, 7
Newspaper test, 189, 191
NIGP's Code of Ethics, 18
NLC (National League of Cities), 36
No-cost termination agreement, 184
Non-appropriation of funds, 215
Non-appropriations clause, 101
Non-binding estimate of cost, 143
Non-competition agreements, 197
Non-Conforming Response, 164, 212-213
Non-consideration of an offer, 103
Non-disclosure rule, 76
Non-Inherently Governmental Functions, 26
Non-performance, 99, 157, 177-178, 215
Non-profit organizations, 46
Non-responsive, 137, 213
Non-selection, 24
Non-solicitation, 197
Non-substitution Clause, 153, 215
Non-voting members, 138
North Carolina, 4, 28, 43
Northlake, IL, 17
Not-for-profit, 2, 5, 13, 15
Notice of Intent, 76, 164, 168
Notice of termination, 216
Notice, written, 97

- O -

O'Hare Truck Service v. City of Northlake, 16
Objection, written, 162
Objective performance measures/performance requirements, 131
OECD (Organisation for Economic Co-operation & Development), 105, 107, 133
Offeror contacts, 86
Offerors, unsuccessful, 136, 165
Offeror's
   actual cost, 90
   employees, 85, 87, 94, 96
   experience, 220
   proposal, 145
   relevant past performance, 137
   response, 146

service, 92, 96, 165
Office of Management & Budget (OMB), 3, 21, 35, 37, 47, 51, 74
OFPP (Office of Federal Procurement Policy), 111, 122, 133
Oklahoma DRS (Dept. of Rehabilitative Services), 129-130, 133
OMB (Office of Management & Budget), 3, 37, 42
Ombudsmen, 167
On-site inspection, 123
On-Time Delivery, 174
One-Time Conversion Costs, 36, 39, 41-45
One-year term, 187
Ongoing service contracts, 188
Ontario, Canada Provincial Government, 121
Ontario Reality Corporation (ORC), 121
Open records statutes, 71-72
Option of renewal, 101-102
Oral presentations, 139, 141-143, 146, 218, 220
ORC (Ontario Realty Corporation), 121
Oregon, 28
Organisation for Economic Co-operation and Development (OECD), 105, 107, 133
Osborne, D., 21
OSHA (Occupational and Safety Health Administration), 91
Outcome
  analysis, 180
  definition, 108
  measures, 180
  Monitoring, 180
  performance, 110, 114, 124, 129
  /Quality, 31, 108-110, 114, 117, 124, 129-130
Outcomes, measurable, 109
Outgoing contractor, 197
Output
  measures, 177-178
  performance specifications, 110, 114
  /Quality, 107, 110, 117, 124, 129
Outside Consultants, 50, 63, 65, 207
Outsourcing
  agreements, 159
  Institute, 174
  Manager, 20, 179

process, 190
Overlapping contracts, 197

- P -

Parallel process, 63, 65, 207
Parker, D., 1, 20
Parker D. & Hartley, K., 57, 74
Partial contracting, 195
Partial payments, 183
Partnering, 192-194, 197
Past performance, 119, 137, 212
Payment
  Bonds, 84, 99-100, 156
  incentives, 120
  methods, 174
  Procedures, 84, 99
  terms, 99
PBSA (Performance-Based Service Acquisitions), 118-119, 122, 133
PBSC (Performance-Based Service Contracting), 133
Penalties, 50, 64, 68-69, 119-122, 157-158, 177, 180, 207, 216-217
Pendleton, A., 9-10, 21
Pennsylvania, 4, 52, 54
Percent inspections, 122-123
Percentage of cost, 105, 124, 214
Perception of wrongdoing, 190
Performance
  Bond, 99-101, 156, 195-196, 209
  failures, 122, 175, 182
  guarantee, 175, 208
  inadequate, 173, 180
  indicators, 107, 177, 179
  measure/performance requirement, 117-118, 120, 123, 131, 217
  monitoring, 82, 123, 173, 176, 180
  outcomes, 107-108, 122, 157, 180
  penalties, 107, 118-119, 121-122, 158, 177, 180, 216
  quality levels, 110, 118
  specification, 113, 118
  standard/AQL, 118-120, 123, 217
  unacceptable, 97-98, 184, 216
Performance-based
  contracts, 18, 38, 105, 111, 113-115, 119, 121-122, 127-130, 157
  pricing, 174
  service, 94, 105, 109-111, 114-

116, 122, 127, 133, 173, 217
Statements of Work (SOWs), 38, 94, 112-115, 117-118, 128, 217
Periodic inspection, 116, 122-124, 176
Perkins, S., 54
Permatemp, 193
Permit costs, 46
Personal bond, 100, 209
Personnel Qualifications, 84, 96, 148
Philadelphia, 4, 53-55, 62
Phoenix approach, 20, 73
Phoenix AZ, 3, 10, 36, 43, 51-54, 57-58
Pinellas County, FL, 132
Point values, 98, 144, 146, 220
Policy Office, 24-26, 47, 79, 109, 111, 122, 133
Political Opposition, 49, 56, 61, 206
Poole, J.B., 6, 21
Poor Performance, 96, 122, 142, 173, 176, 180-182, 216
Portland, OR, 28, 46, 53, 62, 73
Post-award orientation, 175
Power of Attorney, 156
Pre-bid conference, 86, 210
Pre-Proposal Conference, 83, 85-86, 88, 102
Pre-solicitation conferences, 164
Preventive maintenance, 116, 123, 178
Price
  adjustments, 125, 157
  Considerations, 84, 101
  escalation, 188
  fixing, 213
  proposals, 76, 84, 102, 143, 151
  Ranking of Offerors, 84, 103
PricewaterhouseCoopers Endowment, 63
Principle/agent theory, 105
Principles of Partnering, 187, 194
Priority statements, 144
Private contractors, 5, 7, 68, 195
Private Sector
  Competitiveness, 49, 56, 59, 61, 206
  competitors, 50, 66-67, 72
  contractors, 5, 7, 68
  costs, 7, 39, 52, 64, 71, 207
  Delivery, 7, 26-27, 50, 66-68
  employee benefits, 50, 64, 67, 207
  Interest, 49, 56, 58-59, 61, 206
  service delivery, 7, 26, 50, 66-68

Wage Scales, 5, 50, 64, 66, 207
Privatization
  Assessment Workbook, 28, 32-34, 46, 204-205
  /contracting, 1-4, 17-18, 33, 50, 55, 59, 61, 67
  practices, 12, 19, 79
  Profile Scoring Form, 32
  Profile Summary Form, 32-34, 49, 204-205
Procurement
  Evaluation team, 213
  method, 78-79, 92, 138
  of goods, 78, 86-87
  of services, 77, 86-87, 136, 190
  officer, 92, 138, 151, 161, 163-164, 167, 185, 196
  ordinances, 190-191, 210
  Procedure Manual, 144, 146, 158, 220
  process, 50, 53, 55, 66, 81, 136-137, 140, 161-162, 165, 190
  regulations, 88, 131, 138, 149, 164, 191, 210, 215
  staff, 79, 86, 138
Producer's Price Index, 102
Professional associations, 103
Professional Engineers, 17, 153
Progress payments, 120, 129-130, 169, 183
Project
  Manager, 80, 96, 136, 142, 148, 181, 192, 218
  Procurement Officer, 164
  team, 96, 194, 219-220
Proposal
  delivery, 52, 136
  disadvantages, 77
  Document, 75, 150
  Evaluation, 135, 139, 165
  method, 78, 149
  non-responsive, 137
  price, 144, 147
  solicitation, 75-76, 210
  Team, 79
Proposals,
  acceptable, 137, 142, 149, 182, 188, 194
  technical, 25, 143, 148-149
  unacceptable, 137, 142, 149
Protest,
  Avoidance Strategies, 167
  filing, 162, 166
  language, 163-164
  procedures, 161-162, 166, 170
  written, 162, 166-167

Protests And Disputes, 151, 161, 163, 167, 170
Public
  employee unions, 17, 59-60, 62
  inspection, 79
  management, 4, 19-21, 47, 54, 74, 107, 180
  managers, 19, 55, 180
  private competition, 20, 53, 58, 63, 66, 74
  -Private Competition Checklist, 49-50, 61-62, 206
  -private competition policy, 50, 55, 63, 69
  -private partnership, 21, 74
  sector service contracting, 10, 15-16, 24, 28, 45, 52-53, 57, 110, 128
  service delivery, 8, 18-19, 21, 23, 50, 68, 74
Purchase-Order Contract, 151-152
Purchaser and Provider Functions, 50, 66, 70-72

- Q -

QAP (Quality Assurance Plan), 175
Qualifications section, 87
Qualified immunity, 16
Quality
  Assurance Plan (QAP), 115-116, 122, 175-176, 217
  Control(QC), 84, 95, 180
  performance specifications, 110, 114, 118
Quasi
  –procurement, 51
  -contract, 68
  -judicial capacity, 169

- R -

Random sampling, 122-123
Rao, N. & Young, K., 7, 21, 60, 74
Re-offer, 135, 187, 196
Re-solicit, 102, 216
Re-solicitation, 102
Re-submission of a protest, 162
Reason Foundation, The, 36, 73
Reason Public Policy Institute, The, 20, 47, 54, 73, 78, 185
Recording secretary, 139, 142
Recovery of Money clause, 215
Register of Proposals, 79

Regulatory powers of government, 26-27
Reimbursement contracts, 38, 111, 127
Rendell, E., 4, 21, 55, 74
Renewal
  clause, 102, 188
  offer, 101, 189
  option, 188
  period, 101-102
  pricing, 101, 188
  provisions, 101
  requirements, 99
Request For Proposal (RFP) Document, 75
Requirements, technical, 84, 91, 94, 155
Response
  technical, 139, 147
  time, 82, 97, 140, 180, 211
  written, 166-167, 211
Responses, late, 165, 211
Responsible bidder, 77-78, 103, 143-144, 211-212
Responsible offeror, 78
Responsive bidder, 77-78, 103, 143-144
Restrictive competition, 94, 164
Revenue Enhancement, 128, 130
Review process, 76, 83, 140
RFI (Request for Information), 167, 213
RFP (Request for Proposal), 96
RFP
  boilerplate, 87-88, 161, 210
  document, 75, 154, 161
  Draft, 83
  Outline, 83
  requirement, 146, 149
  solicitation, 75, 79, 86, 103, 154
  team, 79-80, 82, 99-102
  technical specifications, 150
Riccucci, N., 4, 21
Richardson & Walker v. McKnight, 16
Right to Audit clause, 216
Right, unilateral, 96, 157, 216
Rimmer, S., 3, 7, 19
Risk
  acceptable level, 178
  assessment, 37-38
  factors, 30, 38
  levels, 137
  management, 37, 47, 180
  of nonperformance, 99, 178
Rogin, R., 112, 133
Royalties, 25, 88, 215

- S -

San Bernardino, CA, 191-192
San Diego County, CA, 4, 19, 43
Satisfactory performance, 102, 184
Savas, E.S., 1-2, 21, 47, 74
Sclar, E., 10-11, 21
Scope/Statement of Work, 75, 84, 91-92, 139, 145, 152, 157-158, 189
Score value, 145
Scorecard system, 176
Scores
  technical, 147
  weighing, 145
  weighted, 34
Scoring
  forms, 141-142
  Method, 77, 148, 218
  methodology, 142
  of oral presentations, 146, 218
  proposals, 220
  system, 146-147
Scottsdale, AZ, 27
SEA, (Service Efforts and Accomplishments) Reporting, 108-110
Sealed
  Competitive bids/tenders, 78
  price proposals, 76, 143
  proposal, 72, 76-79, 96
Secondary contractor, 195
Security clearances, 25, 94
Security Controls, 84, 94
Segal, G., 17, 21
Segmenting services, 57
Selection process, 77, 165
Selim, G., 37, 47
Separation of Purchaser and Provider Functions, 50, 63, 66, 70-72, 207
Sequential process, 63, 65, 207
Service
  Complaints, 84, 97, 122, 176, 178, 190
  contracting—the process, 135-136, 151, 167
  Definition, 97, 115-116, 217
  delivery area, 36, 123
  delivery costs, 36, 41, 44, 71
  delivery mode/method, 30, 44, 67, 210
  delivery plan, 52
  delivery site, 86
  delivery systems, 6, 57, 60, 65
  disruption, 30, 100
  experience, 82, 87, 96, 180
  levels, 7, 107, 133, 209
  monitors, 79, 114
  outcomes, 31, 94, 107-108, 110, 114, 180
  performance, 84, 90, 97, 100-101, 113-114, 120, 132, 135, 158, 176, 180-181, 208
  provider negligence, 99
  providers, 9, 59, 82, 96, 99-100, 164
  quality standards, 114
  requirement, 90-91, 108
  Segmentation, 49, 56-58
  solicitation, 79, 87, 96, 99, 102, 208
  Tasks, 91, 114-115, 217
  unacceptable, 95, 98, 208
Services Most Frequently Contracted, 12-13
Services of consultants, 65
Settlement, 169-170, 182, 214
Share-in-Savings Contracting, 128, 130-131
Shaw, K., 70, 74
Sherman Antitrust Act, 212
Shetterly, D., 11, 21
Short-Form Contract, 151-152
Sign-off sheet, 83
Signature of the protestor, 164
Smaller dollar value, 36, 38
SMEs (Subject Matter Experts), 79-80
Smith, G., 8-9, 21
Soft Services, 38, 49, 56-57, 112
Solicitation
  method, 101, 136-137
  original, 101-102, 144, 156
  response, 100, 210-212
SOW (Scope/Statement of Work), 75, 94, 142
SOW/RFP (Scope/Statement of Work/Request for Proposal), 173
SOW
  sample, 89
  strategy, 91
  team, 90, 93-94, 99-100, 103, 136, 154, 166, 175, 196
Special clauses, 87, 210
Special Conditions, 87, 99, 209
Specifications, 57, 75-77, 84, 91-94, 103, 110, 112-114, 116-118, 124, 150, 164, 177, 210, 217
St. Paul, MN, 112
Staffing requirements, 66
Stakeholder support, 29
Stand-Alone Versus Interrelated Services, 49, 56-57
Standard
  Boilerplate Clauses, 87-88
  clauses, 210, 215-216
  -Form Contract, 151, 153
Start-up costs, 5, 59
State
  contracting, 13, 16, 46-47, 73, 112, 126, 185
  employees, 4, 8, 16-19
  engineers, 17
  laws, 87, 163, 190, 213
  of Texas Approach, 41, 44-45, 64, 67, 207
  statutes, 76, 92, 100
  Supreme Court cases/decisions, 16, 18
Statement of
  objectives approach, 115-117
  Purpose, 85
  Work Checklist, 84, 92
  Work clause, 214
  Work Exhibit, 154-155
  Work team, 136, 164, 211
Statement/Scope of Work (SOW), 75, 84, 91-92
Statutory time limit, 164
Step-down method, 40
Step-Up/Step-Down Incentives, 120
Stevens, B., 10, 21, 59, 74
Stone, M.N., 6, 21
Stonecash, R., 7, 19
Strategic partner, 178
Struyk, L., 7, 19
Sub-national governments, 51, 62
Sub-standard performance, 106
Subject Matter Expert (SME), 79
Submission, in-house, 65-66
Submissions, late, 88, 136, 212
Suggs, R., 9, 21
Sunshine laws, 76
Surety bond, 100, 165
Surety company, 99-100
Surprise inspections, 176
Survey of contractors, informal, 179
Surveys, 13-15, 122-123, 176-177
Suspension and Debarment, 182
Sydney, Australia, 54

- T -

Targeted service, 52, 79, 82, 91, 123
Task Description, 83, 88-89

Task specification, 117-119, 123
Team leader, 96
Team members, 79-80, 93, 192, 218
Technical
  Exhibits, 84, 103
  merit, 140, 149
  /Price Proposals, 84, 102
  responsiveness, 219
  specification, 196
Temporary stopping of work, 157
Tender, 76-78, 136, 139, 150, 191
Term
  cost, 7, 31, 40
  extension, 101
  penalty clause, 98
  performance, 97, 117, 120
  proposal opening, 78-79
  renewal, 101, 187
Terminate, 5, 153, 183-184, 195, 216
Termination
  action, 184
  clauses, 153, 182
  date, 189
  for Convenience clause, 216
  notice, 185, 216
  of the contract, 153, 157
Terms and Conditions, non-conforming, 88, 212-213
Terms/Conditions/Boilerplate, 83, 213
Texas, 28, 41, 44, 47, 67
Thai, K.V., 150, 159
Third party, 99, 153, 178
Third-party certification, 116, 122-124
Third-Party Monitoring, 123-124
Thoma, T., 58, 74, 117, 133
Thompson, L. & Elling, R., 26-27, 47
Time value of money, 142
Time-and-materials contract, 127
Timing Considerations, 84, 101-102
Total cost, 7, 39-41, 125-126, 142, 154
Total quality management (TQM), 11
Total scores, 143, 146, 220
TQM (Total Quality Management), 11
Trade-Off Analysis, 144, 148-149
Trade-offs, 78, 149
Training of in-house staff, 81
Transition
  costs, 16, 50, 64, 67-68, 207
  period, 196
  plan, 196
Transitions, employee, 180

Transitional Contract Issues, 187, 196
Treble damages, 213
Two one-year renewal options, 187

- U -

U.S. Congress, 107
U.S. Federal Procurement Policy, 106
U.S. General Accounting Office (GAO), 1, 36, 52, 54, 105
U.S. Office of Management and Budget (OMB), 21, 35, 37, 51
U.S. Supreme Court, 16-17
UK (United Kingdom), 54, 63
Unambiguous SOW, 84, 93
Unbundling, 10
Unilateral clause, 101, 157
Unit cost, 38, 41, 130, 151
Unit price, 38, 151, 154-155
United Kingdom (UK), 54, 63
University of Sydney, Australia 54
Urban Institute, 20, 112

- V -

Variable Weights, 144, 148
Vendor, 150, 174, 179
Victoria, Australia, 51
Vinson, E., 112

- W -

Waine, B., 54
Walker, B., 59, 74
Walker v. McKnight, 16
Walsh, K., 3, 7-10, 21-22, 36, 47, 51, 55, 59, 62, 74
Walzer, N., 8, 20
Warning notice, 97
Weights, 34, 145-148, 158, 204-205
Willoughby, K., 110, 133
Wilson D. & Game, C., 7, 22, 70, 74
Wimmer, S., 108, 133
Withdrawal, 88, 211

- Z -

Zorn, K., 37, 47

About the Authors

Lawrence L. (Larry) Martin, MBA, Ph.D. is Professor of Public Affairs at the University of Central Florida in Orlando. Dr. Martin has published extensively in the areas of public procurement and contract administration including performance-based contracting. His work has been published by the National Institute of Governmental Purchasing, the International City/County Management Association, the National League of Cities, the IBM Center for the Business of Government, the Reason Foundation and others. His works have been translated and reprinted in: Chinese, French, Korean, Portuguese, Russian and Mongolian. Dr. Martin has provided consultation and training to a number of state governments (e.g., Arizona, Florida, Nebraska, New Jersey, Texas); municipal governments (e.g., Boca Raton, FL, Houston, TX, Phoenix, AZ, Portland, OR,); county governments (e.g., Maricopa, AZ, Orange, FL, Palm Beach, FL) and special district governments (e.g. Phoenix Transit Administration, South Florida Water Management District). He has also lectured and made invited presentations to governmental and non-governmental organizations in Canada, France, Germany, Sweden and Mongolia.

John R. Miller, CPPO, is responsible for procurement services for the Harford County Public School System in Maryland. Prior to joining Harford County Schools in 2000, Mr. Miller was the Purchasing Agent for the City of Baltimore in Maryland. From 1981 until 1995 he served as Deputy Director and then Director of the Baltimore County Office of Central Services. He began his procurement career at Towson University in Baltimore, Maryland, where he served as Director of Purchasing and Material Management. Mr. Miller authored the NIGP textbook, "Contracting for Services" in 1996 and co-authored this textbook and "Alternative Dispute Resolution" for NIGP in 2002 as part of the NIGP LEAP curriculum. He served as an adjunct faculty member for Harford Community College, Maryland and the University of Virginia. He is a member of the U.S. Community Advisory Board. Mr. Miller received his Masters in Governmental Administration (MGA) from the University of Pennsylvania and his BS degree in Finance from the University of Baltimore.

Other books published by
NIGP: The Institute for Public Procurement

INTRODUCTION TO PUBLIC PROCUREMENT

LEGAL ASPECTS OF PUBLIC PROCUREMENT

DEVELOPING AND MANAGING REQUESTS FOR PROPOSALS IN THE PUBLIC SECTOR

CONTRACT ADMINISTRATION IN THE PUBLIC SECTOR

SOURCING IN THE PUBLIC SECTOR

STRATEGIC PROCUREMENT PLANNING IN THE PUBLIC SECTOR

ALTERNATIVE DISPUTE RESOLUTION

FUNDAMENTALS OF LEADERSHIP AND MANAGEMENT IN PUBLIC PROCUREMENT

LOGISTICS AND TRANSPORTATION

CAPITAL ACQUISITIONS

RISK MANAGEMENT IN PUBLIC CONTRACTING

CONTRACTING FOR CONSTRUCTION SERVICES

WAREHOUSING AND INVENTORY CONTROL

NOTES: